Opening the Scriptures

Genesis

OPENING THE SCRIPTURES

Genesis

Cornelis Vonk

Translated by
Theodore Plantinga† and Nelson D. Kloosterman

General Editors
Jordan J. Ballor and Stephen J. Grabill

GRAND RAPIDS · MICHIGAN

© 2013 Christian's Library Press
An imprint of the Acton Institute for the Study of Religion & Liberty
98 East Fulton   Phone: 616.454.3080
Grand Rapids, Michigan 49503   Fax: 616.454.9454
www.clpress.com

Originally published in Dutch as *De Voorzeide Leer. Deel I^a. De Heilige Schrift. Genesis.* 3rd rev. ed. (Amsterdam: Buijten & Schipperheijn, 1991).

ISBN: 978-1-938948-29-9

Scripture quotations not referenced by chapter and verse are translated from the author's Dutch translation or paraphrase.

Unless otherwise indicated, Scripture quotations referenced by chapter and verse are from the ESV® Bible (The Holy Bible, English Standard Version®) copyright © 2001 by Crossway, a publishing ministry of Good News Publishers. Used by permission. All rights reserved.

Scripture quotations marked JB are from THE JERUSALEM BIBLE, copyright © 1966 by Darton, Longman & Todd, Ltd. and Doubleday, a division of Random House, Inc. Reprinted by permission.

Scripture quotations marked NRSV are from the New Revised Standard Version of the Bible, copyright © 1989, by the Division of Christian Education of the National Council of the Churches of Christ in the United States of America. Used by permission. All rights reserved.

Scripture quotations marked RSV are from the Revised Standard Version of the Bible, copyright 1952 [2nd edition, 1971] by the Division of Christian Education of the National Council of the Churches of Christ in the United States of America. Used by permission. All rights reserved.

Cover image: Map of Jericho (14th-century Farhi Bible by Elisha ben Avraham Crestas), public domain.

Cover design: Peter Ho

Printed in the United States of America

1 2 3 4 5 6   18 17 16 15 14 13

Contents

Abbreviations   ix
The Uniqueness of Opening the Scriptures   xi
Introduction   xv

Orientation

1. How Jesus Christ and His Apostles Viewed Holy Scripture   3
2. The Torah   17

The Book of Genesis

3. The Dating and Structure of the Book of Genesis   37
4. In the Beginning   59
5. A Look Back and a Look Ahead   83
6. Rebellion   113
7. Cain and Abel   143
8. Continuing Corruption and Repeated Restoration   155
9. A Promise with Worldwide Scope   213
10. God's Covenant with Abraham   223
11. The Life of the Patriarchs   241

Name and Subject Index   249
Scripture Index   257

This series in English translation is provided by
John and Jenny Hultink
as their legacy to their children and grandchildren,
for generations to come.

*"I have no greater joy than to hear that my children
are walking in the truth." (3 John 4)*

Abbreviations

Old Testament

Gen.	Genesis	Song	Song of Songs
Exod.	Exodus	Isa.	Isaiah
Lev.	Leviticus	Jer.	Jeremiah
Num.	Numbers	Lam.	Lamentations
Deut.	Deuteronomy	Ezek.	Ezekiel
Josh.	Joshua	Dan.	Daniel
Judg.	Judges	Hos.	Hosea
Ruth	Ruth	Joel	Joel
1–2 Sam.	1–2 Samuel	Amos	Amos
1–2 Kgs.	1–2 Kings	Obad.	Obadiah
1–2 Chr.	1–2 Chronicles	Jonah	Jonah
Ezra	Ezra	Mic.	Micah
Neh.	Nehemiah	Nah.	Nahum
Esth.	Esther	Hab.	Habakkuk
Job	Job	Zeph.	Zephaniah
Ps(s).	Psalm(s)	Hag.	Haggai
Prov.	Proverbs	Zech.	Zechariah
Eccl.	Ecclesiastes	Mal.	Malachi

New Testament

Matt.	Matthew	Rom.	Romans
Mark	Mark	1–2 Cor.	1–2 Corinthians
Luke	Luke	Gal.	Galatians
John	John	Eph.	Ephesians
Acts	Acts	Phil.	Philippians
Col.	Colossians	James	James
1–2 Thess.	1–2 Thessalonians	1–2 Pet.	1–2 Peter
1–2 Tim.	1–2 Timothy	1–3 John	1–3 John
Titus	Titus	Jude	Jude
Philem.	Philemon	Rev.	Revelation
Heb.	Hebrews		

Old Testament Apocrypha

Add. Dan.	Additions to Daniel	Pr. Man.	Prayer of Manasseh
Add. Esth.	Additions to Esther	Ps. 151	Psalm 151
Bar.	Baruch	Sir. (Ecclus.)	Sirach
Bel	Bel and the Dragon		(Ecclesiasticus)
1–2 Esd.	1–2 Esdras	Sg. Three	Song of the
Jdt.	Judith		Three Jews
Let. Jer.	Letter of Jeremiah	Sus.	Susanna
1–4 Macc.	1–4 Maccabees	Tob.	Tobit
Pr. Azar.	Prayer of Azariah	Wis.	Wisdom of Solomon

General

ESV	English Standard Version
Heb.	Hebrew
JB	Jerusalem Bible
KJV	King James Version
NRSV	New Revised Standard Version
RSV	Revised Standard Version

The Uniqueness of Opening the Scriptures

Opening the Scriptures is not a new series of technical commentaries that explain the Bible word for word, although this series of volumes does rest upon careful exegesis. Nor is it a collection of sermons, although now and then the authors shine the light of Scripture on our modern world. Actually, there is no familiar category of Bible studies that serves as a suitable classification for Opening the Scriptures. This series has a unique character. It offers devout church members a series of popularly accessible primers, with no display of scholarly expertise, so that the average churchgoer can easily grasp them.[1]

As far as their approach is concerned, these volumes begin by telling you about the structure of the biblical book that you want to study. This is because an overview of the whole enhances insight into the parts. After all, Scripture is not a loose-leaf assortment of essays or a collection of isolated

---

1. [*Translator's note:* In keeping with this purpose and where the flow of argument does not suffer, footnotes appearing in the original as well as some more technical references in the text have been omitted from this translation, since they refer primarily to Dutch and German literature, which for most readers of this series will be inaccessible.]

texts. Therefore the ABC of the authors of this series is this:
pay attention to the text, the context, and the canonical place
of the biblical book (or the other way around). What is the
scope of a particular book, and how is it organized? What
is its place in the totality of Scripture? For example, what
ties Joshua, Judges, Samuel, and Kings together? What does
Lamentations have to say to us today? In short, Opening the
Scriptures resembles a museum guidebook that opens your
eyes to the beauty and meaning of the treasures, large and
small, being exhibited.

The organization of this series follows the four main sec-
tional divisions of Holy Scripture (Luke 24:44). For the Holy
Spirit has joined together all the books of the Bible into an
imposing edifice. The Torah, or the five books of Moses, is the
foundation upon which the entire Scripture rests. Therefore
this section of the Bible is discussed most extensively in Opening the Scriptures. The many prophetic books form the walls.
The Psalms and Wisdom books are the windows. Over all of
this the Holy Spirit has laid the golden dome roof of the New
Testament. The authors of Opening the Scriptures would like
to guide you through this immense building. They will ask,
"Have you seen this, and did you notice that?" And when you
respond, "Surely the Bible is a wonderful book, and I would
like to know more about it!" then they will have achieved
their purpose.

Genesis, the book beginning the series, constitutes the introduction to the Torah. After telling us about the perfect
creation and beautiful garden, human rebellion and divine
graciousness, the flood and the Table of Nations, Genesis
speaks extensively about Abraham's salvation and God's
covenant with him and the other patriarchs. This covenant
is not just one among a number of topics that the Bible talks
about. Nor is it an isolated subject in theological dogmatics.
God's covenant with Abraham exists still today. It consists of
God's *solidarity* with us in the Lord Jesus Christ, and thereby it

forms the basis beneath all our living, and it is the air that we breathe. We walk, we sit, we eat, we drink, we sleep, we work, we live, and we die *within and in terms of* that regulation-saturated and sanction-filled treaty relationship with Almighty God. The authors of Opening the Scriptures are constantly showing that Holy Scripture is from A to Z the Book of God's covenant with his people.

In his faithfulness to this covenant, the LORD delivered Israel out of Egypt, and in addition to the first covenant he established a second covenant. He even came to dwell among these people. Therefore, the Torah of Moses, which deals with this, is hardly a dry collection of antiquated laws. It teaches us to know Yahweh the LORD as the God who despises sin and death, and heartily loves life, especially the life of us human beings. He loves life so much that he sent his Son into the world to restore it. The entire Torah sparkles with that divine love of life. The tabernacle with its worship and all of God's life-enhancing statutes and ordinances bespeak that love.

The prophetic books (Joshua–Malachi) show what Israel did with God's covenant and his Torah. They show how Israel received the promised land of inheritance, but also how Israel forfeited and lost the land. God honored the covenant, however, by means of Israel's return from the Babylonian captivity, so that the Messiah could be born one day from this nation and in that land.

God reveals himself as the God of life even more clearly and powerfully in the New Testament than in the Torah, the Prophets, and the Psalms. For he proclaims that he so loved human life that, in order to save it, he sent his Son Jesus Christ to earth to be born as a son of Abraham. God did so in order that through faith in Jesus Christ he might grant eternal life not only to Jews, as in the old covenant, but now in the new covenant, to believers from every nation. And this is precisely as he had promised earlier under oath to Abraham, as we learn in Genesis.

Tracing the unfolding of this plan, then, is the design of Opening the Scriptures.

Frans van Deursen

Introduction

This volume is the first in a series on which we have been at work for some years now. A number of volumes have already appeared in Dutch, and the books are now appearing in English as well.

We are calling the series Opening the Scriptures. The series is not intended to present a kind of Bible history, nor is it a set of commentaries. Our purpose is somewhat different.

Suppose a friend of yours was about to make his first visit to a historic city that you knew well. Wouldn't you want to tell him a few things about the city and give him some pointers on what to look for? Or suppose your friend was off to a museum to look at a famous painting that you consider one of your favorites. Wouldn't you want to discuss the painting with him and give him your impressions of it?

Our purpose here is to address some such remarks to you as you begin reading one of the Old Testament books or one of the New Testament epistles or a favorite passage. We want to tell you something about the structures of that book, what its main thrust is, and so forth. We want to give you some information and open some perspectives for you so that you will quickly be able to grasp and enjoy the message that comes through in the book of the Bible you are reading.

The obvious place to begin is with the "Law of Moses," for it forms the basis for all the teaching contained in the Old and New Testaments. Because it is the basis for what follows, we have found it necessary to discuss the Law of Moses in more detail than we will devote to some of the later books.

In our treatment of the books of the Bible, we have drawn freely on the insights of other scholars. Our debt to them is acknowledged especially in the notes to the Dutch edition, which do not all appear in the English edition. But here in this introduction we would like to acknowledge a couple of people with gratitude. At the same time we will draw the reader's attention to a fundamental theme not just in the Law of Moses but in the entire Bible, namely, the meaning of the name YHWH or LORD.

Most of our English Bibles translate the Hebrew name YHWH as LORD (to be distinguished from Lord, which is used in the Old Testament to translate a different divine name). Because Hebrew was originally written without vowels, there has been some confusion as to what vowel sounds to put with YHWH in order to produce a pronounceable name. In the Middle Ages, the pronunciation "Jehovah" won wide acceptance, while in our time "Yahweh" is gaining ground. (The Jerusalem Bible, for example, uses Yahweh where most other English Bibles use LORD; we will have more to say about this matter in our discussion of the book of Exodus.)

What is the meaning of the name Yahweh, or LORD? For a long time it was assumed that this name means "the One who is." It also has been suggested that the name brings God's covenantal faithfulness to expression in a special way, which is a view we once affirmed in an earlier publication.

We have since abandoned this interpretation of the name, despite the healthy covenant emphasis it reflects. Our reasons for this as well as our reason for not accepting the earlier view will be spelled out in detail later. For the present we propose only to tell the story of how we came to a change in position on this matter.

It was the work of Prof. Benne Holwerda that made the difference. Through his writings we became convinced that it is not correct to interpret the name Yahweh as referring especially to God's covenant faithfulness. And Holwerda also showed in a convincing manner what meaning we should ascribe to this name instead. The name spoke to Israel of the power and force God had used to deliver the children of Abraham from the danger of death in Egypt. Yahweh is the name God gave himself in order to make himself known from then on as the God of life.

We do not mean to say that Holwerda was the first one to suggest this interpretation. Given the references he makes to other works, this clearly was not the case. We mention Holwerda here only to indicate how we came to embrace this interpretation, which by now has won acceptance in a somewhat broader circle.

Subsequently the correctness of this interpretation was confirmed for us when we became acquainted with a somewhat older work that was published in the first half of the previous century—K. C. W. F. Bähr's book *Symbolik des Mosaischen Cultus* (2 volumes, 1837 and 1839). If there is one point Bähr wants to make in this work, it is that the Lord chose to make himself known to Israel as the *God of life*.

The way in which Bähr talks about the Lord's name is already remarkable. Here and there he does speak of "Jehovah" as "the One who is," which may have had something to do with the philosophical convictions he had chosen, whether knowingly or unknowingly. According to F. Friedrich, one of his opponents, he was a Hegelian (not only Hegelians use such language: compare, for example, Herman Bavinck's treatment of the name YHWH in his *Reformed Dogmatics*, 4:944, s.v. Yahweh, YHWH).

But on some occasions when Bähr talks about the "name," "essence," and so forth, of the LORD, Scripture overpowers his philosophical commitments. We read, "Death and corruption are the most complete expression and revelation of finite and transitory being over against the true being of God, which is *absolute life and holiness*" (2:497; italics added). And what can one say about a short sentence in which Bähr again talks about the "infinite being" of God but then throws in innocently, in parentheses, "*to put it in concrete, Eastern terms—true life*" (2:462; italics added)?

We hear the sounds of theological and philosophical chains rattling as a man deeply under the impression of the liberating Word of God tugs at them. Here Bähr almost let go of his system of thought as he spoke in scriptural terms of the LORD as the God *who lives and gives life.*

What was Bähr's book all about? If we disregard the unscriptural language about God as the "infinite being" and "absolute being" and focus on the careful study this author has made of the instruction about himself that the LORD gave Israel by means of the "shadow-like" rituals, we must recognize that the author is a Bible scholar who, like the owner of a beautifully furnished home, shows us all sorts of things both old and new.

According to Bähr, the tabernacle and all that belongs with it preaches this message in particular: God abhors death and takes pleasure in life! As we see it, he has backed up this thesis in a convincing way with a great mass of evidence, although of course one may choose to disagree on this or that point. We will be drawing freely on Bähr's material in these volumes.

From Holwerda we learned something about the meaning of the name Yahweh, or LORD, and from Bähr, about the meaning of the shadowy worship. Were not the two pointing in the same direction? Could this direction not be extended to cover the entire "Law of Moses"? Doesn't the whole Law of Moses depict Yahweh as the living God who thoroughly abhors death and deeply loves life, which he freely gives to his people?

And if this was the truth that the work of Bähr and Holwerda unfolded, did that truth always receive the attention it deserved?

Take our Easter sermons, for example. Could not Easter

sermons be based on Old Testament texts that weren't part of the Scripture passages to which we are directly referred through the addresses of Peter and Paul in Acts 2 and 13? Instead of preaching on Genesis 3:15 (the "mother promise") or 12:3; 22:18; and 26:4 (the promise to Abraham and Isaac) or Psalms 2, 16, and 110, could we preach on Exodus 28 (the garments worn by Israel's priests) or Leviticus 4:1–5:6 (Israel's sin offering)? Wouldn't such sermons express God's abhorrence of death and the pleasure he takes in the life of his children?

Someone might respond by asking whether we haven't heard of the young goat that is not to be boiled in its mother's milk. Of course we have. In our earlier years we would have seen no possibility of preaching a sermon on this text (Deut. 14:21c), let alone an Easter sermon. At that time we were not yet acquainted with the idol Mot, the god of death, whose disfavor the Canaanites tried to avert by the sprinkling of milk, which is ideal nourishment. You can make further applications on your own. We will come back to this text later.

But isn't the application of such texts obvious? What else has God ever done than to show his great love for life, especially for our human life?

God gave life at the time of creation (Gen. 1) and already protected it in the garden by warning our ancestors against death. And when they chose evil anyway, and thereby death, it was again God's hand that powerfully pulled Adam and his wife (at that point seen together as a unit) back after they had crossed death's boundary. He laid upon them a judgment abundant with grace when he made them bring forth the human race in pain. What else could it have been but God's promise that inspired Adam to call the woman God had given him Eve, that is, life (Hebrew *khawwah*, Greek *zoē*, Gen. 3:20)? God warned Cain against the very thought of murder. And how he grieved when he decided he would have to punish the world with the flood! He also saved Abraham from death by drowning, this time in a pool of paganism. Through the birth of Isaac he showed that he is the God who has the power to make the dead come to life and who loves to awaken new life to laughter.

Abraham's descendants experienced the deliverance from Egypt. This was an unparalleled deed, and from that time on, God wanted Israel to know him as Yahweh, as *the One who lives and who gives life*. It is almost impossible to overestimate the importance of this historical lesson, since it is the basis for all the instruction we find in Scripture. It is even the basis of the book of Genesis, however strange this may sound at first.

To these same descendants of Abraham, this same God—Yahweh—made his hatred of death and pleasure in life known at Mount Horeb by means of a number of visible and tangible symbols so beautiful that many an attentive Israelite could not get enough of looking at them. He saw the gleam of the metals and the language spoken by the colors. He saw the garments worn by the priests, rich with meaning. And then there was the ceremonial garb of Israel's high priest, the man who was never allowed to mourn and who could not marry a widow. What unique regulations! They all spoke jubilantly of *life*. And the same message was heard or read in the commands that the same Yahweh had given with regard to sin and guilt offerings, death, and leprosy.

Everywhere in the books of Moses we meet this deep "abhorrence of death"—if we may use such language—and the LORD's heartfelt pleasure in life. We even see this to some extent in Genesis, which forms a prelude to the Law, but it comes through especially in Exodus, Leviticus, and Numbers, which together form the heart of the Pentateuch. It even comes through in the epilogue to the Pentateuch, the book of Deuteronomy, where Moses says to the church that had been led out of bondage, "You are the sons of the LORD your God. You shall not cut yourselves or make any baldness on your foreheads for the dead" (Deut. 14:1).

The prophetic books come next. How the LORD would have loved to bless his chosen people with life, and he would have done so if only they had clung to his lovely Torah. The prophetic books tell us about the wrong choice the people made—a choice in favor of death and against life. If it were not for the fact that God is Yahweh, there would have been no life left.

The writings in the third section of the Old Testament, the Wisdom literature, show us what a good and beautiful life Israel would have had with Yahweh if they had kept the Torah. And there were indeed times when Israel did enjoy something of that life—that real, true life.

Please do not spiritualize the word *life*. To find out what the good, genuine life of a faithful people with their God Yahweh is like, we must read a book like Proverbs. In the keeping of Moses's Torah lay a guaranteed length of days and years of life (Prov. 3:2), of medicine for the body and renewal for the bones (3:8), of prevention of adultery along with the injury and shame it brings in its train (6:20–7:27), of prevention of death and alienation from the church (5:1–23), and in place of these evils, safety (3:23), sound rest at night (3:24), and more such exquisite things. Wisdom makes us walk in Yahweh's law. Thereby wisdom becomes a genuine "tree of life" (3:18).

When we turn to the New Testament, it doesn't surprise us that our Lord Jesus Christ hated death and loved life while he was here on earth. He came to bring us life. He called himself the life, and he was life (John 1:4; 6:35; 14:6). He was angry when he was at the grave of Lazarus. He was deeply incensed and deeply moved as he stood there by his grave, weeping about death (11:33, 35).

Think also of the answer Jesus gave the Sadducees, the people who accepted only the books of Moses as Scripture. They thought they could corner Jesus with their question about the resurrection of the dead, which was a doctrine they denied. Isn't it striking that the Savior should answer them with an appeal to those same books of Moses? He appealed to the very thing that we mentioned earlier in this introduction:

God's aversion to death and the deep pleasure he takes in life. Christ said, "As for the resurrection of the dead, have you not read what was said to you by God: 'I am the God of Abraham, and the God of Isaac, and the God of Jacob'? *He is not God of the dead, but of the living*" (Matt. 22:31–32; italics added).

It is unnecessary to rely on all sorts of tricks and acrobatics to bring in Christ whenever we deal with large portions of the Pentateuch. Christ is immediately in the picture when we hear the voice of the LORD, who abhors sin and death but loves life.

Neither do we need to follow the lead of the rich fantasies of the ancient typologies, which seemed able to make almost anything of any passage. One of the old typologists named Herman Witsius actually said that it was better to find Christ everywhere than nowhere. This sounds almost comical in our ears, but when we really think about it, we see that it is a tragic ploy.

Is this sort of thing really necessary? No. The Law of Moses is full of gospel! It preaches the LORD, who had such good intentions for his people Israel (which includes us). The "Law" is not dead and dry. The chapters that are rarely read need not remain a closed book to Christians as long as people see the main theme to which we have pointed in this introduction: *God's awful hatred of death and his heartfelt good pleasure in life!* If we once grasp this point, we will be careful not to concern ourselves only with a fraction or a thimbleful of the rich ocean of the Word in the form of a few favorite texts from the New Testament.

We want to show just as much respect for the New Testament as anyone else, but it does form only a part of Scripture, not more than a quarter. And the New Testament is based on "Moses, the Prophets, and the Psalms."

"Moses," then, is the basis and beginning. And this Law of Moses is not at all dull or tiresome. Genesis often sparkles with humor. (Think of the puns it contains.) The heart of the Torah (which includes Exodus, Leviticus, and Numbers) overflows with light and life. It acquaints the church of today with her God, Yahweh, the Creator and Giver of life, who also has shown himself to be a Lover and Preserver of life, of genuine human life. We know that he loved life so much that he sent his own Son so that we might have life.

Orientation

CHAPTER 1

How Jesus Christ and His Apostles Viewed Holy Scripture

No one who picks up a Bible supposes that he is the first one to do so. Many generations have read the Bible before us. Yes, just as in the old days—before modern fire engines—buckets of water were handed from person to person to put out a fire, so previous generations have passed on our Bible to us, as it were. The presence of the Bible in this world has been an undeniable fact for centuries.

The various parts of the Bible originated one by one, a process that obviously took centuries. Subsequently those portions, consisting of letters and books, were arranged and bound together. Then they were copied and recopied. They were translated, and translated again. Finally people began to print Bibles. Even then it took a long time before we got today's Bibles, so beautifully laid out and packed individually in boxes so that we can easily wrap them and give them to each other as gifts.

That book, the Bible, which we hope you take in hand every day, did not simply fall from the sky one fine day. It has been passed down to us through the hands of countless people who have contributed in some small way or other to its final form. There are a lot of interesting books you could read on the subject: for example, think of the ancient manuscripts of Isaiah and Habakkuk that were found in the wilderness of Judea some years back.

Even more interesting is the question of how all those earlier generations viewed the Bible. What value and significance did they attach to the Bible? Surely we should not be indifferent to the views of the great men in the history of the Christian tradition.

What did Augustine think about the Bible? How about Thomas Aquinas, Luther, and Calvin?

Still more important by far is the question of what Christ and his apostles thought about the Bible. In comparison to their judgment, the views of the greatest and noblest of our forefathers and predecessors count for very little. Therefore we should all be silent and listen respectfully to the voice of Jesus and his earliest disciples.

Jesus Christ and the Bible

How did our Lord Jesus Christ regard the Bible? Strictly speaking, one could reply that this question is impossible to answer. When our Savior was on the earth, there was no Bible yet.

But such a reply would be somewhat too literal. Naturally, when we hear the word *Bible*, we immediately think of the handy little Bible that fits in our coat pocket, or of the big family Bible in which many dates of births and marriages are recorded. The Bible, for us, is that well-known collection of 66 books, 39 of them comprising the Old Testament, and the remaining 27 the New Testament.

It is true that the complete collection did not yet exist in the days when Christ was on earth. But most of those books (i.e., the ones that make up the Old Testament) were already in circulation. And the Old Testament constitutes three-quarters of our present complete Bible. Looking back, we can see that those Old Testament books were longingly ready for the completion they finally received in the form of the New Testament.

Christ's evaluation of the Old Testament is actually rather difficult to separate from his evaluation of our New Testament. We would like to comment on that rather narrow point and then say something as well about the division between Old and New Testaments.

What did the Lord Jesus Christ think about the Old Testament, the part of our current Bible that was already in circulation, during the days when he was on earth?

In those days the 39 books were not yet called the "Old Testament," of course, just as we do not speak of an "old" highway or an "old" church before there is a new one. And the 39 books were not yet called "the Bible" either. Since the name Bible really has little meaning, this fact is of little importance. The name is simply derived from a word that means "book," and we know that there are thousands and thousands of books in the world!

We much prefer to speak of the Bible as the "sacred Scriptures," for this name at least says something. The name is modeled after the language used by the apostle Paul, who reminded Timothy that he had been acquainted with the "sacred Scriptures," or sacred writings, from childhood on. What the apostle meant, naturally, was the 39 books of the Old Testament.

It is well established that the "sacred Scriptures" of the Jews were in circulation during the time of Christ and the apostles. They were organized into a certain arrangement, divided into groups, and regarded as together forming a unit. (We will come back to this later.)

The sacred Scriptures of the Jewish people had already been translated into a foreign language by Jesus's time. The Old Testament books—or most of them, at least—were originally written in Hebrew. A few chapters were written in Aramaic, a language closely related to Hebrew and spoken by the Jewish people in the time of Jesus. In the synagogues the Scriptures were read aloud in Hebrew, and the rabbis would then explain them in Aramaic. Just as we could only understand someone who spoke the English of 400 years ago with difficulty, the Jews who spoke Aramaic could hardly understand the Hebrew of earlier centuries.

In Palestine, then, which was the Jewish fatherland, it is not surprising that people knew little Hebrew and were fluent in Aramaic, since for years they had been away from the ancient fatherland. Evidently many members of the Jewish nation had never set eyes on that fatherland, and at least had never spoken the language of their ancestors. Here we face that remarkable phenomenon known as the Diaspora, the great dispersion. Not just thousands but millions of Jews had spread all over the known world by the time of Christ's birth. From China to Spain, Jews were engaged in commerce, and there were many Jews in Egypt especially.

The language most commonly spoken among these Jews outside Palestine was Greek. Greek was to the lands around the Mediterranean Sea what English is today to so many parts of the world.

For the sake of those Greek-speaking Jews, the "sacred Scriptures" of the fathers were translated into Greek. The translation was already completed about three centuries before Christ. It is called the Septuagint, after the Greek word for seventy. According to a legend, the translation was done by a group of seventy men. Therefore it sometimes is referred to in abbreviation, by means of the Roman numeral LXX. We will have more to say about the Septuagint when we discuss the apocryphal books.

Let's first take up the question of what the Old Testament of Jesus's time must have looked like. We have already noted that it was not called the Old Testament in those days. There was no single exclusive name for Scripture. It usually was referred to in one of three different ways: (1) the Law, (2) the Law and the Prophets, (3) the Law, the Prophets, and the Psalms.

1. Examples of the first of these designations are found in John 12:34; 15:25; and 1 Corinthians 14:21. The word *law* is used there in the broader way in which it is also used in Psalms 19 and 119: "The law of the Lord is perfect." There the term simply means all that God had taught Israel.

2. Examples of the second designation are found in Matthew 7:12; 11:13; 22:40; Luke 16:16; Acts 24:14; and Romans 3:21. Sometimes there are also references to "Moses and the Prophets." The best example, perhaps, is the story of the travelers on the road to Emmaus. The Lord Jesus made it clear to them what the Old Testament had said about the Messiah: "And beginning with Moses and all the Prophets, he interpreted to them in all the Scriptures the things concerning himself" (Luke 24:27). Think also of Luke 16:31: "If they do not hear Moses and the Prophets, neither will they be convinced if someone should rise from the dead." Paul also spoke of "Moses," for example, in 2 Corinthians 3:15, where he was talking about the reading of Scripture by the rabbis in the synagogue on the Sabbath day: "To this day whenever Moses is read a veil lies over their hearts."

3. Finally, there is also the designation of the entire Old Testament by the threefold name "the Law, the Prophets, and the Writings." This third designation is already reflected in a certain writing that existed before the New Testament was written: the apocryphal book known as Ecclesiasticus. This book was originally written in Hebrew by a certain Jesus Sirach. Around 132 BC it was translated into Greek by a grandson of Jesus Sirach. This grandson added an introduction to the book in

which he tells us that his grandfather, Jesus Sirach (his name was really Jesus, the son of Eleazar, the son of Sirach), had devoted himself zealously to the study of "the Law, the Prophets, and the other books of the fathers." Here the grandson used language strikingly parallel to the third designation for the Old Testament.

We find basically the same way of speaking in the New Testament, for example, in the story of Jesus's resurrection, in which our Savior said to his disciples, "These are my words that I spoke to you while I was still with you, that everything written about me in the Law of Moses and the Prophets and the Psalms must be fulfilled" (Luke 24:44).

This threefold name is also reflected in current editions of the Bible in the Hebrew language. Thus the division of the Old Testament into three parts stems from the Jews. Part 1 is the Torah or the Law, including the books Genesis through Deuteronomy. Part 2 is the Prophets, which are in turn divided into two sections: the Former Prophets and the Latter Prophets. The Former Prophets include Joshua, Judges, Samuel, and Kings (4 books in all, since Samuel and Kings each count as one book). The Latter Prophets include the three great prophets (Isaiah, Jeremiah, and Ezekiel) and the twelve Minor Prophets (Hosea, Joel, Amos, Obadiah, Jonah, Micah, Nahum, Habakkuk, Zephaniah, Haggai, Zechariah, and Malachi). The twelve Minor Prophets often have been regarded as forming one book together, so the Latter Prophets is also made up of four books.

The rest of the Old Testament belongs to Part 3: Psalms, Proverbs, Job, the Song of Songs, Ruth, Lamentations, Ecclesiastes, Esther, Daniel, Ezra, Nehemiah, and Chronicles. The writings in this third group are referred to together by the grandson of Jesus Sirach as "the other [or remaining] books of the fathers." Sometimes they are also called "the Writings," following the lead of the rabbis responsible for the Hebrew edition of the Old Testament. Our Savior referred to them by the title of the first book in the series, "the Psalms," just as today we sometimes use the name of the first essay in a collection of essays as the name of the entire book. Our Lord spoke, then, of "the Law, the Prophets, and the Psalms."

No doubt it has struck you that the arrangement of the Bible books mentioned above differs somewhat from the arrangement we are accustomed to. Later we will come back to this difference. First we will take up the question of which books belonged to the Old Testament our Savior referred to when He spoke of "the Law, the Prophets, and the Psalms."

Did the apocryphal books belong to that Old Testament? These books are listed in Article 6 of the Belgic Confession. They are found in Roman Catholic Bibles (e.g., the Jerusalem Bible) and in some older Protestant Bibles as well.

The grandson of Jesus Sirach tells us in his introduction to his grandfather's book:

> It was in the thirty-eighth year of the late King Euergetes, when after my arrival in Egypt I had already spent some time there, that I found a work of more than common instructional worth [by which he simply means what Paul later referred to as "sacred Scriptures"], which convinced me of the urgency of applying myself in my turn with pains and diligence to the translation of the book that follows (Ecclus. 1:1 JB).

His grandfather had written that book so that he would tell others about the wonderful books he read so zealously himself and enjoyed.

The grandson's comment is very valuable. Bear in mind that the book of Ecclesiasticus is the oldest of all the apocryphal books. Thus we hear Jesus Sirach's grandson admitting that the apocryphal books did not form part of what we might call the official Jewish Bible, or what the Lord Jesus called "the Law, the Prophets, and the Psalms."

Israel's Bible in the days of the Savior did not include the apocryphal books, not even the book of Ecclesiasticus, even though it was originally written in Hebrew. Thus the other apocryphal books, which arose later—many of them written in Greek rather than Hebrew—certainly were not seen as part of the Old Testament.

It is likely that our Savior spoke and understood Greek, but in his preaching he surely used Aramaic, which, as we saw, comes close to Hebrew. And when he read from the Scriptures in the synagogues at Nazareth and Capernaum, we can be sure he was not reading from Greek texts. He was reading Hebrew, the same Hebrew that we encounter in our current Hebrew editions of the Old Testament.

Here we see something of the scope of the Old Testament that our Savior must have known and recognized. As the humble Servant of Yahweh, he showed deep respect and obedience before the Law, the Prophets, and the Psalms, as we can easily see from a couple of examples. Our Lord Jesus Christ was slandered, and so were some of his followers, like Stephen (Acts 6:13). The false accusation made was that they were attacking what was regarded as sacred in Israel. In order to deny such slander directed at his Master, Matthew, the author of the first gospel, passed on to us Christ's well-known statement that he did not intend to abolish even the smallest bit of the Law and the Prophets (5:17–18); on the contrary, he was angry that this "word of God" had been rendered powerless by the scribes and Pharisees through devices of their own that they had imposed on the poor people in the synagogues (Mark 7:13). Our Savior also appealed repeatedly to the Old Testament in support of his preaching and as containing the program the Messiah would carry out.

For our Lord Jesus Christ, the Old Testament was a source that proved his legitimacy; it provided him with his credentials. He urged people to test his words and works by the Old Testament (John 5:39).

When we today receive that same Old Testament, made up of the same books from the hands of the previous generation, and accept it as the Word of God, we are following the example of the One who is above all suspicion: Jesus, our Lord and Master. In his company we can feel safe and at rest.

The Apostles and the Bible

If we respectfully accept the Old Testament as the Word of God, we are following not just the example of Christ but also the example of his apostles and other disciples. They too refer to the Old Testament frequently and quote from it. They often appeal to the Old Testament in support of what they write. They do this so often that it would be an endless task to list the examples. Anyone can easily find them for himself. If all the New Testament's quotations from the Old Testament were printed in bold in our Bibles, many pages would be printed in heavy black type.

The writers of the New Testament gave evidence in other ways of their respect for the Old Testament, not only by quoting from it but also by their explicit comments about it. The apostle Peter, for example, honored the Old Testament as the prophetic Word that is really due not to men but to the Spirit of God, who drove holy men to prophesy. That Word (the Old Testament), said Peter, has now been established even more firmly because of the coming of the fulfillment in the form of Jesus Christ (2 Pet. 1:19–21). The apostle Paul, likewise, not only quoted repeatedly from the Old Testament but also spoke openly about it. Earlier we saw that he referred to the "sacred Scriptures." Timothy, as a man of God, a servant of the gospel, was instructed to value the Scriptures highly, for all Scripture is given by God. What Paul said, in literal terms, is that Scriptures were "breathed out" by God (2 Tim. 3:14–17). By this he was referring to the driving power of the Spirit of God.

How did the apostles regard the New Testament? Strictly

speaking, you could say that this question cannot be answered, because the Bible had not yet been completed in the days of the apostles. They themselves were the ones who wrote the last books.

However, such reasoning is a bit narrow. We know that certain apostolic writings were already being circulated while their authors were still alive. Paul even gave express orders that one of his letters be circulated (Col. 4:16). And Peter made reference to some letters of Paul that were in circulation (2 Pet. 3:15–16).

Although we cannot speak of an explicitly formulated judgment of the apostles concerning a finished New Testament, there is an indirect expression of their views. We saw earlier that our Savior relied on the Old Testament to legitimize himself as the Messiah sent by God; he viewed the Old Testament as a divine document testifying to his calling. If that is the case, then the New Testament can be regarded simply and only as testifying to Christ's legitimacy. We therefore could speak of it as a collection of writings testifying about Jesus as the promised Messiah.

As we know, after his suffering the Savior was taken up from the earth to heaven, where he lives in glory that cannot be described. But once he arrived in heaven, he did not follow the example of Pharaoh's butler, who forgot all about Joseph after he had been restored to his position of honor. Our Lord could not do that, for he said he would love his followers right to the end (John 13:1). Moreover, he had given them a special promise: once he was in heaven, he would ask his Father to send another Paraclete, or Counselor—namely, the Holy Spirit (14:16–17). The Spirit would lead them in all truth and make them recall everything Christ had taught them when he was still on earth as their Counselor. The Spirit would then make use of Jesus's disciples to advance the cause of Jesus in the face of the world represented by the Jewish authorities that had rejected him. Through his disciples the Spirit would testify that Jesus was indeed the Messiah, the Christ (15:26; 20:31).

Christ kept that promise faithfully. He had hardly been exalted in heaven, where he received the Spirit in the richest measure, when he shared the Spirit with his disciples (Acts 2:33). They were completely baptized by the Spirit (1:5), and through the Spirit they were made able to become witnesses of Jesus. The word *witness* should be understood in its real sense, the sense in which we serve as witnesses when called upon to do so by the police or the courts. On such occasions we are called on to communicate what we have seen with our own eyes and heard with our own ears.

The apostles now stepped forward as ear- and eyewitnesses of everything they had personally experienced in connection with the intensely reproached Jesus of Nazareth (Acts 1:8). Before the people and the authorities, they testified about his baptism in the Jordan by the universally esteemed John the Baptist. They also testified about his preaching, about the miracles he had performed, about his suffering and death, about his resurrection and his many appearances afterward, and finally about his ascension into heaven and the promise of his return.

The apostles were familiar with all those facts, and now they understood their meaning. Jesus himself, between the time of his ascension and his resurrection, had taught them out of the Old Testament. Through that instruction their eyes had been opened to Christ's coming and work, his humiliation and exaltation. What had already been announced in the Old Testament, they could now see for themselves. And when Jesus himself took leave of them, the Holy Spirit took over the leadership. He equipped them to understand the Scriptures more fully and to view in the light of the Scriptures everything they had experienced with Jesus. Thus they were enabled to testify of these things before the people and the authorities.

Listen to how Peter talked already at Pentecost! The same Peter, who had fearfully denied his Master about a month and a half before, in the presence of several servant girls, testified boldly of Jesus as the true Messiah. The Spirit of Christ enabled him to do this. The Spirit gave him the wisdom to take the Bible of those days in hand, as it were, so that the people could hear what the Bible had to say about the Messiah in Joel 2 and Psalms 16 and 110. Against this background Peter showed them what had happened to Jesus of Nazareth. The people could check out the facts for themselves. It all fit together neatly.

In this initial period the disciples testified for Jesus only orally. Later they began to put their testimony on paper. Perhaps some of them dictated their thoughts to someone who could write. That's how the apostolic letters and stories (the so-called Gospels) came into existence. The purpose was always to testify about Jesus as the Messiah. The Spirit equipped them for this and drove them to do it—the Spirit sent by the Savior. Therefore we could say of the New Testament what Peter said of the Old Testament, namely, that the Spirit of God was behind its origin.

Those who trace the course of events that led to the existence of the New Testament will have to agree that we owe the New Testament the same kind of respect that Christ and his apostles showed the Old Testament, for one and the same Spirit is behind both Testaments. In the New Testament we must recognize and honor the testimony of Christ's apostles, whom the Holy Spirit motivated and equipped.

The demand for respect flows from the course of events as sketched above. But the respect is expressly commanded by the apostles themselves. We have seen that they dared to demand that their writings be read to the congregations and even be sent around (Col. 4:16; 1 Thess. 5:27). And we have reason to believe that the Letter to the Ephesians was also such a circular letter.

The apostles also dared to demand that people subject themselves to what they had written. Paul, for example, told the Thessalonians that his epistles were not to be misused or disobediently shoved to the side (2 Thess. 2:2; 3:14, 17). As for the apostle John, he did say that both those who read the Revelation of John aloud to the congregation as well as those who heard the reading were blessed (1:3), but he also dared to threaten with fearful punishment anyone who took anything away from his book (22:18–19). Thus he certainly wrote with authority.

And so we see how our Bible has come to us. We also see what a great benefit God conferred upon us when he gave us that Bible. We are no longer dependent on the oral tradition of the stories handed on by the apostles and other eyewitnesses. But much of that apostolic tradition—the parts we need—has been preserved for us in black and white. We would have had to believe even without the written testimony, but now we are as fortunate as the "most excellent Theophilus" for whom Luke wrote his two well-known books, Luke and Acts, "that you may have certainty concerning the things you have been taught" (Luke 1:4).

We have not yet said everything there is to say about the origin of the Scriptures, for we have not even touched on the origin of the individual books of the Bible. One could talk, for example, about Hezekiah's men busily gathering the proverbs of Solomon (Prov. 25:1), or about Paul with his flashing eyes and bruised fingers writing the Letter to the Galatians, this time with his own hand (Gal. 6:11), and the Letter to the Romans, which he dictated (Rom. 16:22). Nor have we said anything about how Luke the physician scrupulously gathered information from all kinds of sources to put together his large, two-volume work.

There are all sorts of stories behind the individual books. The word *Bible* reminds us that the Bible is made up of a number of little books that together add up to an impressive library. Just try copying them all by hand!

Now that this library is complete, we are struck that it is not a chaotic collection. No, all the volumes, great and small, are bound together in an eloquent arrangement. Behind this great compilation is an undeniable unifying conception.

Looking back at it, we recognize this from its structure. The
Spirit of God managed to take all that material that had been
brought together through the hands of a great many people
over the centuries and make a harmonious whole of it. The
Spirit's hand introduced form and style to this project. The
Architect kept his plan in mind and worked steadily toward
his goal.

First he laid the Mosaic foundation. Next he built some
prophetic walls on that foundation, and then he opened some
windows of wisdom in those walls through which people
would receive perspective and insight. Finally, this convincing architectural whole was capped off before our eyes by the
dome of the New Testament that covered the whole edifice.

It is true that the Bible is a library, but it is not a library
in which books are arranged in random order. This library
clearly forms a unity, for it is one book, a unique book.

The more you know about this book and the more you
subject yourself to it, the more its origin, content, and central
thrust will win your confidence. You must bow before this
book as before God's own voice. Such a guarantee comes to
you from no one less than Jesus Christ and his apostles.

The honesty of God's Spirit is at stake here. Through this
great book, the Spirit stands up for the rights and good name
and honor of Jesus Christ, who was despised by people but
given by God to the world as life. On this claim the book either stands or falls; and were it to fall, it would fall as a piece
of daring imagination, indeed, as a horrible lie.

CHAPTER 2

The Torah

The Division of the Bible into Four Sections

Earlier we indicated that we prefer to view the Bible as made up of four parts or sections. We wish to make two more comments on this subject.

First of all, we do accept the usual division into Old Testament and New Testament. Whether this is a division that Scripture itself points to is not entirely clear. Even 2 Corinthians 3:14, where there is mention of "read[ing] the old covenant," is not clear in this respect; opinion is divided on this matter. But whatever the case, the division into Old Testament and New Testament may never be used to destroy the unity of Scripture.

It is with Scripture as it is with the church. There is nothing wrong with speaking of an Old Testament church and a New Testament church—as long as we do not lose sight of the unity of the church. There is only one church. The church gathered among the Gentiles is engrafted into ancient Israel (Rom. 11:17–29, esp. 24).

The New Testament, then, is not a new Bible alongside the Jewish Bible that had already existed; rather, it forms the indispensable capstone of the "sacred Scriptures" about which Paul wrote to Timothy. And this affirmation has implications and consequences. If we view the Scriptures in such terms, we cannot regard the Psalms as songs we have outgrown, songs that are somehow not good enough for us anymore. We must then view them as songs given by God's Spirit to his one church, our church.

In the second place, in addition to the division between the Old Testament and the New Testament, there are divisions within the Old Testament, as we saw.

The division of the Old Testament into the Law, the Prophets, and the Psalms or Writings is scriptural. It was used by our Savior himself. It is still used in current editions of the Hebrew Old Testament.

The arrangement we propose to use, then, is the following:

A. The Law of Moses (Genesis through Deuteronomy)
B. The Prophets, made up of (i), the Former Prophets, namely, Joshua, Judges, Samuel, and Kings, and (ii) the Latter Prophets, made up of Isaiah, Jeremiah, Ezekiel, and the book of the twelve minor prophets (Hosea, Joel, Amos, Obadiah, Jonah, Micah, Nahum, Habakkuk, Zephaniah, Haggai, Zechariah, and Malachi).
C. The Writings, made up of Psalms, Proverbs, Job, Song of Songs, Ruth, Lamentations, Ecclesiastes, Esther, Daniel, Ezra, Nehemiah, and Chronicles.
D. The New Testament (Matthew through Revelation).

An Old Arrangement and a New Arrangement

The arrangement above is not the one we are used to from the Bible we possess, the Bible with which we were raised. How did the arrangement get changed? The changes go back to the men of the Septuagint, the Greek translation of the Old Testament that was made before the time of Christ.

Those translators did some strange things. They left section A, the books of Moses, virtually unchanged, although they did give these books new titles. (We will have more to say about this matter later.) But in sections B and C they made all sorts of changes. They took the books of section C and scattered them among the books of section B. Ruth came to follow Judges. They put Chronicles after Kings, followed by Ezra and Nehemiah. Then came Esther, Job, Psalms, Proverbs, Ecclesiastes, and Song of Songs. After Jeremiah they placed Lamentations, and they put Daniel after Ezekiel.

In short, they gave the books of the Old Testament the arrangement we are all accustomed to. This Greek Bible, the Septuagint, was later translated into Latin, which was the language of the West. This Latin translation was known as the Vulgate. The Vulgate became the dominant translation for the church in the West; Roman Catholics still use it today. Via the Vulgate, the Greek arrangement of the Bible books was carried over into our Bibles.

But there's still more to the story. The men of the Septuagint were like children who pick up a handful of sand and scatter it around their sandbox. Then they pick up another handful of sand and do it again, and then again.

Fortunately, the men of the Septuagint did this only twice. We have already seen what they did the first time: they took the books of section C and scattered them among the books of section B; that is, they scattered the Writings among the Prophets.

When they scattered for the second time, they grabbed a number of other books that they apparently found good and instructive and scattered them throughout section B. They put the Wisdom of Solomon after the Song of Songs and followed it with Ecclesiasticus. Ezra and Nehemiah had already been thrown in behind Chronicles, and now came some additions to Esther, Judith, Tobit, and the four books of the Maccabees. After Jeremiah came Baruch, and after Lamentations the Letter of Jeremiah came next. After Ezekiel and Daniel came

Susanna and the story of Bel and the Dragon. In this way the apocryphal books were given a place within the Bible.

Centuries later the apocryphal books were taken out of the Bible again. Actually, this took place later than most people think—generations after the Reformation era opened. The Roman Catholic Church has never dropped the apocryphal books from its Bible. Even in Protestant circles there were people who clung to those apocryphal books.

Some earlier Bibles used to have the apocryphal books in the back, but modern Protestant Bibles do not include them at all. In the Jerusalem Bible they are still to be found right where they were placed in the Septuagint and the Vulgate.

The second sprinkling by the men of the Septuagint has practically been undone, bit by bit, and not in an elegant way. Yet nothing was done about the first sprinkling. The disorder and confusion created by the men of the Septuagint among the books of the Old Testament has been left just as it was. In fact, everyone is so used to it by now that we would probably find the original arrangement a bit strange at first. But by now we can see which one is the old arrangement and which is the new arrangement.

We trust you can now understand why we also propose to disregard that first sprinkling and return to the original arrangement of this treatment in the Bible books. First the Law of Moses, then the Prophets, and then the Psalms or Writings. In time it will become apparent that there is good reason for going back to the original arrangement.

The Word *Torah*

We have spoken a number of times of the "Law of Moses." In this regard we have followed Scripture's own lead, for there are a number of references to the "Law of Moses" (see, for example, Deut. 31:9; Josh. 1:7; Dan. 9:11, 13; Luke 24:44; 1 Cor. 9:9).

In the Hebrew Old Testament, the word used for law is *to-rah*. And the primary meaning of this word is instruction. The Greek New Testament uses the word *nomos*, which is simply the Greek word generally used for law. The "Torah of Moses" is translated the "Law of Moses."

But if someone should suppose we always know exactly what we mean when we use the word *torah*, he would be mistaken, even if the reference is to the "Torah of Moses." This we can easily see from the following story.

When Kings Manasseh and Amon reigned, the temple of the LORD in Jerusalem was frightfully neglected. God's house was desecrated abominably. But then the throne came to Josiah, who did what was right in the eyes of the LORD. Josiah restored the temple. He had money collected among the people and saw to it that the funds raised were carefully guarded and used for the intended purpose. Hilkiah, the high priest, personally kept an eye on the situation.

One day when Hilkiah was in the chamber of treasures, he "found" a book that plays an important role in the story to be told here. Therefore we should ask ourselves exactly what is meant by the word *found* in this context. Our own view is that one should not make too much of this little word. In those days it was not very unusual to store books in a chamber of treasures (see Ezra 6:1). Also, the high priest would naturally have free access to the room where the money for the temple restoration was kept. Therefore we do not believe that one needs to interpret the word *found* to mean that Hilkiah one day, unexpectedly and to his great amazement, came across a book in the chamber of treasures that he had never seen before and of whose contents he knew nothing.

To interpret the word *found* in such a way would be to force an interpretation on the passage. That the situation was different becomes clear from the story. In Hebrew, the language of the high priest, the book is immediately called the *torah* that Yahweh gave to his people by way of Moses (2 Chr. 34:14). We saw earlier that the word *torah* has the broad meaning of teaching or instruction. Because it was generally known that the LORD had made use especially of his servant Moses, who was highly honored in Israel, to instruct his people, we may assume that the title of this book was in agreement with its contents. If so, the book could not be totally unknown to a functioning high priest in Israel.

Now, in those days not everyone could read and write as well as most people today. It is true that we should not underestimate the abilities of the people in the ancient Near East in the centuries in which the Old Testament originated. It is not true that almost all the people were illiterate in those days; we know better from the excavations that have been made.

Actually, we should respect Near Eastern civilization, for we owe to that society our ability to write. Our alphabet comes to us from Phoenicia, Israel's neighbor, by way of the Greeks. The main innovation of Phoenicia was to greatly simplify writing.

Originally, writing was not at all simple. This must be one of the reasons why the art of reading and writing was not more widespread in the land during the centuries on which we are now focusing our attention. Indeed, there were certain people who made a calling of it: the scribes. The king, of course, had his own scribe; today we would speak of a private secretary.

When Shaphan, the private secretary of King Josiah, had a talk with the high priest Hilkiah one day, he found out about the book. Hilkiah let him see the book and even let him take it along to read. Shaphan in turn showed it to the king and read to the king from the book. Or did he read the entire book to Josiah? We read, "When the king heard the words of the Book of the Law, he tore his clothes" (2 Kgs. 22:11).

So the question arises at this point: What is meant by that "Book of the Law of the LORD given through Moses" (2 Chr. 34:14)? There seem to be two possibilities. Kings and Chronicles mean either the entire collection that the New Testament refers to as "the Law," "the Law of Moses," or "Moses" (in other words, Genesis through Deuteronomy); or they mean only a part of this material.

The first possibility seems less likely to me. The story speaks of a book (singular). It hardly seems possible that the five books (Genesis through Deuteronomy) would all be inscribed on one scroll and thus form one book. And even if one thought in terms of more than one scroll, we can hardly imagine the scribe Shaphan walking over to the king's palace with a couple of those heavy scrolls in his arms (which he would need if all of Genesis through Deuteronomy were recorded on them). Moreover, we read in 2 Kings 23:2 that King Josiah either read or had someone read "all the words of the Book of the Covenant." If we take literally especially that word *all* in this phrase, then we cannot possibly think in terms of the complete first five books of the Bible. It would have been quite a job to read all that material aloud!

Thus we can much better think here in terms of only part of this material. Then the question immediately arises: Which part? Assuming that we must settle on something within those first five books of the Bible, our thoughts go at once to Deuteronomy. In that book we encounter nothing but *torah*—that is, teaching, instruction. Moreover, it is *torah* given through Moses; it is the teaching he gave Israel shortly before his death.

It is not impossible that the book referred to in our story was not the entire book of Deuteronomy but rather only a part of it. We read in Deuteronomy 31:24–26 that Moses spoke certain words, wrote them down, and commanded the Levites to preserve that written material alongside the ark. Perhaps this writing of Moses or a copy of it was later stored in the ark in the temple in Jerusalem. Perhaps it was kept there over the centuries so that every newly crowned king would be able to copy it over, which was what Moses had commanded (Deut. 17:18). Perhaps during the time of the high priest Hilkiah it was still preserved carefully in the temple, although for practical reasons it may not often have been taken from its place. Deuteronomy contains virtually no regulations for the practical service of the priests in the sanctuary, as, for example, Exodus and Leviticus do.

Perhaps the high priest thought that no one had made King Josiah aware of Moses's wish that each new king in Israel was to have a copy of this writing made for him. Because of the unfaithfulness of Josiah's predecessors, this rule may well have been neglected. Later it became apparent how much Josiah feared the LORD. Perhaps when, on a certain day, Hilkiah saw the book in the place where it was kept in the temple, he thought to himself, "This is really something that our current king should read." Then he sensibly drew on the help of the chief scribe to bring that matter to the king's attention. Perhaps the "finding" of the book by the priest Hilkiah means that it was due to the impact this book made on Josiah that we have a book of Deuteronomy in our Bible. Maybe Hilkiah's copy was used by the collectors who were responsible for putting together the large body of writings that our Savior and his apostles referred to as "the Law of Moses" or simply "Moses." Perhaps those collectors made a copy of this writing (see Deut. 17:18; Hos. 8:12) and added to it what they thought was necessary.

We have deliberately used the words *maybe* and *perhaps* here and there in telling this story in order to make it clear that one must be careful not to jump to conclusions in this area. We cannot simply say that the Torah is the Law of Moses (or simply "Moses") and that the Law of Moses is Genesis, Exodus, Leviticus, Numbers, and Deuteronomy. It's not quite that simple.

The "Pentateuch"

The books of Genesis through Deuteronomy were passed on to us by Israel, the Old Testament church, as a unity. Think of the passages where these five books are referred to together as "the Law" (or "the Law of Moses," or simply "Moses"). In their own language the Jews would refer to "the Law" as "the Torah." They all accepted the Torah as Scripture—even the

Sadducees did. The Samaritans also accepted the Pentateuch as Scripture.

But one might go on to ask whether the Old Testament Israelites also made use of the five names for these books that we now use—Genesis, Exodus, Leviticus, Numbers, and Deuteronomy. These five names were introduced by the men of the Septuagint, whom we discussed earlier.

Those Septuagint translators certainly have a good deal to answer for. First, they jumbled the Prophets and the Writings together. Secondly, they scattered some apocryphal books among the Prophets and the Writings. Thirdly, they introduced the names Genesis, Exodus, Leviticus, Numbers, and Deuteronomy. Most of these Greek names have come down to us in Latinized form via the Vulgate, the Latin translation of the Western church. Those Latinized Greek names are part of our heritage in the Western church.

As long as we are discussing Greek names, this may also be the place to talk about another important name that is of Greek origin—Pentateuch. It is a handy name, for it enables us to refer to the first five books of the Bible with one word. It is used often as a noun: we speak of the Pentateuch. Originally it was used mainly in an adjectival way.

The idea behind the first part of the word is "fivefold" (*pente* is Greek for five). But what about *teuchos*? Some believe that *teuchos* means "book," but there are others who understand it to mean a case or container or wrapper, like that in which the scroll was put for safekeeping after it was used. If so, the Pentateuch is not the fivefold book but the book with a fivefold wrapper.

We do not propose to try to settle this issue here, but would point out that in either case, the use of the singular points to the unity of the five books. It is either the fivefold book or the one book enclosed in a fivefold wrapper. Even the Greek-speaking Jews, then, saw the books of Genesis through

Deuteronomy as a unity, which fits in with the thinking of the Jews back in their original homeland, who spoke of the books as the "Law of Moses" or simply "Moses."

It is another question whether the Jews in Palestine recognized any division of the Law of Moses into five books before the rise of the Septuagint. It is not clear whether or not they did, but it is certainly possible. In any event, they surely accepted such a division later. And they gave names to those books in the same way that we still tend to give names to songs and hymns, that is, by their using the first words. Luther's great Reformation hymn begins, "A mighty fortress is our God . . ." We usually refer to it simply as "A Mighty Fortress." Thus the name the Jews gave to the first book of the Bible was not "Genesis" but "In the beginning" (*Bere'shit*).

There is more to be said about the division into five books by the Jews before the rise of the Septuagint. There probably was such a division, but established in a different way than we are used to—not quite as striking but just as meaningful. When we read attentively, we see that the conclusion of one book always points to the main theme in the next one. At the end of Genesis we read that Joseph, before his death, ordered that his bones be taken along when the descendants of Jacob left Egypt. Exodus then begins with the departure from Egypt. And Exodus in turn ends with some chapters about the tabernacle. Leviticus picks up this theme at once and carries it further, speaking especially in its opening chapters about all sorts of things that have to do with the sanctuary. Leviticus concludes with a reminder about what happened at Mount Sinai. Numbers then begins with "the wilderness of Sinai." Numbers ends by referring to the commandments the Lord gave to Israel through Moses. Deuteronomy promptly picks up Moses's preaching about the "ten commandments."

Are there sharp lines between the various books, then? No, what we find instead are gradual transitions. That way the books were not crudely separated but left bound together. A kind of division was made in such a way that the various parts would still fit together neatly, preserving the unity.

Some later hands (conceivably the men of the Septuagint again) went to work in an unpolished way, perhaps out of a "Western" need to make sharp distinctions. The books were separated.

Since that time there is hardly a book in the world that has been so extensively carved up and sliced into pieces as the Pentateuch, even though it unmistakably presents itself to us as an unbroken unity. Have people paid enough attention to the climate in which the Old Testament arose? Have people kept in mind that the literary customs in the Old Testament world may have been rather different than in our world? In the Semitic world, for example, a book would often take its title from the words with which it began. Perhaps in that world it was also a stylistic concern to write in such a way that a second book would present an outworking of the theme with which the first book ended.

Why is "the Law" referred to in Scripture as "the Law of Moses"? We often speak of the "five books of Moses." The Germans speak of 1 Moses, 2 Moses, 3 Moses, and so forth, when they refer to these books.

What do we mean when we say "of Moses"? No one will deny that a large portion of the Pentateuch is closely bound up with the figure of Moses. This by itself should be sufficient reason for using his name in connection with the Pentateuch as a whole, for we speak of the book of Joshua and the books of Samuel in much the same way. We do not mean to say that Joshua and Samuel personally wrote everything we find in those books. That could not be, for some events described in those books took place after their death. Second Samuel, in particular, speaks of events long after the death of Samuel. And Moses could not have written the entire Pentateuch, for he could not have described his own death (see Deut. 34).

We are told explicitly in various places in the Pentateuch that Moses himself wrote this or that (see Exod. 17:14; 24:4; Num. 33:2; Deut. 31:9, 24). Such passages leave us with the impression that other parts of the Pentateuch do not come to us from Moses's hand. (We will come back to this subject later.)

For the present we would simply point out that the phrase "the Law of Moses" should not lead one to jump to any conclusions. It certainly does not justify assuming that Moses was the author of the entire Pentateuch as we find it in our Bible today. What it means is simply that no one is as prominent a figure in the Pentateuch as Moses. A great many of the events described in the Pentateuch formed part of his life history, and he played a dominant role in most of them. He described many of them in his own handwriting. How many? We will come back to that question later. For the present, we may confidently assert that no one is in a position to answer such a question very precisely.

The Central Theme of the Torah or Pentateuch

The word *torah* has the general meaning of instruction, teaching, doctrine. But when we speak of the Torah (with a capital *T*), we mean the Pentateuch. This should not surprise us, for the instruction Israel needed in order to know and faithfully serve the LORD, her God, while living in Canaan among the heathen, she received in the Pentateuch. We will have more to say about this matter later, but for now we would simply ask: What is the instruction in the Pentateuch mainly about? On what matters did the Pentateuch itself focus its attention?

Does the Pentateuch deal mainly with the creation? Was this great work composed for the primary purpose of instructing the people of that time as well as later generations about the creation of heaven and earth?

We can safely say that the Pentateuch was not written to deal mainly with the event of creation. True, the Pentateuch does speak of this subject, right on the very first pages. But that's the most obvious place to speak of it; it would hardly make sense to begin speaking of the creation halfway through, or at the end.

But if we take a closer look at the part of the Pentateuch that deals with the creation (Gen. 1–2), we see that it is only a very small segment. In Kittel's Hebrew edition of the Bible, it takes up only 77 lines.

Could it be that the central theme of the Pentateuch is the fall into sin? Is the Pentateuch concerned chiefly with the disobedience of Adam and Eve in the garden? This can hardly be defended either: there are only 39 lines devoted to this matter (ch. 3).

And so we could go on to Genesis 4–11, which deals with the increasing corruption, the flood, the saving of Noah and his family, God's covenant with Noah, and so forth. Finally we come to Terah, Abraham's father. We do not know how many years belong to the period covered in those chapters, but it must have been a long enough time that we can regard Genesis 4–11 simply as dealing with events by way of a brief summary.

Then we come to Abraham, who is dealt with in Genesis 12–25. These chapters cover the period from his calling in his own land to his death—fourteen chapters in all, comprising 500 lines in the Hebrew Bible. The entire history of the three patriarchs covers Genesis 12–50, some 39 chapters consisting of about 1,600 lines, a fairly lengthy treatment. If we compare Genesis 1–3 with chapters 12–50, we see that the ratio in terms of length is about one to fourteen.

On the other hand, we know it's not really a question of length. Length is a formal matter. But these numbers do give us some indication of where we are to seek the Torah's center of gravity.

What is that long section (chs. 12–50) really about? It is

about the covenant God made with Abraham and confirmed repeatedly. Everything in the second half of Genesis fits within the framework of that covenant relationship: it tells us how the LORD kept his covenant and what people did with that covenant.

What about the rest of the Pentateuch? What do Exodus, Leviticus, Numbers, and Deuteronomy deal with? In light of these four books, Genesis looks like an introduction that first raises the subject that the rest of the Pentateuch deals with at considerable length. Exodus, Leviticus, and Numbers show us how God kept his covenant with the long-deceased patriarchs by delivering his children from Egypt, leading them to Sinai, making a covenant with them there, taking up residence among them, and teaching them how he wished to be honored and served in the sanctuary, that is, through which regulations and commandments. The Pentateuch devotes more space to these matters than to anything else.

This explains why Paul, when he later spoke about the Law in Galatians 3, could have in mind mainly these shadows (the ark of the covenant, the mercy seat, the altars, the sacrifices, and so forth) and why he could call Israel the people of the covenants (plural, see Rom. 9:4), in contrast with the Gentiles, who were strangers to the covenant (Eph. 2:12).

We need not say anything more about Deuteronomy here. We all know that this book is full of a retrospective vision of God's deliverance of Israel, Abraham's blessed seed, and God's covenant with Israel made at Sinai. Even if the *torah* in the story of King Josiah is not the entire Pentateuch but only the book of Deuteronomy, or perhaps part of this book, Deuteronomy goes down in history as the book that provides a summary of the teaching of Moses. Therefore it is referred to as "the Book of the Covenant" (2 Chr. 34:30).

So the Pentateuch is chiefly intended to give instruction about the series of covenants God made with Abraham and his seed. The emphasis falls on the seed. The Pentateuch may first give a rather extensive account of God's covenant with

Abraham, Isaac, and Jacob in Genesis, but when we compare this account with the treatment of God's covenant with Israel at Mount Horeb, the chapters in Genesis do not add up to all that much after all. We see that they function chiefly as an introduction to what follows. The covenant made at Horeb is discussed much more extensively than anything that comes up in Genesis. It is almost as though the Pentateuch does not really begin until Exodus.

The Reason for King Josiah's Sorrow

At this point we return to King Josiah. Earlier we noted that when Shaphan read to him from the book "found" in the temple, King Josiah became very upset and was overcome by such great sorrow that he tore his clothes in mourning.

Even if the book Shaphan read to the king was not Deuteronomy as a whole but only the heart of this book, the words Josiah heard must have clearly expressed what we had seen earlier as the heart of the Pentateuch, namely, God's covenants with Abraham and his seed. The book in question is referred to, after all, as "the Book of the Covenant" (2 Chr. 34:30). So it must have contained something about the blessings the LORD would shower on his people if they kept his covenant, and also about the covenant wrath that would strike them if they showed contempt for his covenant. God would visit them with drought, hunger, war, the loss of their children to a life of slavery, and even the deportation of the entire nation to a life in exile (see Deut. 28–29).

If King Josiah heard all these things in the book read to him, it must immediately have occurred to him how many of those threats had already been fulfilled. There had already been a great drought under King Ahab (1 Kgs. 17). Once, in Samaria, a woman had eaten her own child because of her extreme hunger (2 Kgs. 6:29). Now Josiah was hearing that such punishments had long ago been held before Israel as a threat.

Jewish children had also been taken away by bands of enemy raiders, as we can see from the presence of the Jewish slave girl in the household of the Syrian commander Naaman (see Deut. 28:32, 41; 2 Kgs. 5). Samaria, the capital of the kingdom of the ten tribes, had been captured long before Josiah's day, and many of the people had been taken away into exile.

All this had happened about a century before Josiah's time, and the king knew all too well that in his own realm, the southern kingdom, the LORD had been scorned just as much. He only had to think back to what had gone on during the reign of his father, Amon, and his grandfather, Manasseh.

Josiah now understood the situation that he and his people faced. With devastating clarity he could read the hands on the clock of God's failing patience. Because the people of Judah showed the same contempt for the same covenant with the same God, they could expect the same punishment.

And that's indeed how things turned out. The punishment was not long in coming. Josiah himself died at a relatively young age. About twenty years after his death, Jerusalem was destroyed and Judah went into exile.

We have no need to discuss this matter any further here. We brought up this story only to show the relationship between the Pentateuch and the Prophets. In "the Law of Moses" we are given a look at covenants with which God blessed his people in Old Testament times, and in "the Prophets" we are shown what Israel did with these covenants. Israel did not keep the covenant as she had promised. We are then shown how the LORD, like a father with seemingly inexhaustible patience, called his children back to himself and to his covenant.

The Law of Moses and the Bible as a Whole

As you will recall, we used the comparison of a house with its foundations, walls, windows, and roof when we spoke of the structure of our Bible. The Torah of Moses is to be regarded as the foundation of the entire Bible. In the Torah the LORD acquaints us with the beginning of his efforts to restore the human race. Humanity had taken the side of the devil and death, but God protected humanity against itself and protected its life. He always had good intentions for humanity. He promised Noah that the catastrophe of the flood would never be repeated. He delivered Abraham from heathendom and gave him a promise, which the LORD confirmed with the covenant and by swearing an oath to the effect that Abraham's descendants would be a blessing to all the peoples of the earth. That is why, since that time until Christ's return, a people of God will always exist, despite all the measures taken against that people and against the earth. The basis for this faith is what the Pentateuch tells us about the agreement God made with Noah and Abraham.

In this Pentateuch we have the foundation of the Scriptures. All the rest of the Bible's contents are determined by it. After the Pentateuch there can be nothing completely new.

In the Prophets God described what Israel did with God's covenant. We read how the LORD kept his promises faithfully, even though his chosen people repeatedly tried to sabotage them. Century after century the LORD warned his people by means of his prophets, telling them: Back to the Torah (the Law of Moses) and the Testimony (the covenant with the Lord). That's what we read about in the books that make up section B.

The books of section C sing of the blessedness of God's people when they keep his covenant and remember his commands and obey them. Such an attitude toward life is praised as true wisdom. Happy are the people who keep the Torah!

The New Testament is then the roof over this edifice. There we are shown the fulfillment of God's promise to Abraham in his descendants. It is this covenant of which Mary and Zechariah sing at the time of the birth of our Savior (Luke 1:55, 72–73). The gospel of this covenant is later brought to the Gentiles (Gal. 3:8–9, 14), and not the gospel of the Horeb covenant, however wonderful that covenant was in itself. Paul later declared that this wall between Israel and the other people, this wall consisting of ordinances, was torn down (Eph. 2:14). The shadows of the law (the sacrifices, the altars, the Sabbath, etc.) were fulfilled in the coming of Christ (Col. 2:17; see also Heb. 10:1).

The New Testament forms only a relatively small part of Scripture as a whole—about one-fourth. But in this relatively small portion, the entire edifice of Scripture is capped off and climaxed. All the rafters come together in this capstone, this roof. In the New Testament the prophetic Word is crowned as true and reliable (2 Pet. 1:19).

The Book of Genesis

CHAPTER 3

The Dating and Structure of the Book of Genesis

Headings, Chapters, and Verses in the Bible

We speak of the Bible in casual terms. "There's a Bible over there, on the table," we say. We may be referring to a beautiful old King James Version, a big pulpit edition with metal clasps. Or perhaps the Bible on the table is a small, modern paperback edition printed on thin paper.

Let's pause here for a moment. Strictly speaking, is it correct to speak of "a Bible over there, on the table"? Not really, for the book we are pointing at is actually a translation of the Bible.

Let's take such a "Bible" in hand and open it. We find ourselves in the middle of the Letter to the Romans. When we page back to the beginning of the letter, we see the following words printed above it: "The Letter of Paul to the Romans." It all looks so nice and neat. But it would be a mistake to suppose that the apostle himself put those words above his letter. Neither this heading nor any of the other headings above 1 and 2 Corinthians, Galatians, Timothy, or Hebrews stems from Paul. They were all placed there later by other people.

If we page a little further in the Bible we use every day, we see that many of the books and letters it contains are divided into chapters, and the chapters into verses. There have been Bible readers who believed that these divisions within the text were introduced by the writers of the letters and books themselves, an illusion that must have had an adverse effect on their Bible reading. Again, it's not so. Originally the Bible was without these divisions into chapters and verses.

Are we suggesting that the divisions into chapters and verses be eliminated? They do have a certain practical value, for we can use them to refer to a particular passage we have in mind. By means of these numbers people can go right to the words and sentences we mean without having to read through a long passage to find them. We simply say, for example, "Look in chapter 4, verses 11 and 12."

But there is also something to be said against this system. In the old days, if someone wanted to refer to a passage in the letter of the apostle James, for example, he would first have to indicate in a few words what the apostle was talking about in that part of the letter. Only then could he zero in on the phrase or sentence he was referring to. Thus people had to be much more at home with the contents of the Bible than they are today. They had to remember the context in which the passage they were referring to occurred. When it became possible for people to mention only a few numbers (e.g., "Look in chapter 3, verses 5 or 6"), there was a much greater danger that Scripture would be quoted out of context. But enough on this subject of the division into chapters and verses. Suffice it to say that it's not an ideal system.

In the course of time there have been divisions other than the ones we now use. Jewish rabbis, early on, divided the Law into *parashot* (sections), while Greek writers of the fourth century introduced a series of *kephalaia* (headings or titles) into the Gospels.

Not until the thirteenth century was our division into chapters introduced. The division into verses came still later—probably not until the fifteenth century for the Hebrew Old Testament, and the sixteenth century for the Greek New Testament. And the new divisions were not accepted right away. Some writers, like Guido de Bres, the author of the Belgic Confession of the sixteenth century, used the chapter divisions but not the verse divisions. He used a different system instead. In his system, "a" meant that the sentence in question occurred in the first part of the chapter, "b" meant that it was somewhere in the middle of the chapter, and "c" that it was near the end of the chapter. A reference to Romans 5a, then, meant that you would find the sentence referred to somewhere in the first part of Romans 5. Through this method people were forced to bear the context in mind much more than when numbers are used for the verses.

But our present division into chapters and verses has been widely accepted. To not make use of this system would be foolish and lead only to confusion.

My main motive for discussing this matter here is to make it clear to the reader that these divisions should not be regarded as actually forming part of the Word of God. They are not worthy of such honor. In fact, there are even discrepancies between the numbers we assign to the various chapters and verses and the numbers used in the Hebrew edition: Leviticus 6:1–7, for example, is Leviticus 5:20–26 in the Hebrew Bible.

The Authorship of Genesis: Who, When, Where

Until now we have not focused on the book of Genesis. Instead we have talked about a larger whole of which this book forms a part—the Torah or Pentateuch. We observed that no one can be really sure who is responsible for the Pentateuch in its present form; we are given no information on this matter.

This is not an isolated phenomenon, for the same can be

said of various other parts of Scripture. This may well be due to prevailing literary customs in the ancient Semitic world. Anonymous writings are unusual in the modern world, but they seem to have been the rule in the ancient Near East.

Perhaps there are readers for whom this comes as something of a surprise. They may well want to hear a bit more about it. They may have been under the impression all their lives that Moses is the author of the entire Pentateuch because they so often have heard mention of "the five books of Moses" and "the Law of Moses" or simply "Moses." They have come to the conclusion that the entire Pentateuch—Genesis 1:1 through Deuteronomy 34:12—comes to us from the pen of Moses. But now this nice dream is shattered.

Yes, *dream* is the proper word for it. We saw earlier that an expression like "of Moses" does allow us to conclude that Moses had a great deal to do with the Pentateuch, if only because we are told so much about him there. We also saw that various parts of the Pentateuch are indeed identified as coming from Moses's hand. But this does not allow us to jump to the conclusion that he is the author of the Pentateuch as we now possess it. Think again of Deuteronomy 34, where we are told about the death of Moses. The fact that we are informed expressly that this or that passage was written by Moses can better be seen as an indication that Moses is not the author of the entire Pentateuch.

There are other considerations that come into the picture as well, such as the way certain place names are used in the Pentateuch. In Genesis 14:14 we find a reference to Dan, but in Judges 18:29 we learn that this northern city received the name Dan in the time of the judges, long after the death of Moses. It has also been pointed out that the background of Genesis 36:31 ("These are the kings who reigned in the land of Edom, before any king reigned over the Israelites") is clearly a time in which Israel already had kings, which would have to be a time long after the death of Moses. Let's take one more example from Genesis. In the account of the burial of the patriarch

Jacob, Abel-mizraim, a place east of the Jordan, is spoken of as lying "beyond the Jordan" (50:11), from which one might conclude that the person who wrote those words lived west of the Jordan. Since Moses was never west of the Jordan in his entire life, how could he have written those words?

It is true that arguments like these have more or less validity for various people. But we might also approach this issue from a little different angle and ask: Are we somehow called and obligated to acknowledge and defend the view that Moses is the author of the entire Pentateuch?

There have been scholars who thought so. The well-known German exegete, C. F. Keil, maintained Moses's authorship of the Pentateuch from the beginning of his commentary right to the end. In his concluding remarks he observed:

> With the exception of the last chapters of the fifth book, which are distinctly shown to be an appendix to the Mosaic *Thorah*, added by a different hand, by the statement in Deuteronomy xxxi. 24 sqq., that when the book of the law was finished Moses handed it over to the Levites to keep, there is nothing in the whole of the five books which Moses might not have written. (C. F. Keil and F. Delitzsch, *Biblical Commentary on the Old Testament*, trans. James Martin, vol. 3, *The Pentateuch* [Edinburgh: T&T Clark, 1867], 517)

It seems to me that this is going too far. Even though some scholars have gone much too far in arguing that Moses is not the author of some passage or other in Deuteronomy, Keil is going too far in the opposite direction. To defend his drastic conclusion, he has to say some drastic things about certain passages. He identifies the city of Dan referred to in Genesis 14:14 not as the Laish that is renamed Dan in Judges 18:29 but as the Dan in Gilead, mentioned in Deuteronomy 34:1. He sees the comment in Genesis 36:31, about there being kings in Edom even before there was a king ruling over Israel, as referring to Edomite kings in the time before Moses. As for a king in Israel, he explains this in terms of Moses's unshakable faith in the promise made to the patriarch Jacob that kings would be born of him one day (Gen. 35:11). We find this a pretty far-fetched interpretation.

If we embraced Keil's standpoint, we would also have to assume that Moses wrote the following comments about himself: "The man Moses was very great in the land of Egypt, in the sight of Pharaoh's servants and in the sight of the people" (Exod. 11:3). And this: "Now the man Moses was very meek, more than all people who were on the face of the earth" (Num. 12:3).

We know that people in ancient times were not as squeamish as they are today and were not at all shy about announcing their own virtues (think of how Homer's heroes praised themselves), but that a wise man like Moses would have written such lines about himself—no, that's a bit too much to swallow.

There are other scholars who join Keil in accepting the Law of Moses as part of Scripture but do not go along with him in regarding Moses as the author of the entire Pentateuch as we now possess it. G. C. Aalders, for example, does accept the Mosaic origin of part of the Pentateuch, but he believes that the time in which the Pentateuch received its present form could not have been any earlier than the reign of King Saul. J. de Groot speaks of the "Palestinian background" of the Pentateuch. A. Clamer, a Roman Catholic scholar, writes, "Doubtless this or that passage in the Pentateuch is to be ascribed to Moses, as we saw earlier, and nothing would seem more obvious than to recognize literary activity on the part of Moses; what we know about the literature of Egypt and Mesopotamia, of Mari and Ugarit, leads us to accept the talk of literary work of Moses handed down." But that's as far as Clamer goes (Louis Pirot and Albert Clamer, eds., *La Sainte Bible: texte latin et traduction française d'après les textes originaux: avec un commentaire exégétique et théologique*, vol. 1, *Genèse. Exode* [Paris: Letouzey,

1946], p. 56). P. J. Hoedemaker wrote an engaging study of the Mosaic origin of the laws in Exodus, Leviticus, and Numbers in which he lists many church fathers who already regarded the Pentateuch in its present form as postexilic, that is, as coming from the time after Judah's return from Babylonian captivity in 539 BC. Hoedemaker also mentions various seventeenth-century Reformed scholars who joined in the discussion of this question as to what extent and in what sense Moses can be regarded as the author of the Pentateuch.

Turning now to the book of Genesis, we see that there is quite a difference between this book and the other books that make up the Pentateuch. When we look at Exodus, Leviticus, Numbers, and Deuteronomy, we can see that some parts of them, at least, stem from Moses. There are passages that simply state this. But this is not the case with Genesis. The book itself gives us no indication of its authorship. Of course this does not rule out the possibility that Moses wrote some parts of Genesis.

On the basis of considerations mentioned earlier, it seems to me that we should conclude that Genesis in its current form does not come from Moses's hand. But this does not mean that Moses did not do some preparatory work toward this book during the time that he led Israel as her shepherd (Isa. 63:11). Whether he might have done so orally or in written form we just do not know, nor do we know what sources he might have had at his disposal. It is quite possible that in the days of Moses, Israel already possessed some very old written records that had been handed down from generation to generation.

That this may very well have been the case is illustrated by the Babylonian flood story of the priest Berossus, a contemporary of Alexander the Great. He reports that those who survived the flood took not only decorative gold and silver objects with them on board the ark but also some writings they wanted to preserve. This fits in with the repeated assurances in

Babylonian literature that there was indeed scholarship before the flood. King Assurbanipal liked to pride himself in reading stones that dated from the time before the flood.

Why would not Israel, and especially Moses, a man who had received an outstanding education at a school at the Egyptian court, have possessed and made use of very old written records as well? And if he did, we can understand that another person who lived much later, when Israel dwelled west of the Jordan, would gratefully have made use of Moses's preparatory work. But such a view cannot be proven, unfortunately.

If someone were to ask how to picture the process that led to the writing of the book of Genesis as we have it today, we would answer as follows. (Note that we are referring to the book of Genesis that now forms part of the Pentateuch.)

We believe that the Pentateuch consists of three parts:

A. an introduction, i.e., Genesis;
B. a central section, i.e., Exodus, Leviticus, and Numbers; and
C. a conclusion, i.e., the book of Deuteronomy.

First, some comments on part B. There is a great deal of material brought together in this central section of the Pentateuch, material that we are told stems from Moses himself. This must have come about through the work of one or more collectors, including perhaps Moses, who then shaped it into a whole. The order used was neither logical nor chronological. In other words, the material was not arranged in the kind of order we now prefer in a book. The intention was rather that everything that was useful would be included. The chief goal was completeness. By collecting in this way, the books of Exodus, Leviticus, and Numbers assumed their original form. This also explains why some subjects are dealt with more than once. The annual feasts, for example, are dealt with first in

Exodus 23:14–19, then in Exodus 34:18, 22–26, once again in Leviticus 23, and finally in Numbers 28 and 29. That's the sort of thing that can easily happen in a collection of writings.

This collection should be viewed as the core of the entire Pentateuch. The Pentateuch is to be seen as a work that was not brought into being first and foremost for us as twentieth-century readers, but for Israel. This collection of writings talks about the basis for Israel's existence; it describes how Israel was made the LORD's private possession. The Horeb covenant and the inauguration of the Levitical worship is the midpoint around which everything revolves.

When this great body of written material was finally there, or at least reached a certain stage prior to its present existence, it was obvious that the book of Deuteronomy should be added to it. We are not provided with any details about this course of events, but we do know that Moses wrote down the sermon he delivered in the plains of Moab and gave the written version to the Levites to be safeguarded in the ark. That was no doubt the beginning of our present book of Deuteronomy. But we know nothing more about the how and when. In any event, the book of Deuteronomy, perhaps after some editing, found its proper place as an epilogue for the collection of writings that we are familiar with as Exodus, Leviticus, and Numbers.

This great body of material still needed a prologue, an introduction. That prologue is Genesis.

Note that we are not trying to nail down the exact chronological order in which parts A, B, and C of the Pentateuch, or even their prototypes, were written. We can merely make educated guesses about this matter. My concern is much more with the contents of the various parts of the Pentateuch, and how their contents fit together. Genesis could just as well have been put together at the same time or even before the other parts of the Pentateuch. We do not intend to pass judgment here on this question.

Genesis has received a fitting place at the beginning of the Pentateuch, which is clear when we bear in mind the fact

already emphasized earlier that this book, or perhaps an earlier form or prototype, was not written first and foremost for
a reading public that lived after the birth of Christ, but for
people who lived long before then. Genesis was intended for
Israel. The book records the familiar traditions that had already been handed down from generation to generation about
the patriarchs as Israel's forefathers, God's covenant with the
patriarchs (especially Abraham), God's covenant with Noah,
and the saving of man and of other living creatures from the
flood. Genesis goes back even further and deals with the deep
corruption into which humanity had plunged itself. Finally,
it deals with the beautiful beginning of all things—the wholly
good creation—through which God was completely justified.

In the creation story we already have a clear indication
that it was written for Israel. The creation story is put into
perspective through an ordinance that Israel received from
the mouth of the LORD at Horeb, where Israel was told that
the people were allowed to rest every seventh day in imitation of their God, who also rested on the seventh day after six
days of creation. That was why later, at Horeb, God made the
seventh day Israel's Sabbath day or rest day, a day set apart
(sanctified) and blessed (Gen. 2:3).

This, in general outline, is how we should look at the origin of
the book of Genesis and its place in the Bible. But we have said
very little to this point about the nature of the book.

It is not to be denied that Genesis also has the character of
a collection. That may be the reason why the explanation of a
personal name or place-name is sometimes repeated (see, for
example, Gen. 21:31 and 26:33, where the name Beersheba is
explained). On the other hand, when we look at such examples,
we should not forget the widespread use of repetition in Semitic
literature as a matter of good style. Westerners do not appreciate
repetition, but Hebrew poetry makes extensive use of it. (Think
of the famous parallels between successive lines of verse.)

Hebrew prose also makes use of repetition. In the famous Table of Nations in Genesis 10—which is certainly a prosaic passage in Western eyes—we are told in verse 5, after the Japhethites are summed up, ". . . each with his own language, by their clans, in their nations." These words are repeated almost verbatim in verse 20, after the Hamites are summed up; again, in verse 31, after the Shemites; and once more, in verse 32, after all three sons of Noah are mentioned—four times in all.

We mention this in order to warn against too hasty an appeal to the repetition argument. But even if we eliminate repetition as an argument, the hypothesis that Genesis has something of the character of a collection is hardly a reckless one. Genesis 14, for example, gives the impression of being an independent document. It is generally regarded as a very, very old document.

Even though Genesis seems to have been put together originally as a collection, it is not a loosely composed work. The structure of the book betrays the presence of a mastermind. The person who put the book together may well have made use of various documents and sources, both oral and written, but he added his own exquisite touch to it. Therefore we should not deny Genesis its own character as an independent book, for it has its own unique and remarkable structure. We will have more to say about this matter later.

First, a few comments about the time and place of the book's origin. We cannot give a specific answer to the question of who is chiefly responsible for putting Genesis together as a book. Later we will see that the book of Genesis as we now possess it has such a unique structure and style that we cannot help but suppose that a single individual is behind its composition, someone who set his stamp on the book. But exactly when such a man might have lived we do not know. And even if we call him the author, it is possible that later editors changed things here or there and permitted themselves a few liberties. We do not know for sure whether there was any editing, and, if so, when it finally stopped.

We saw earlier that some scholars believe that the finishing touches were not put on Genesis until the time of the kings. Since Genesis bears the character of a prologue and was placed as a prologue to the main body of the Pentateuch when this was essentially complete, and since the completion of Exodus, Leviticus, and Numbers is not usually assigned an early date, scholars are generally inclined to look to a period some distance into the time of the kings as the time of the origin of Genesis.

We do not believe that it is possible to be certain the one way or the other about this matter. The Pentateuch no doubt underwent some growth and development. Surely it was not originally written in the form in which we now possess it. At the very least, we should leave open the possibility that some comments were inserted later for clarification. We will see that some later editors apparently did dare to make certain changes in the material.

But if we admit this, we are not ruling out the possibility that Moses is responsible—if not in formal respects, then surely in material respects—not only for the chief part of the Pentateuch (i.e., Exodus, Leviticus, and Numbers) but also for the conclusion (Deuteronomy) and the introduction (Genesis). We can easily imagine that someone with an education like the one Moses received and with a shepherd's heart would want to take care to take the words of God that had been directly entrusted to him and pass them on to later generations in pure form. In Joshua's time there already appears to have been a collection of "Mosaic laws" (see Josh. 1:8; 8:31). If this collection was assembled in Moses's own time, it seems entirely possible that Genesis was also written at that time as an introduction to these laws—or at least a preliminary version that included the main lines of the book.

It appears that we cannot be any more certain than this when we address the question of where the book of Genesis was written. As we saw earlier, there is a passage that suggests it was written west of the Jordan, within the promised land (see Gen. 50:10–11). However, this may be due to some editor working in Palestine who put the finishing touches on the book, which would not exclude the possibility that someone who lived before him had actually composed the book. We have no way of knowing whether that might have been Moses himself. This possibility should not be ruled out.

In the discussion earlier, we did not argue that Genesis was written only after the chief part of the Pentateuch (Exodus, Leviticus, and Numbers) had received its current form. The one certainly could have occurred simultaneously with the other. But we did not reject the first possibility entirely, namely, that Genesis was composed after Exodus, Leviticus, and Numbers.

The suggestion that Genesis is not the first book in terms of origin need not be a cause for amazement. It's all too easy to assume that the book with which the Bible opens, the one that deals with the very earliest events in human history, must also be the oldest. But a book that deals with very early events could have been composed either earlier or later than a book that deals with later events.

Take the New Testament as an example. It is generally accepted that the Letter of James is one of the oldest—if not in fact the oldest—of the writings included in the New Testament. It is older than the Gospels, for example. But this letter was not placed at the very beginning of the New Testament, before the Gospels. Instead it was placed close to the end, and the Gospels, which were written later, came first. The Gospels were put at the beginning because of their content, of course, for they tell us what happened to our Savior while he was on earth. What better place for them than at the beginning? But this does not tell us anything about when they were written.

The books of the Bible are not arranged in order of their age. Genesis could easily have been assigned its place as prologue after the large center of the Pentateuch (or at least an early form of Exodus, Leviticus, and Numbers) had already been written and after Deuteronomy had been added as an epilogue.

Finally, we should bear in mind that the matters under discussion here—the place and time of authorship—are not of ultimate importance, however much they might contribute to the understanding of Genesis. The most important thing we must concern ourselves with when reading Genesis is the question of what the book teaches us about God, and especially about how he brings fallen mankind back to life.

The Structure of Genesis

If we had to select an emblem to symbolize the book of Genesis, we would do well to choose a branch. Why a branch? Just take a look at one of the main branches on a tree, with the various branches and twigs that grow out of it in turn as offshoots. Look especially at the two-pronged forks you see wherever the branch and one of its offshoots divide. Those forks are worthy of attention; you find them wherever the new comes forth from the old.

But what about those buds themselves, which you can still see, for example, on a dead bamboo stick? Are we to view the bud as a beginning or an ending? Actually it is both, for where you find such a bud you have one piece of the branch ending and something new beginning.

The book of Genesis is like a branch with buds that signal a new beginning. Unfortunately, this is not so clear from the current form of the book, especially if you have to use a translation instead of reading the book in Hebrew. Your translated version will include the division into chapters and verses, which we discussed a little earlier, and the chapters and verses will draw your attention away from buds on the branch.

These divisions introduced in the book of Genesis did not

take those buds into account but tended to obscure them. Genesis did not need major divisions, for it already had them, but this fact seems to have escaped the people who broke the book up into chapters.

The man who gave Genesis its present form, which makes it one of the most beautifully arranged books of all, introduced ten transition points into the work. Those transition points are what make me think of the buds and forks on the branch of a tree. Because of them, Genesis really should be seen as comprising eleven parts, parts that fit together closely. The division markers should not be seen as introducing separations into the text. They can better be viewed as joints tying the parts of the book together.

Let's briefly survey those joints in the book of Genesis. If you take the trouble to mark them in red or blue in your Bible as we go through them, they will help you later in your reading.

The first joint comes in Genesis 2:4. What comes before is the account of the creation of heaven and earth, and what comes after is a story that makes it apparent what has become of this beautiful work of God. We learn what place God gave to man, how he elevated man and was good to him, and how he gave man the garden as his dwelling place and woman as his companion. But we also learn how these two good gifts were drawn into the rebellion that followed: it was in the garden and through the woman that man rebelled against the LORD, which led to God's curse striking the earth. Even despite God's redemptive breaking of the alliance between man and the devil, humanity split into a godless line and a God-fearing line—the descendants of Cain and the descendants of Seth. Dividing these two passages of Scripture, then, are the following words: "These are the *toledoth* of the heavens and the earth when they were created" (2:4).

The second transition comes in Genesis 5:1. There the writer throws in a reminder about what came before, namely, the beautiful creation of Adam. He speaks of Adam as the father of Seth, in whom God gave renewal and deliverance in the face of the wickedness of Cain and his line. But then he has to show how the seed of Seth showed contempt for God's grace. Seth's people intermarried with Cain's people.

The godlessness of humanity became so widespread that the LORD was sorry he had ever created man. He decided on the horrible punishment of the flood, but Noah found grace in the eyes of the LORD. Between the story of Seth and his originally pious generation and the story of the corruption and apostasy of Seth's line stands Genesis 5:1, which reads, "This is the book of the *toledoth* of Adam," that is, as father of the new line, the line that is saved, Seth's line. But then we see what came of that line.

The third transition comes in Genesis 6:9. Noah had found grace and God had begun anew. But during Noah's lifetime we have the beginning of the cursed line of Cain. In this we see a branching off: "These are the *toledoth* of Noah."

The fourth transition is 10:1: "These are the *toledoth* of the sons of Noah." What became of Noah's sons? Even after the flood upon the world that had been spared, there seems to have been apostasy in the human heart, right down to the farthest generation. A typical example is the building of the tower of Babel. Again there is an offshoot, a fork between two branches.

The fifth transition is 11:10: "These are the *toledoth* of Shem." The (Israelite) readers are asked to focus attention on Shem and his descendants. The line runs from Noah to Shem to Terah.

The sixth transition comes in 11:27: "Now these are the *toledoth* of Terah." But we need not look for a story about Terah here. That's not what Genesis gives us, nor does it tell us about all his descendants. It tells us only about that one son of Terah, Abraham. Through Abraham God again sent out a new branch, new life. He even promised that the descendants of Abraham would be a blessing to the peoples of the earth. Ishmael was also a descendant of Abraham, but the promise of blessings for the entire world through the descendants of Abraham was tied in with Isaac in a special way (21:12). Unfortunately, Ishmael was not willing to bow before this decision on God's part. Again the lines branched off in different directions.

The seventh transition (25:12) shows us where Ishmael came from and where he wound up: "These are the *toledoth* of Ishmael."

The eighth transition also focuses our attention on a further split: "These are the *toledoth* of Isaac" (25:19). The promise of serving as father to the many descendants through whom the world of nations would be blessed is now passed on to Jacob. This is a divine decision before which Esau does not wish to bow.

Therefore there must be a ninth transition: "These are the *toledoth* of Esau (that is, Edom)" (36:1). By way of a series of names that must have spoken much more clearly to the Israelite readers than it does to us, we are shown what became of Esau.

The thrust of the entire book of Genesis begins to become clear. Then the tenth transition: "These are the *toledoth* of Jacob" (37:2). From that point on, Genesis has very little to say about the other descendants of Adam and Noah. It focuses almost exclusively on the family of the patriarch Jacob, who found refuge in Egypt after following a path of much suffering. Then comes the transition to the next book, Exodus.

What we have presented above is a brief survey of the ten transitions or joints in the book of Genesis. We trust this survey is clear enough for you to be able to see what sort of division this first book of the Bible already contained before our present division into chapters and verses was introduced into it in such a careless way centuries later. The division into eleven sections that was already there was completely ignored. The remarkable structure of the book of Genesis was missed.

Were the men of the Septuagint aware of these divisions? It does not look that way. They must have had an excellent knowledge of the Hebrew language; otherwise, they would hardly have undertaken such a translation project. And there was no division of Genesis into chapters as yet to distract them and draw their attention away from the division that was already present.

If they did bear these divisions in mind, did they reflect them in the title they gave to the first book of the Bible? They gave it the name *Genesis*, a Greek word with an English counterpart, meaning origin or development. In selecting the name *Genesis*, were they trying to echo something of what they heard in the Hebrew word *toledoth*, which occurs in the ten passages mentioned previously?

We cannot be sure either way, but it does not seem likely. The full title they gave this book of the Bible was *genesis tou kosmou*, that is, the "genesis of the world." Since they seem to have been under the impression of the Greek mind, they would have understood the term *kosmos* (world) as referring to what we call the creation, that is, everything created. If this is indeed what they had in mind, we would have to conclude that they did not choose a very appropriate title, for we saw earlier that it was not the primary purpose of the first book of the Bible to inform the Israelites about the creation of heaven and earth. Genesis devotes relatively little attention to this matter.

But if our supposition is wrong and they did want to use the Greek name *Genesis* to echo the Hebrew *toledoth*, what then? If that was indeed the intention, we must still shake our heads, for the Greek word *genesis* is hardly a suitable rendering of *toledoth*. Yet the idea of *genesis* is not entirely foreign to the word *toledoth*, for it does contain the idea of "bringing forth." The Hebrew word *toledoth* means more than that, since it refers not just to the process of bringing forth (the genesis) but also to the result, that which is brought forth. If we wanted to translate the word *toledoth* into English, we probably would have to use two separate words to capture the two aspects, perhaps *genesis* and *product*.

Because the word defies translation, we must use a variety of terms to describe the idea. Some translations use the word *descendants*. It fits some contexts, but not all. When Genesis 2:4 speaks of "the *toledoth* of the heavens and the earth," we cannot very well translate, "the descendants of the heavens and the earth." The words *history* and *genealogy* and *generations* have also been used to translate *toledoth*. There are problems with some of these terms as well. Can we speak of "the history of Isaac" in Genesis 25:19 when most of that history is already behind us? And if a *toledoth* is simply the story or history of this or that person, why do we nowhere find the "*toledoth* of Abraham" and the "*toledoth* of Joseph," both of whom are dealt with at length in Genesis?

Perhaps we should consider leaving the word *toledoth* untranslated, just as some other Hebrew words are taken over into our Bibles untranslated (e.g., "shittim" wood in the KJV). Such words become part of our Christian vocabulary with surprising ease and speed. Think of such words as *Sabbath*, *Immanuel*, *parousia*, and *Christ*.

What would be the advantages of leaving *toledoth* untranslated? For one thing, Bible readers could not help being struck by the occurrence of this word. They would notice that this word comes up at various places in Genesis—ten in all. They possibly might underline it each time and thereby develop an appreciation of the structure and divisions in the Bible's first book. They probably would also notice that Genesis was trying to show its original (Israelite) readers what kind of a God the LORD is—in a word, the God of life. Was it not the LORD who was responsible for the astounding act of the creation of heaven and earth as a perfect world and who, after death and corruption had forced their way into this world, continued to watch over life, giving the human race, despite its repeated disobedience, new opportunities as new generations arose and also new perspectives that all pointed toward the one goal, the blessing of the entire world of the nations?

Maybe these perspectives would have broken through a bit more. It is not an exaggeration when we say that Genesis is all too often regarded as a book that anyone who has some interest in history thinks he could use to map out the entire family tree of the human race on a large sheet of paper. On the basis of these "genealogies" in Genesis, all sorts of interesting calculations could be made. Hypotheses have arisen regarding matters such as the age of the earth and the human race, as though the author of Genesis had written his book for exactly that purpose. The way he organized his book clearly testifies to an entirely different purpose. We will come back to this point later.

If in fact he had had the former purpose in mind (and there is nothing wrong with such a purpose in and of itself), he would have had to give us an entirely different kind of book. The question can be raised, for example, whether the genealogies are complete. Scholars have pointed out that it is not uncommon for such genealogies to skip a generation, as for example when a man dies before his father, with the result that the grandson becomes the direct heir of the grandfather. What reason do we have to suppose that the lists and family trees contain all the names through the ages? (We will discuss this matter further in connection with Gen. 11:10–32.)

We must not ascribe to the author of Genesis a plan that probably never entered his mind for a moment. The thrust of his work seems to indicate that he had entirely different purposes in mind: he wanted to give Israel instruction, *torah*. The people who had entered the Horeb covenant spelled out in the heart of the Torah (Exodus, Leviticus, and Number) and also in the epilogue to the covenant (Deuteronomy) were in need of instruction. To provide this, he wrote a prologue, an introduction to the four books mentioned above. The idea was not to tell Israel something new. The entire book contained the truth handed down from the fathers about the LORD and his work. The people were to read that work and hear it read. In this way, they would learn to trust in the reliability of the instruction they were being given. It was obviously within the scope of the author's rights to offer this instruction in the beautiful literary form that he gave to the book of Genesis.

CHAPTER 4

In the Beginning

By now the reader will have noticed that one of our cherished notions is that the entire Pentateuch, including the book of Genesis, was not written in the first place for readers who would live after Christ, but for ancient Israel. Hence a few comments in relation to the Sabbath are in order.

Written for the People for Whom the Sabbath Was Instituted

Men and women and children, large and small—all the Israelites at Mount Horeb—heard God's own voice when he proclaimed the ten words of the covenant. This unique event must have made an unforgettable impression on them (Exod. 20:18–21; Deut. 5:23–31).

Among these ten words was the fourth commandment, the one about the glorious Sabbath. Now, we do not find anything like the Sabbath among the pagans. The Sabbath was not an international institution and never became one either. The Sabbath had been instituted as a sign of God's covenant with Israel (Exod. 31:16–17), that is, as a sign of the Sinai covenant. The Sinai covenant with its beautiful Sabbath was one of the reasons Israel could sing, "He declares his word to Jacob, his statutes and rules to Israel. He has not dealt thus with any other nation; they do not know his rules. Praise the LORD!" (Ps. 147:19–20). The Sabbath had pervaded all of Israel's life; all "ecclesiastical" activities were based upon it. Think of the three great feasts, for example, which were true Sabbath feasts.

The pedagogical effect this Sabbath decree had on Israel should not be underestimated. The Sabbath spoke to the simplest of the Israelites. When the harvest season came, the heathen farmer would think to himself that all his toil and labor would induce Baal (whose name means "Lord") to provide a good future for him. But when the Sabbath day came during good harvest weather for the Israelite farmer, he could fold his arms and look out over his fields without running here and there. The LORD, who was truly God over heaven and earth, sun and rain and fields, was also his God. After Egypt, the LORD no longer wanted to see his people in the clutches of slavish labor. He wanted to call a regular halt to their work. Every seventh day the people on whom he had bestowed his love would rest, in imitation of their heavenly Father: "In six days the LORD made heaven and earth, and on the seventh day he rested and was refreshed" (Exod. 31:17).

In Israel's later history, unfortunately, and also among the Christians, people lost sight of the true character of this Sabbath command. The Sabbath day became a trial, an irritant, which was directly contrary to its original purpose. Moses, apparently, was highly esteemed, but the commentary he gave on the commandments, including the fourth, the one about the Sabbath (Deut. 15:1–16:17), which was so full of healthy insight and wise counsel, was ignored.

If there was anyone who was acquainted with God's purposes, surely it was Moses. He had certainly spoken often with the LORD person to person. We should bear in mind especially that Moses's explanation and application of the fourth commandment does not even use the word *Sabbath*. The only place in the book of Deuteronomy where the word *Sabbath* is used is in 5:12–15, where the fourth commandment is quoted.

It may seem strange that the word *Sabbath* is not used elsewhere in Deuteronomy, but that was a freedom Moses could take. He was indeed that familiar with God's purposes. Yes, he even took the liberty of changing the words God had used at Horeb: "Rest on the seventh day, for that's what I did after six days of creating." Moses took the reminder about the creation that God had used, and substituted his own reminder about God's great deeds in Egypt, about the time when the LORD delivered Israel from slavery, from succumbing to death and the grave. "Therefore keep the Sabbath!" Moses declared. "Be thankful for the life the LORD gave you, the life he spared." Because God's children are precious to him, he does not want to see them working continuously. He is like a husband who says to his busy wife in the evening, "It is enough."

The explanation Moses gives of the Sabbath commandment in Deuteronomy 15 and 16 is gospel through and through. Love speaks in this explanation. Because the LORD loved you, he delivered you from Egypt's house of bondage, so show your gratitude by walking the path of love to others. For example, be good to your poverty-stricken countrymen. Be faithful in bringing the LORD the first fruits, to which he has a double right since the days in Egypt. Appear with full hands before the face of your God on the appointed feast days, to praise him and to support the priests and Levites, who are his servants.

That was the place that Moses—expressing God's intentions—assigned to the Sabbath in Israel. It was a very high place indeed, for the Sabbath was to be a sign of the covenant for every day, every week, and every season and year. The Sabbath was to be at the very center of Israel's life—in her heart and thoughts.

⟳

We have already made it clear that we do not ascribe Genesis—at least in its original form—entirely to Moses. We see no need to argue for Moses as author through thick and thin. On the other hand, we did leave open the possibility of Mosaic authorship. Suppose Moses is indeed the author of Genesis. Then it should not surprise us at all that Genesis already speaks of the Sabbath on its very first pages (see 2:3). Moses could well have been the one who chose to look at the events of Genesis 1 from a Sabbath perspective.

But if someone other than Moses is the author of Genesis in its early form, the mention of the Sabbath at the very beginning of the book is still a highly remarkable fact. What we encounter here, then, is an unmistakable Israelite emphasis, the strongest such emphasis conceivable. The stamp of the Sabbath is placed on every day and all of life! This early Sabbath reference is an eloquent indication of what was to be the main theme of Exodus, Leviticus, and Numbers: the calling of all the Israelites to serve the Deliverer of their lives with grateful hearts.

The author of Genesis knew the audience he was writing for. He was writing for the Israelites, for the people of the Sabbath. Hence a short reference to the Sabbath made in passing was sufficient: "So God blessed the seventh day [at Horeb] and made it holy, because on it God rested from all his work that he had done in creation" (2:3).

The World of the Story

"A short reference to the Sabbath made in passing," we just said. We also pointed out that it was not the intention of the author of Genesis to tell his readers anything they had not heard before. But perhaps there are some who would like to hear a bit more about this.

We are strongly convinced that even without the written instruction provided in the form of the Torah, the Israelites had a certain amount of knowledge of their own history and of the history of other peoples. Israel was part of the Semitic family of nations in what we now call the Near East. Despite all the military and political maneuvering, those nations were strikingly similar to one another in mores and customs. Apparently not even the modern "blessings" of the West (technology, the press, radio, etc.) have been able to put an end to these similarities.

Just think, then, of how things must have been in the days when there was still very little—or nothing—being written down on papyrus and animal skins and clay tablets. Those days must have been the golden age for the great storytellers of the ancient Near East.

The people of the ancient Near East loved stories, stories, and more stories. The stories told were always typically Eastern and generally moved along at a pace too slow to suit us. But in the thirsty lands where such stories originated, they were received like cold water on a hot day.

For example, there were the names of previous generations. We can be sure that the Israelites, in typical Near Eastern style, knew the names of their forefathers and that they carefully preserved the patriarchal stories century after century and carried those stories century after century with them as the very flesh and bones of their history. People of the Western world might be inclined to be skeptical or dubious about such assertions, for we are often indifferent about our ancestry. There are many people who hardly know the names of their eight great-grandparents. Do you know yours?

You can still meet people in the Near East today who can recite lists of ancestors. Inscriptions and documents have been found that contain extensive family records. Even the wandering Bedouins in the desert near Syria have kept careful track of their ancestors. Some of the documents go all the way back before the time of Christ.

Israel shared the earliest phases of her history with the nations around her. The memory of those days was probably kept alive among the Israelites by the power of the story, a power that is still operative in families today and should not be underestimated. That power must have been very prominent indeed by ancient Israel's homes and city gates. Moreover, despite the isolation of the Israelites, Scripture makes it clear that they did have contact with the trade routes along which the caravans passed. We can be sure that when the travelers sat around their campfires at night, they exchanged stories with the Israelites. An Old Testament scholar, W. H. Gispen, even delivered a lecture once on "Israel's compulsion to tell stories."

That Israel's own history was not entirely unknown to the nations around her is apparent from the story of Jephthah. When Jephthah, at the beginning of his career as judge, reminded the Ammonites of the story of the Israelites' conquest of the land east of the Jordan, he was presupposing a certain amount of knowledge of these events and hoping that this brother nation that had always been so hostile to Israel would see things his way (Judg. 11).

At God's own command, storytelling assumed a fixed place in Israelite circles at the annual celebrations of the Passover (Exod. 12:26–27). We read similar commands in Deuteronomy 6:7 and Psalm 78:3–4. Think also of Israel's priests. These men not only had cultic duties that we can discuss in connection with Leviticus; they also had the task of instructing the people in the words and deeds of the LORD, in remembrance of his name (Exod. 20:24; Pss. 45:17; 105:1). How could they have carried out these duties apart from oral instruction? We think also of the difficult cases involved in the administration of justice, for such cases could also be brought to the priests (Deut. 17:8–13). The judgment rendered would not be handed down in dry, legal language, as in our society: "In accordance with Article 38, Section 4 . . ." Instead of this dry, administrative approach, the case at issue would be judged in relation to the concrete history handed down in oral tradition.

We can be sure that storytelling also played a very important role in Israel when it came to preserving the treasure of the Word. For centuries it was kept in the holy safe-deposit box of believing Israel's memory, which was a secure place of refuge for it since the Israelites, unlike modern Westerners, had to make heavy use of memory.

We have also seen that it is generally accepted that the relatively early possession of written documents on the part of Israel and the patriarchs is not to be ruled out. True, we do not know anything concrete about such a written inheritance. We have no idea how many there may have been, how old they may have been, and what subjects they may have dealt with. But such an inheritance does seem to shine through in Scripture here and there in a natural way.

In Numbers 21:14, for example, we find that a quotation is drawn from "the Book of the Wars of the LORD." This is done in a natural, rather casual manner in passing. Scholars suggest that this book was a collection of songs. That may well be. What nation is there that has not used songs as an outstanding means of giving instruction in history? And Genesis 14, the story of how Abraham freed Lot, has sometimes been viewed as a document that first existed on its own and then was made part of Genesis. Thus it would be a Palestinian document! Even this should not be thought to have been impossible.

In recent years, the labors of archaeologists in Palestine have yielded results that make it abundantly clear that there is no reason to think of ancient Palestine and related cultures as primitive. Moreover, we should not forget that when Moses did the written work that somehow played a role in the birth of the Pentateuch, the palaces of Mesopotamia and Egypt already contained extensive archives. And Moses was "instructed in all the wisdom of the Egyptians" (Acts 7:22). Since Egypt, for centuries on end, laid claim to sovereignty over Palestine, imagine the geographical and ethnological knowledge of Palestine that an Egyptian prince like Moses must have possessed even before he got anywhere near the promised land.

It would be good for us to keep all these things in mind. Whether Moses is the primary author behind the book of Genesis or not, they are relevant. It may really be that the preparatory work done by Moses was later used by someone in Palestine to put the book of Genesis into the form in which we now possess it.

The Reason for the Writing

Because of the remarkable structure of the book of Genesis, we have argued that it should be thought of in terms of a single individual or author who set his stamp on the book. Therefore we have spoken simply of the "author of Genesis." Whether it was Moses or someone else we do not know. Later changes in the book made when Israel was already living west of the Jordan have somewhat blurred the original stamp set on the book.

At this point a question naturally arises: What drove this author to the work of writing Genesis? We must be careful not to misunderstand this question, for it does not ask about God's motive for the appearance of the book of Genesis. We need not be in the dark about God's motive for even a moment. The apostle Peter writes, "The prophets who prophesied about the grace that was to be yours searched and inquired carefully" (1 Pet. 1:10). In his second letter he speaks even more directly: "We ourselves heard this very voice borne from heaven, for we were with him on the holy mountain. And we have the prophetic word more fully confirmed, to which you will do well to pay attention as to a lamp shining in a dark place, until the day dawns and the morning star rises in your hearts, knowing this first of all, that no prophecy of Scripture comes from someone's own interpretation. For no prophecy was ever produced by the will of man, but men spoke from God as they were carried along by the Holy Spirit" (2 Pet. 1:18–21). And when Paul wrote to Timothy about the sacred

Scriptures given by the inspiration of God's Spirit, he must have been thinking first of all of the book of Genesis, for it was from Genesis that he derived his knowledge of the first Adam, Christ's counterpart, whom he so often mentioned in his letters (Rom. 5:12–14; 1 Cor. 15; 1 Tim 2:13–14).

The writer of Genesis was also used by the Holy Spirit as his instrument, the Spirit who testified of the suffering and glory that would come upon Christ (1 Pet. 1:11). He, too, was used by God "for our instruction, that through endurance and through the encouragement of the Scriptures we might have hope" (Rom. 15:4). But this divine motive does not exclude the possibility of inquiring into particular human motives that may have played a role in moving the author of Genesis to take up his work.

What reason did the author of Genesis have, then, for writing such a book? We do not have the same certainty here that we have with regard to God's motive, but there are at least two considerations we should bear in mind.

To begin with something general, what gives the hearts of believers greater delight than seeing their children walk in the path of the truth (3 John 4)? Here we should understand the word *children* in the broader Near Eastern sense, which includes *disciples*. What God-fearing father or pious teacher in Israel did not want to teach his children in such a way that they would come to know the LORD and learn to cling to him? Abraham did so (see Gen. 18:19). Moses gave orders that this be done (Deut. 6:7; 11:19), and he did it himself, as we see from the book of Deuteronomy as a whole. And what if that same Moses was the author of Genesis? The possibility cannot be ruled out.

Thus we should seriously consider the possibility that Genesis was written for "children." A number of questions would not seem nearly as forbidding if this possibility were simply taken seriously once. Think of it: Genesis written for children to keep them near the LORD and his covenant and his people! This could already be reason enough why the writer of Genesis should choose to write such a book.

In the second place, there is something more particular to bear in mind. If the writer of Genesis was none other than Moses, we may attribute to him great knowledge of the geography and people of Palestine, as we saw earlier. But if it was not Moses himself, but someone who had actually lived in the land Moses yearned to see, the author would have seen with his own eyes the urgency and necessity of sounding a warning against the danger to God's people in those days, that is, the danger of Canaanite religion. This could have been a second, more concrete reason for writing Genesis.

This possibility is drawing a good deal of attention nowadays. In earlier eras people were not exactly ignorant of the ancient Canaanite world, but in our day much more information is available than before. (We will have more to say about this in connection with the book of Exodus.)

At this point a few observations are in order about the origin of Canaanite religion and what that religion is related to. Canaanite religion is one of the branches of an enormous religious stream that spilled into Palestine from the East. Striking similarities have been found between the Assyrian and Babylonian tales of the gods and goddesses, on the one hand, and the ones that circulated in Canaan, on the other. Excavations have brought some remarkable things to light. They have shown us what was believed in the Mesopotamian world about the origin of the gods and of the world from primordial material, and about a great flood. At the same time they have proved that the Babylonian creation story and flood story were known far and wide in the ancient world. Moreover, there were many peoples who believed that original principles of good and evil stood over against each other in the beginning and continued to do battle with each other to gain dominance in the world and over men.

According to the ancient Babylonians, the gods came forth from Apsu and Tiamat. Apsu was the original primordial ocean, while Tiamat was the sea conceived of as a monster. The god Marduk engaged in a titanic struggle with Tiamat, whom he overpowered and killed. He then created the earth from pieces of her body. There is good reason to suppose that such ideas penetrated the land of Canaan at an early stage and were in circulation when the Israelites arrived there.

The Epic of Gilgamesh, which is familiar to many people even in our time, is a poem about heroic figures, among whom Gilgamesh is central. The Epic of Gilgamesh included a flood story that was not just found in the library of King Assurbanipal of Assyria virtually in its entirety, but was also found in Sumerian, early Babylonian, Assyrian, and Hittite fragments. This shows that the Epic of Gilgamesh was known for a period of at least fifteen centuries in Mesopotamian cultural circles, an area that stretched all the way from Asia Minor to the Persian Gulf.

What does this mean for the land of Canaan in particular? One scholar has observed that one of the most important archaeological discoveries in Palestine itself is the finding of a tablet in the ruins of Megiddo with part of the Gilgamesh epic in Middle Assyrian script. This discovery showed that this poem was indeed directly known in pre-Israelite Canaan, which raises the possibility that the ancient Israelite writers (and we think immediately of the author of the stories in Genesis) oriented themselves in relation to this material in order to oppose these ideas.

Could the chief author of Genesis have been driven by a polemical motive, then? Could this have been one of his reasons for writing? We should at least take this possibility into account seriously. The author of Genesis may well have been doing battle with the spirit of the age. He may have been opposing the Babylonian and Canaanite spirit, which can really be regarded as one and the same, given the great cultural unity of the ancient Near East. It may be that he wanted to assure his own children and his people that the world did not begin with a chaos or with primordial matter from which the gods (*'elohim*) were then brought forth, but that God (*'Elohim*), whom the Israelites later came to know as the LORD, had created heaven and earth (Gen. 1:1–2). Then he could go on to show that the sun, moon, and stars did not have to be worshiped as though they were gods. They were only created entities and had been given to man by the LORD so that they could serve man in indicating the seasons, days, and years (1:14). It was not supposed to be the other way around: man was not supposed to serve the sun, moon, and stars.

At any rate, this is a possibility to be considered as we read Genesis. Perhaps this was a special motive for the man who gave the creation account a place at the very beginning of his book.

But who was this man? Was it Moses himself? As a well-educated "Egyptian," he would have been familiar with the Canaanite religious world. Or was it an Israelite living in Palestine? Such a man would have known the Canaanite religion even better.

In any event, we know the author was a man who celebrated the Sabbath every week, a man who was familiar with the covenant sign between the LORD and Israel that put its stamp on all of Israel's life, as long as Israel followed the right path. But Israel did not always follow the proper route. There were already complaints about laxity even in the days of Moses and Joshua. Thus there was good reason to warn the church of the future and to strengthen her by assuring her of the reliability of the ancient truths that had been preserved intact in the treasure chest of the memory of the forefathers, and to fortify this memory all the more powerfully by writing down these ancient stories.

The Heading (Gen. 1:1)

"In the beginning, God created the heavens and the earth." These words, which may represent the best-known sentence in all of Scripture, actually form a heading. The heading tells us what subject the first part of Genesis deals with.

Does this heading say anything about an original chaos? In Christian circles the view has slowly begun to take hold that God first, in an instant, created a great chaos and then, over a period of six days, brought rank, order, and structure into the creation. On this view, the real creation activity of God did not take six days but was actually completed in that instant.

Scripture, however, does not speak of the world as created in an instant. And on Mount Horeb God spoke of the work he did during those six days of creation. That should be good enough for us. If the writer of Genesis could hear us using the word *chaos* in connection with creation, we can certainly imagine that he would look disappointed and ask, "Surely you do not want to go in the Babylonian direction?"

The writer of Genesis simply speaks of "the heavens and the earth" without any further explanation. Thus he assumed that his Israelite readers and hearers would immediately understand what he meant. But do we understand him? When you hear these words, does not the concept of "the universe," a term we use daily and also read regularly in the newspaper, come to mind? The ancient Hebrews did not even have a word for "universe."

What is meant by "the heavens" is not explained directly—neither here nor elsewhere. The author did not regard this as necessary, as we saw earlier. But from 1:8 we can gather what he had in mind: by "the heavens" he meant the firmament. And what he meant by the earth becomes clear from verse 10: he meant the dry land.

Because we are modern people, it takes us a little while to get accustomed to such usages. Whenever we hear the word *earth*, we think of the entire globe. The Hebrew word used in this passage is *'erets*. When a simple farmer's son like Gideon (and Genesis 1 was written for simple people) heard the word *'erets*, he thought of the ground beneath his feet. In Judges 6 we read that the ground (*'erets*) under Gideon's feet remained dry, while the fleece became wet; the LORD saw to it that the situation was reversed the next night at Gideon's request.

There are many places where our English versions translate *'erets* as "land." Here is one: "The land [*'erets*] shall not be sold in perpetuity, for the land is mine" (Lev. 25:23). What if we were to translate *'erets* as "land" in Genesis 1:1? "In the beginning, God created the sky and the land." Is there anything wrong with that translation?

Just try reading the heading above Genesis 1 this way. The author was not telling his public (children, farmers' sons, and so forth) about a primordial chaos or a globe; he was simply saying that the sky and clouds that people looked up to night and day in Palestine, and also the land from which Israelite fathers and mothers and children lived and harvested were created by God "in the beginning."

Perhaps someone would want to interject, "But if the author of Genesis wanted to warn his Israelite readers against Babylonian fantasies about chaos and gods arising from the chaos, why was not he more direct about it? Why did not he call a spade a spade?" It is entirely understandable that someone would ask such a question. In response we would point out that the Israelites had been commanded not to mention the names of the idols if they could possibly avoid it (see Exod. 23:13; Ps. 16:4). Beyond that, perhaps the error could be overcome best by remaining silent about it and instead speaking the truth.

The Transition (Gen. 1:2)

The first verse of Genesis, as we have seen, is to be read as a heading to the creation story. But before the author proceeds with the creation story, he makes a remark that is also intended to be of an introductory character. That remark is Genesis 1:2.

We would propose to translate this verse, placing a few

words in parentheses, as follows: "Now that land (at first, indeed) was desolate and empty. Also, there was (indeed) darkness above (the) flood. But (fear not, for) the Spirit of God rose up (high and mighty) above the water." That's how we would translate this text, and this also shows how we would interpret it. But there is more to be said about what the author wanted to get across in this text.

Genesis 1:2 talks further about the *'erets*—not the heavens, then, but the earth, for all people need to live on the earth and from the earth. Thus he first says something more about the earth. He will come back to the heavens later.

God had to make the *'erets* habitable for man. Without his creating hand, we would not have been able to live upon the *'erets*. Not even animals or plants could have lived there, for at the outset the *'erets* was uninhabitable—desolate and barren. There was not yet a division between ground water and rain water, and there was no light. These conditions for life did not appear by themselves. God had to take care of that.

He did all this faithfully. When we speak here of the flood (*tehom*) and the water (*mayim*), we should not think in terms of that gruesome Babylonian story about a Tiamat, even if that word is related to the Hebrew word *tehom* and reminds us of it.

We should not believe in a frightening primordial mass from which both gods and men arose through a horrible battle. That's all speculation, fantasy, even if some elements of the truth are interwoven with it. Though some truth was passed on, its form was twisted. The simple truth is that the *'erets* was uninhabitable at first—barren, dark, unproductive. But this does not mean that God had to conduct a horrible war against a dangerous power. No, the Spirit of God was ready to make a beginning of his work. Even today, all creatures owe their continuing life and existence to him (Job 33:4; Pss. 33:6; 104:30). He was "*merakhephet* above the water."

This is the same sort of language we might use in connection with a bird. Think of how the eagle proudly soars high in the sky over our heads. That's how it was with the Spirit of God. There was no need to do battle with any primordial monster of chaos or mass of water. There is no such suggestion of this in Genesis. Unshakably powerful as he rose up above the work of his hands, he was ready to shape the relationship between earth and water in such a way that we could live here as human beings among many other creatures.

Genesis 1:2 should be read as a postscript to the heading of Genesis 1:1 and, at the same time, as a transition to the creation story itself. We will now find out how God made the earth a suitable dwelling place for humanity.

The Story Itself (Gen. 1:3–2:3)

Yes, a dwelling place for humanity. Just as verse 2 was not focusing on the heavens but rather on the earth—the land—the verses that come after it are not about the sun and moon and stars in general or about other creatures great and small, but are intended to lead up to the human race. Genesis tells us about things that concern humanity: Eve and Paradise (ch. 2), and the initial rebellion (ch. 3), and so forth. By way of the history of the patriarchs, it prepares us for the story of Israel at Horeb.

Among Israel and for it, the work of God through which he made the earth habitable is now described for us in Genesis 1. Thus it follows an order of seven, the very order of which God himself had spoken at Horeb: "In six days the LORD made heaven and earth, the sea, and all that is in them, and rested on the seventh day." In this respect there is no difference between Genesis 1 and Exodus 20:8–11.

Genesis 1 thus speaks of a first day, a second day, a third day, a fourth day, and so forth. The author uses these numerals as ordinal numbers, then. With each day, part of God's works is explained. But the author did not pretend that his account was complete or exhaustive. Who could ever compile a complete catalogue of everything God did "in the beginning"? Even if we limited ourselves to the *'erets*, it would be impossible. Of course there were many more things that happened than what we read about in Genesis 1. Genesis simply surveys these events, touching only on the main points.

The writer uses the word *create*. It has become customary to reserve the word *create* for the events described in Genesis 1. This custom no doubt stems from a distinction that has been drawn, a distinction that really amounts to a separation of the creation of God from the providence of God.

The doctrine of providence as now understood has been promoted considerably by what we read in the Heidelberg Catechism. Lord's Days 9–22 give us an explication of the Apostles' Creed, article by article. The Catechism goes about it somewhat freely, not always limiting itself to what the particular article under discussion deals with. For example, the Answer to Question 57 ("What comfort does the resurrection of the body offer you?") not only deals with the resurrection of the body but goes on to talk about "the soul," even though the Creed itself says nothing about soul and the Catechism's own question did not raise the subject either.

Even more remarkable is what the Catechism does in connection with Question 26 ("What do you believe when you say: 'I believe in God the Father, Almighty, Maker of heaven and earth'?"). As in the case of Question 57, the words to be explained are set off in quotation marks. But Question 26 is followed by two questions about "the providence of God." The Catechism, however, does not set this phrase off in quotation marks, and for a good reason: the Apostles' Creed does not speak of "providence" any more than it speaks of "the soul." Thus the Catechism is somewhat free here.

What if Lord's Day 9 (Question 26) and Lord's Day 10 (Questions 27 and 28) had been made one unit? Then we would have one Lord's Day devoted to the first part of the Creed, the part that deals with God as Creator. That way we would stick much closer to the text of the Creed we are supposed to explain, and the word *providence*, which most likely is pagan in origin, could be avoided. The good things of which Lord's Day 10 speaks could then be placed under the heading of the scriptural term *create*.

We should not get the impression that what the Scriptures mean by the word *create* is something that God does not do any more today. It may be understandable that some people think along such lines, but this view finds no support in Scripture and is in fact contradicted by Scripture. The word *bara'*, which means "create" and is used in the Bible in relation only to God, does appear a number of times after Genesis 1:1 (in 1:27; 2:3; 5:1–2; and 6:7) and not just to remind people of God's work as Creator as explained in Genesis 1. It is used in relation to creation in Isaiah 40:26 and 28, but in other passages it applies to later work on God's part (see Ps. 51:10; Isa. 45:7; 65:17–18; Jer. 31:22; Amos 4:13). From this we learn that what the LORD did (according to Genesis 1) and still does (from moment to moment he makes air for us, waters the mountains from on high, and causes grass to grow for the animals, as we learn from Ps. 104:13–14, 30) may all be referred by way of that one word, *create*.

It would have been much better if Lord's Days 9 and 10 of the Heidelberg Catechism had taken this approach, for we are always best off when we stick close to the language of Scripture. There is also this difference, that Genesis 1 speaks of the beginning of God's works. That's why the author used "In the beginning" for a heading. And he ends the story by telling us that the world as we see it around us, with all its regularities and ordinances for nature, was made by God "in the beginning." God continues to work with both the heaven and the earth to make the earth a dwelling place for plants, animals, and people. All this activity began with Genesis 1.

It was in this way that God created the heavens and the earth, making the land suitable for human habitation. It was especially the latter point that the author of Genesis wanted to get across to Israel. He did so in a way that must have appealed to the Israelites as poetic. Listen to the repeated refrain: "And there was evening and there was morning, the (first, second, etc.) day." (The evening is mentioned first in accordance with Israelite custom.)

Such repetition was appealing to Semitic ears. The busy Westerners of our time, people of paper and pencils and numbers, would no doubt want to make a short factual report of Genesis 1: "On the first day this; on the second day that . . ." The narrative style of Genesis wins little appreciation in the Western world. But we saw earlier that we must leave room for a variety of literary styles and tastes.

Here we have the answer to the question Israel must have asked, "Where did it all come from?" When the Israelites looked around them, before they arrived in Canaan and afterward as well, they saw God's work everywhere. First of all, they saw the light. Ask someone from the East sometime what light is. They simply abhor the darkness.

The Israelites also admired the rain and dew God sent; without such moisture, a land like Palestine would dry up during certain seasons of the year. They saw the streams and creeks and rivers that refreshed the land and were connected with the ground water, which is indispensable for the growth of trees. They saw shining heavenly bodies. Yet they did not speak of them in astronomical language as "heavenly bodies": they referred to them simply as the sun and the moon. Sometimes they even used the word *moon* in the plural, no doubt because there is always a "new" moon that appears (Deut. 33:14). They were also familiar with the stars in the sky. They viewed the sun, moon, and stars as servants of God, assigned to give man light (Ps. 119:91).

But they were not to bow down in worship before this "host of heaven." God had handed over "all the peoples under the whole heaven" to such practices (Deut. 4:19; see also Rom. 1:25), but Israel was to view the rising and setting of the sun as a work of God and was not to worship the moon-god Sin. Instead they were to believe that day and night, God gave them what they needed. All these things were set underway "in the beginning": they were "framed" by God (see Heb. 11:3 KJV).

But when the Israelites looked at the creatures around them, they asked not only where they came from; they also asked, How? Genesis gave them the answer. The people had heard it with their own ears at Horeb (in the fourth commandment), and now the same answer was given to them by the author of Genesis in more detail.

This man who composed his book so capably gave them a beginning that was not lacking in style and narrative continuity. He explained how God had made a beginning in his six great works by causing the light to shine, giving a place to the dew and the clouds, creating food for creatures to come, and ordering night and day and the seasons. With poetic elegance the author leads us ahead as though we were climbing a stairway to the climax, God's purpose.

That climax or purpose is indicated toward the end of our passage, when the creation of the human race is mentioned. As we reread the passage, we see that the author has been leading us to this from the beginning. The light was given for humanity (Gen. 1:3–5); dew and rain made the land inhabitable for humanity (vv. 6–8); grain and fruit trees were made to grow on the land to provide food for humanity (vv. 11–13, 29); the lights in the sky had to serve to indicate the times, days, and years of humanity (vv. 14–19); and humanity is given dominion over the creatures of both the water and the land (v. 26), of whose creation we read in verses 20–23 and verses 24–25.

Everything is prepared for humanity. That was how the Israelites were to speak of creation and humanity. "You have made him [man] a little lower than the heavenly beings and crowned him with glory and honor. You have given him dominion over the works of your hands; you have put all things under his feet" (Ps. 8:5–6). The LORD did not create the world to be empty but so that humanity could dwell in it (see Isa. 45:18).

The Main Thrust of the Story

There are two things here that must be distinguished: God's purpose in creating the heavens and the earth, and the purpose of the author of Genesis in describing these things. God's purpose was to work toward the creation of humanity; he was paving the way toward the human race as he performed those great deeds on the five or six days.

But when the author of Genesis began to describe these things and tell us about them, he also had a purpose in mind. What was that purpose?

He tells us the purpose himself when he reaches the seventh step. According to some manuscripts, Genesis 2:2 is to be read as "When God finished the work on the sixth day" instead of ". . . on the seventh day." But this question should not cause us any problems. The author tells us in any case that when God had finished his work and surveyed it all, his eyes found nothing wrong with it. It was very good (1:31). And "he rested on the seventh day from all his work that he had done" (2:2).

Here God's first works are described, and also the rest he enjoyed. But what comes after that? More information about the creation? No, the author now has a chance to do what teachers like to do when they come to a break, namely, point to a lesson. (The author does the same thing in 2:24, after the creation of Eve.) And what is the lesson here?

The lesson drawn from Genesis 1 is that this is how it came to be that God (at Horeb) blessed the seventh day (for us) and sanctified it (2:3). There you have the direction in which the book of Genesis immediately points its Israelite readers: Horeb. It reminds them of the story of the burning bush, when God said to Moses that from then on he would be known in Israel as the LORD (see Exod. 3). Is also reminds them of the covenant made between the LORD and Israel, and of the Sabbath as the sign of that covenant. Only Israel was given this sign (Neh. 9:14; Ezek. 20:12).

This God Is the LORD

The believing Israelites must have listened eagerly and attentively to such language, and also to what followed it. A moment ago we mentioned the name Yahweh. We will deal with this name at some length in connection with the book of Exodus. For the present we will make only a few observations.

We learn from Exodus 6 that God did not make himself known to the patriarchs as Yahweh. (The name Yahweh appears in most English translations of the Bible as LORD.) The first one to hear about the name Yahweh was Moses (Exod. 3). In effect the meaning of this name was a short summary and reminder of Israel's deliverance form Egypt. There especially, God manifested his power and might; he showed that he is the Living One. In the name Yahweh, the gospel of those days came to expression in concentrated form.

It was God's express desire to be known among the Israelites especially by this name from then on. Because this name was so widely used, it crept into the old stories about the days of the patriarchs as they were told and retold in Israel. Strictly speaking, the use of the name Yahweh in those stories was an anachronism, but the name penetrated the tradition anyway, whether oral or written. Thus the occurrence of the name Yahweh or LORD in the Bible before Exodus 3 need not puzzle us.

But there is something more to be said. We are now at the end of the first section of Genesis, the one that runs from 1:1 through 2:3. This section is separated from the second section by 2:4, where the word *toledoth* occurs for the first time.

Genesis 2:4 is the first joint. But in this joint we find a word making its very first appearance in the Bible—the name Yahweh or LORD. Why does this name first come up here?

It seems likely that the author of Genesis had a pedagogical reason for this. In the previous verses he had referred to God by way of the name *Elohim*. Elohim, in the Semitic world, is a word widely used for God. There is some variation in pronunciation: among the Arabs, the word eventually became *Allah*.

It was the obvious thing for the author to use the customary Semitic name for God in the early verses of Genesis. He was presenting a creation story that had originally belonged to all nations, although it later became more and more of a Semitic story, undergoing severe distortion in the process. (Think of the fantastic creation story of the Babylonians.) Only in Israel was the truth about the creation preserved intact, in its simple form without adornment. The story related in Genesis 1 is characterized by its simplicity and clarity.

What this story led to was a sensitive reminder of the events at Horeb. Since he was leading up to Horeb, the author decided to also introduce the name Yahweh, since that name was so closely bound up with Horeb. That's why the name Yahweh appears as early as in 2:4.

But it is introduced in a certain manner. Here and elsewhere (about twenty times in all), the name Yahweh is used in conjunction with Elohim: the reference is not to "Yahweh" but to "Yahweh Elohim," which in most English Bibles becomes "the LORD God."

It's as if the author wanted to impress upon Israel that Yahweh is God, and Yahweh alone (Deut. 6:4). He is the only God. There is but one God, and he is Yahweh. The God of Genesis 1, who is the Creator of all things, and the Deliverer of Israel are one and the same. Hence the double name: Yahweh-Elohim.

It was undoubtedly for pedagogical reasons that this name was repeated a number of times in the early part of Genesis. *Yahweh is the same as Elohim!* In this way a centuries-old treasure drawn from the faith of the fathers (i.e., the creation story) received a powerful stamp and was made Israelite property in a special sense.

Here again we see that Genesis has the character of a prologue. It is an introduction to the *torah* (instruction) about Yahweh's covenant with Israel at Horeb.

CHAPTER 5

A Look Back
and a Look Ahead

It should not surprise the reader that we have chosen to begin a new chapter here, for we are now up to Genesis 2:4, where we read, "These are the *toledoth* of the heavens and the earth." As we saw earlier, Scripture introduces a division here—not a sharp division but really more of a transition. That it is in fact a transition will become apparent from the content of this chapter. Through various remarks to be made below, we will look back at Genesis 1. At the same time, we will look ahead to what is to come, that is, the events in Paradise, including the fall into sin and its consequences.

Not a Second Creation Account

At the end of the last chapter, we were talking about the divine names Elohim (God) and Yahweh (LORD). We explained the use of the name Elohim in Chapter 1, followed by Yahweh from 2:4 onward, and especially the combination of these names in the early chapters of Genesis.

Not everyone agrees with this explanation. On the contrary, the use of these two divine names is the starting point of the famous source criticism of the Pentateuch. Scholars who use this approach focus on the use of the divine name and then attribute one part of the Pentateuch to one source and other parts to some other source. This method has been used to carve up the Pentateuch into quite a number of bits and pieces. And those using this approach could not always agree with each other either. Because of the internal battles they fought, source criticism of the Pentateuch has consumed itself.

On the basis of this method, some scholars have concluded that Genesis 2:4 is the beginning of a new creation story with a different origin and content, which thus brings it into conflict with what we read in Genesis 1. This thesis is to be rejected, for its very starting point is wrong. What is particularly offensive about it is that it completely ignores the structure of the book of Genesis. The book clearly indicates that Genesis 1 (to be more precise, Gen. 1:1–2:3) is meant as an introduction.

The book really begins at 2:4, then, telling us how humanity repeatedly alienated itself from God, and how God repeatedly had mercy on humanity. What we are told about Paradise and the woman from 2:4 onward is not a second creation account, but serves to help us understand the story of Adam's rebellion (Gen. 3). Knowledge of these matters is indispensable if we are to follow the continuing story as it tells of progressing corruption (Cain, Lamech), the great flood, and the mercy God repeatedly showed to the human race (Noah, Abraham).

Created in God's Image

We do not believe, then, that Genesis 2 presents us with a second creation account. But this is not to say that the author of Genesis did not add a few things to the story he had already told in Genesis 1. He had more to say, for example, about the creation of humanity. Before looking at the additional comments he makes, we will pick up a couple of points from Genesis 1 that were skipped over in the previous chapter.

In verses 26–31 we were shown that already the very manner in which the creation of humanity took place indicated that there was something special about this creature. Let's read those verses together. What the text tells us literally is that God said, "Let us make people"—"us," the plural form.

Christian writers of long ago and more recent times have pointed to that plural as proof of the doctrine of the Trinity. This seemed so obvious that Calvin, both in his *Institutes* (1.13.24 and 15.3) and in his commentary on this passage, dismissed all who did not agree as mockers and fools (when he got to Genesis 3:22, he ended up contradicting himself).

Now, we should not be arbitrary in our approach to such matters. Why not take every Bible text in which the LORD is called Elohim as a proof of the Trinity? The word Elohim, after all, can also be taken as having plural meaning—gods. And when this name is used as the subject of a plural verb (which happens in various places), we are not to take this as proof of the Trinity either. Those who know Hebrew are quite aware that in such passages the translators are right in translating both Elohim and the corresponding verb as singular forms. Through such a procedure, the "simple Bible reader" is not burdened with needless problems. For this we should be thankful. But, then, why use a plural form in Genesis 1:26?

There are some who interpret this plural ("Let us") as a royal plural. Think of a stately queen saying, "We are not amused." Yet there are other scholars who want to hear nothing of such a solution. They argue that there was no royal plural in the ancient Near East.

Need we view this as a great difficulty? The word 'elohim is a plural form meaning "gods." But it can also have a singular meaning, "God," for example, when Israel used this name in relation to Yahweh, the LORD, who alone is God. But even when it was used with a singular meaning in relation to Yahweh, the Israelite ear could still hear the echo of a plural form in the name. Sometimes this plural echo was even reflected in speech through the use of a plural verb.

Although the author of Genesis had spoken of "God" with singular verbs in chapter 1, in verse 26 he wrote, "Let us. . . ." Why? It was no more than a simple slip on his part. He really meant "me," and therefore we should translate, "Let me." We routinely make such an adjustment for Elohim itself (also a plural form) even when it is used with a plural verb. Just check the translation of such passages as Genesis 20:13; 35:7; and Isaiah 6:8. Should we not be consistent in such matters? If we translate a plural verb that goes with Elohim as a singular, why should we not follow through when it comes to Genesis 1:26? "Simple Bible readers" would then find themselves facing one less difficulty.

We would therefore propose to translate, "Let me make people." Humanity was intended to be the crown of all that had been created up to then. But humanity was not to be like God; this (pagan) idea is foreign to the Scriptures and is expressly rejected here and elsewhere (see Isa. 40:18). Humanity was only to look like God. A son or a daughter never becomes exactly like the father, but he or she can certainly look like him. "Let me make people in my image and after my likeness."

There appear to be two reasons why the word *likeness* is used after the word *image* has been used. In the first place, the second word (*likeness*) probably weakens the force of the first word (*image*) somewhat. What is at issue is not identity in nature but only similarity. In the second place, the use of the word *likeness* indicates what a grandiose fact it is. The description also had to be ceremonious and grandiose, hence this recourse to the beloved Semitic custom of repetition.

And it was something grand indeed. Whereas God created the plants, trees, and animals by way of the earth where they were brought forth (Gen. 1:11, 24), he created humanity in an entirely different way. And while he created the plants and animals each "according to their kinds"—that is to say, the one this way and the other that way, such that the enormous variation has amazed observers through the ages—he created humanity after his own nature. We do not actually find these words in the text, for the idea is expressed a little differently: "in my image." One could also translate, "as my image."

This is something great and elevated, but at the same time it is passed on to us in a cautious way. Therefore we should be careful not to overestimate its importance. In the Old Testament we find additional explicit references to humanity being created in God's image only in Genesis 5:1; 9:6; and Psalm 8:5. Thus the subject does not come up often.

Yet these Scripture passages are enough to make us understand "in my image" and "after my likeness," especially when we bring in the other Scripture passages that have some relevance to the ones mentioned.

Genesis 5:1–3 presents us with a transition between what happened with Adam and Eve as well as Cain and Abel, and the history of those who came after them (*toledoth*). Therefore the passage first goes back and cites what was earlier said about the creation of Adam and Eve in 1:26–27, namely, that they were created in God's image and likeness and were therefore called "man" (*'adam*). We discover that this name and honor also applied to their descendants who were born to them as a result of God's own blessing. Thus Adam could sire a son "in his own likeness, after his image." Seth is expressly spoken of in those terms, but this should not make us suppose that Cain and Abel were not born as "man." Seth is described this way in Genesis 5 because an overview is to be presented of his descendants. The purpose is simply to assure us that the descendants of Adam and Eve were also "man," and that just as God was able to view Adam as his image, Adam could in turn view his son and his son's sons as his likeness and image.

We should also think here of all the Scripture passages, too numerous to mention, referring to people as children or sons of God. Scripture never refers to any other creature in such terms: no animal is ever called a son of God. And what Scripture often says about those who are in authority over people, namely, that they are *'elohim* or "gods" (see Exod. 21:6;

Ps. 82:1, 6), it never says about animals.

We would also refer you to the many Scripture passages that speak of God's heart, eyes, mouth, nose, ears, hands, and so forth. It is true that we may not make any sort of image of these hands and eyes of God. We may not even try to imagine them. God's hands are divine hands, naturally, and his feet are divine feet. Yet Scripture does speak in such terms about the LORD. We must accept such passages for what they are and not try to eliminate them from Scripture in one way or another.

We can better think back to what we read in Genesis, namely, that a human being, including heart, eyes, mouth, and so forth, was created as the image and likeness of God. But a human being's hands and feet, naturally, are those of a creature; they are distinctly human. Thus they are not to be identified with the corresponding parts of an animal's body. The analogous organs in an animal are of a different nature, and therefore certain languages (e.g., German and Dutch) tend to use separate sets of words depending on whether a human being is meant or an animal. When a human being eats, the Germans speak of *essen*, but when an animal is doing the eating, they call it *fressen*.

Human beings are created in such a way that by the possession and use of their organs and body parts, they may look like God, even if only in a distant, creaturely way. Because it was God's wish, a human being may respond to God as a creature that resembles him.

God expressed this wish on the sixth day: "Let me now make people—creatures in my image, as my likeness." God made those creatures in such a way that they were destined for fellowship and concourse with him. A father does not treat his son in the same way he treats his horse, regardless of how much he may love the horse. The Heidelberg Catechism rightly says in Lord's Day 3, "so that he might truly know God his creator, and love him with all his heart." That's why God created human beings with hearts capable of deep feelings, minds that can understand things, hands to steer things, tongues to sing praises, attentive eyes and ears, legs and feet to walk erect as human beings so that they would be able to walk with God in the garden.

When we are told that Adam was created in God's image, our attention is immediately focused on the great difference between humanity and all the other creatures on earth. That difference is summed up by one biblical scholar this way: "Every other creature or thing remains what it is without forming a center on its own that could be spoken of as independent. The thing (including the animal under this heading for the moment) cannot be addressed and cannot answer either. Therefore it remains completely without responsibility" (Philip Kohnstamm, *Het Oude Verbond*, p. 43).

Because of the special way in which humanity was created, humanity was charged with a unique task. An ambassador or emissary receives honors that are really intended for the king who sent him. God created humanity specifically so that he could entrust humanity with dominion over all his earthly creatures. Humanity was to be God's vice-gerent. The animals could not possibly fill such a role. They had not been created for any such purpose and therefore they did not have the needed capacities. But human beings, thanks to the special way they were created, did possess them.

Against this background the author of Genesis could go on to narrate what those human beings perpetrated against God. Human beings were creatures capable of sin; people could be disobedient and rebel. Plants and animals are not capable of any such things. People can sin precisely because they had been created in God's likeness. That is also why God could have fellowship with humanity and speak with people, and why people could react to God's word with some words of their own, why they could answer God's love with their love, why they could respond to God's promises with faith and to his commands with obedience—or disobedience.

The Garden

The preparatory report about humanity being created according to (or as) God's image is now worked out further. Two
points are added to what was mentioned earlier. First we are
told that God gave humanity a paradise, and secondly that he
gave the man a wife. We begin with the paradise (Gen. 2:8–17).

At first, God the Lord "made the earth and the heavens."
Note the order used in 2:4, where the earth comes first. In
Genesis 1 it was the other way around. God saw to it that
there were fields and meadows so that there would be a basis
for humanity's existence, and also a sun and a moon, so that
there would be some regularity in their life and work, their
sleeping and waking hours. This all happened early on—literally, "in the day that," a phrase we can translate as "when" or
"then" (e.g., in 2:17).

"Then the Lord God made earth and heaven." He had
already created plants and trees, but that was about as far as
he had gone. The order that we take for granted in the world
around us today—here a field of grass, there a field of wheat,
and in the next field nothing but oats—that order was not yet
present. There was no such evidence of culture. The plants and
trees were all mixed together—oats among the wheat, almond
trees among the date trees. No cultivation had been undertaken to turn the land into gardens and fields. Trees of the
same kind did not grow together in groups. There was plenty
of growth among the plants and trees, thanks to the daily dew,
a phenomenon of nature that inhabitants of such lands as Palestine cannot help but regard as indispensable. God had not
yet deliberately sprinkled a particular region with mild rain to
stimulate growth, nor did human hands cultivate certain fields
with irrigation (2:5–6). That work was now first undertaken
by God himself.

The Hebrew text speaks simply of a garden. The Septuagint translated this as *paradeisos*, a word of Persian origin that
really means "park." This word was carried over into later He-

brew (see Song 4:13; Eccl. 2:5; Neh. 2:8) as *pardes* but we do not find it at all in the Hebrew text of Genesis 2 and 3. Thus we have here another occasion where the Septuagint gets in the way and obscures things in the Bible. Changing "garden" into "paradise" does not help matters any, for "paradise" is a rather grandiose term. "Garden" is much more down-to-earth—provided we do not forget the meaning of the Hebrew *gan*.

In this event we have a new indication of God's partiality to humanity. First we are reminded that man was also made from the dust of the earth and that the LORD blew the breath of life into his nostrils. It was only because of this that man became a living *nephesh*, a "living soul" (Gen. 2:7 KJV). The same expression (i.e., "living soul") is used in connection with animals (1:20, 21, and 24).

We also read that the *'adam* (man) was formed by God from the dust of the earth (*'adamah*). The connection is suggested in the two related words: the *'adam* is formed from the *'adamah*. There is an important point behind the emphasis on this connection. Humanity, who was to rise up against God in such an insolent way, is of very humble origin. That Adam went on living and did not immediately turn back into dust, as he would when he finally died (3:19), was due solely to God, from whom he received breath in his nostrils. Only because of what God did could he have life and be a living soul (2:7).

If we understand Genesis 2:7 in these terms, then, we should sense a contrast when we come to verse 8. (Note that Hebrew has a single word that covers both of our English words *and* and *but*.) Thus we should translate, "But Yahweh Elohim planted a garden."

Next comes the story of how the LORD planted that garden. Of course this story was not written down to give modern people a lesson in geography. Genesis simply wants to sketch the beauty and charm of Paradise and it does so through another play on words: the Hebrew word *'eden* means "luxury" (see 2 Sam. 1:24), "delicacy" (see Jer. 51:34), "delight" (Ps. 36:8).

Genesis also acquaints us with the garden by mentioning a couple of well-known rivers. When people in Palestine talked about Paradise in connection with Genesis 2, they stretched their hand toward the east and thought in terms of some sort of oasis in a wilderness, which for the people in the East was indeed something glorious. The word *'eden* is no doubt related to the Sumerian word *edin* and the Babylonian word *edinu*, which are old words that Israel's ancestors had used to refer to steppes. Still pointing in some sort of easterly direction (there was no precision about it, for they had no compass or an exact description of the direction in degrees), one would utter the names of those four rivers, which were fairly well-known names.

The latter two (the Tigris and the Euphrates) were so well-known that no further explanation was needed. But the Pishon and the Gihon were not quite as well-known, and therefore some additional information about them was given. Havilah, a land of trade, was mentioned in connection with the first, and Cush in connection with the second. Both names make us think of Arabia, the extensive area that is now viewed as the birthplace of the Semitic peoples. It was an enormous area that seemed to rise out of Egypt and stretch far to the north-east toward Chaldea. What those four great rivers brought to this area in the way of refreshing moisture was once accomplished by a single river that brought water to God's garden in Eden before splitting up into four.

Such a description certainly touched the minds and hearts of the people in the ancient Near East. It would mean much more to them than to us, for very few of us know what it is to yearn for water. Egypt was always envied for its abundant water supply. Think of the story of Lot, for example, who chose an area for himself before Abraham. "And Lot lifted up his eyes and saw that the Jordan Valley was well watered everywhere like the garden of the LORD, like the land of Egypt, in the direction of Zoar. (This was before the LORD destroyed Sodom and Gomorrah.)" (Gen. 13:10).

That is how glorious Paradise really was. It was truly a region of life, especially because of its water. The cedars, plane trees, and cypresses with their extensive root systems must have soaked up water daily from that abundant supply (see Ezek. 31:8). The lemon trees and date trees must have flourished there. The fruits of Paradise must have been very tasty indeed with all that water available.

It was this area that was given to humanity to live in. All of this was offered to humanity—and at the same time entrusted to them. They were to "work" the land and "keep" it. What do these words mean?

We should not think here of heavy labor and sweat pouring down Adam's face. That comes later (see Gen. 3:19). Moreover, we must remember that humanity had been placed in Paradise. Placed there? In 2:8 we read that God "put" humanity in Paradise, while in verse 15 we come across a word that indicates that God gave Paradise to humanity as a place of rest.

But what about "keeping" the garden? There are some scholars who say that we should translate the word as "guard" instead, and it is indeed true that the Hebrew word used here can mean "to guard." The idea is then that Adam was entrusted with the task of guarding the garden against Satan's attacks.

It should be said at the very least that such a task is not mentioned expressly. We do not read that God gave Adam such orders. Furthermore, it becomes apparent later that Satan was free to come and go in Paradise. And from later Scripture we know that Satan really is not interested in apples and pears at all: he wants to capture human hearts instead.

Could we then not give the word *keep* a meaning that would be in the same general area as work, so that the two could be mentioned together in one breath? Adam was to "work" and "keep" the garden (2:15). "Keeping" the garden would then have nothing to do with the spiritual power of Satan; rather, we would have to think of plants and trees. There was the beautiful work of selecting the best plants, improving the strains, and checking unwanted growth. Cultivating a vineyard and grouping plants and trees together surely should not be thought of as a war. We see no need to make anything more than this of Adam's "working and keeping" the garden. We should respect the restful character of this story and the simple meaning of the Hebrew word *gan* (i.e., garden).

Human beings were allowed to eat anything that was brought forth in this garden, for the garden was for them. The LORD had made only one exception.

In the middle of the garden stood two trees about which we are given some special information. The reason is obvious: the information will help us to better understand the story of the fall into sin.

One of the trees was called the tree of life. We will have more to say about this in a moment, but for the present only one comment is needed. The whole garden, of course, was full of "life." That this tree was spoken of anyway as specifically the "tree of life" must mean simply that it was extra good for a person's health and strength to eat from this tree.

The other tree was called the tree of the choice between good and evil. This, at least, is how we would propose translating the phrase, although many Bible translations speak of it as the tree of the knowledge of good and evil. The problem with the latter translation is that it leaves us with the impression that humanity came to the knowledge of good and evil by eating from this tree, which would be to greatly overestimate the importance of eating.

The word at issue here is an expression that appears more often in Scripture. We come across it in Deuteronomy 1:39, 2 Samuel 19:35, and Isaiah 7:15–16. In these passages the issue is recognizing and choosing between good and evil, whether the person doing the choosing is an old man of eighty or a young child that can hardly say "Father" and "Mother." Because of those passages, we believe that the best translation of Genesis 2:17 is "tree of the choice between good and evil."

We could also use the term *discern* in this context. When a young person is being told what to do by his elders, he may retort that he knows without anyone telling him. He means that he can decide and choose on his own, for he can discern both good and evil.

In connection with the second tree, the LORD issued the following warning: "In the day that you eat of it you shall surely die." We do not need to assume that the LORD meant he would die that very day, for, as we saw earlier, "in the day" could also mean "then" (see 2:4) or "when," as it does here. In other words: If you eat from that tree, you will die.

This, then, is what Genesis tells us about Paradise. If we look back, we must ask ourselves whether it is indeed wise to use that high-sounding word, *Paradise*. It tends to make us think too much of a royal estate, and before long Genesis 2 has been made the basis for all sorts of speculation about culture. The fact of the matter is that the only culture spoken of in Genesis 2 is agriculture. The story is a simple one, and it is intended merely to lead up to the story of the fall into sin. Adam did not fall because the test was too difficult intellectually or morally. It was simply that he disobeyed a down-to-earth command of God concerning a matter that even a child can understand: eating.

The Woman

And now comes the creation of woman (2:18–25). Two things show us that this story is also very practical in nature.

First of all, there is the context. This little passage, too, prepares us for the story of the rebellion that followed, the rebellion in which the woman played such an important role that Paul focused attention on it later (1 Tim. 2:14). The rebellion began with the woman.

The practical nature of this pericope is also attested to by its conclusion. There is something fatherly and pastoral about the conclusion: "Therefore a man shall leave his father and his mother and hold fast to his wife, and they shall become one flesh" (Gen. 2:24). This statement does not come from Adam but from the author of Genesis. He felt he could permit himself to introduce such a statement of application at this juncture. His story about the creation of the world in six days and God's resting on the seventh led him to remark that God had commanded his people Israel at Horeb not to work more than six days in succession, and to rest on the seventh day (2:3). We have something similar in this passage.

Therefore a young man is to leave his father and his mother and cling to his wife, and they shall be one flesh (2:24). What does "clinging to" or "holding fast to" one's wife mean? It can easily be understood in the wrong sense, of course, as when we say of the young couple that they should not cling to each other so much in public. Sometimes a pair of horses is inseparable, whether they are in the pasture or running a race. Because "clinging" is so easily misunderstood, we could better speak here of "remaining faithful." We might translate, "Therefore a young man shall . . . remain faithful to his wife." This is indeed the sense of the Hebrew word *dabaq*, which is used here. It is never used in connection with sexual intercourse, but it is often used for heartfelt love (e.g., Shechem's love for Dinah in Gen. 34:3, and Solomon's love for some of his heathen wives in 1 Kgs. 11:2) and for unbroken faithfulness (e.g., Ruth's faithfulness to Naomi in Ruth 1:14, and the faithfulness of the Judeans toward David during Sheba's rebellion in 2 Sam. 20:2).

Marriage, then, requires faithfulness and devotion. Such a reminder is not only necessary for our time, with its crumbling marriages; it was also necessary for ancient Israel. Moses's commandment with regard to divorce also bore especially on faithfulness in marriage (Deut. 24:1–4).

It is especially important for Bible readers not to get the impression that the "therefore" in Genesis 2:24 is part of an enthusiastic outcry on Adam's part when he first saw Eve, part of his "bone of my bones and flesh of my flesh" speech. Rather, the statement is a wise, sensible comment made by the author of Genesis for the benefit of his readers, a statement that he wove into his story in a fatherly way. (Does this not suggest that Genesis was written for young people?)

But when was the woman created? There is so much tied up in this question that we must interrupt our progress through Genesis and consider this matter. But first some remarks on how creation is described in Genesis.

Science and the Creation Story

It can hardly be denied that there is something poetic about the way the creation story is written. Think of the repetition of the words "And there was evening and there was morning." This would have appealed greatly to the Israelites with their sensitivity to poetry, for such refrains were prized in the Semitic world. In Genesis 1:27 we already encounter the first *parallelismus membrorum* (i.e., set of parallel statements).

This Latin phrase is used for a figure of speech that comes up quite often in Hebrew poetry. Most Bible readers will quickly recognize it as present in the Psalms. Think of Psalm 103:1, where we read:

> Bless the LORD, O my soul,
>> and all that is within me,
>> bless his holy name.

The lines are sometimes also parallel in that they bring the same basic idea to expression, as we see in Genesis 1:27:

> So God created man in his own image,
>> in the image of God he created him;
>> male and female he created them.

But if the creation story of Genesis 1 is clothed in poetic garb, it does not thereby lose its character as reliable knowledge for Israel about God's great works. It speaks in a poetic manner about matters that go far beyond our understanding, but in a way that has won widespread praise for its natural, simple character.

When the author of Genesis spoke about the days of creation, he did not worry much about being misunderstood. He simply went ahead and used the word *day* in a bit broader sense. He worried so little about this term that in 2:4 and 2:8 he used the phrase "in the day that" to mean simply "then" or "when."

That's not the meaning we are to ascribe to the "days" of Genesis 1:1–2:4. The days meant there are just the sorts of days that the Israelite readers had seen coming and going all their lives, that is, days with an evening and a morning. We lift the whole creation story out of its peaceful setting when we assign the word *day* a different meaning than the everyday meaning it had for the Israelites.

The number six need not give us any problem either. Every involved Israelite would immediately be reminded of those familiar words spoken at Mount Horeb: "For in six days the LORD made heaven and the earth, the sea, and all that is in them, and rested on the seventh day. Therefore the LORD blessed the Sabbath day and made it holy" (Exod. 20:11).

It was probably because of the revelation at Horeb that the author could speak of six days of creation on God's part, while he rested on the seventh day. In the creation stories handed down by other peoples at least, these numbers do not appear. Thus we may regard them as peculiar to Israel.

The author of Genesis may have expected his Israelite readers would encounter little difficulty in understanding what he had written, but subsequent readers of the first page of the Bible have faced numerous difficulties. This already began to happen in a time not very far removed from the apostolic age and a land not very far from the land of the apostles. The author and the first readers of Genesis 1 were undoubtedly people of ordinary intelligence and therefore could easily understand that the light they enjoyed every day came from the sun, which was not created until with the fourth day. Yet they had no problem with the creation of light mentioned in connection with the very first day.

Christ and his apostles never warned against the first page of "Moses and the Prophets" because it contained something that did not quite fit. Even so, there were Syriac church fathers who had problems with Genesis, arguing that they could not possibly see how evening and morning could have existed before there was a sun to rise and set. At that point they devised a variety of solutions to this problem.

Later the difficulties have become still more acute as a result of reflection on the age of the universe and especially of the earth. As astronomers investigated the universe with its immense masses and volumes, distances, temperatures, numbers, density here and emptiness there, they became acquainted with such awesome dimensions of both space and time that their largest astronomical unit of measurement, the cosmic year (the time it takes the sun to revolve around the Milky Way's center), was hardly sufficient to measure some of these dimensions. And geologists, especially the paleontologists among them, as they investigated the origin of the Earth, could come to no other conclusion than that the length of time which had elapsed between the first life on Earth and the arrival of the human race must have been greater by far than just a few days.

These difficulties, which seemed to many to be occasioned by the reading of Genesis 1, have given rise to an extensive body of literature and much controversy. Some people, arguing that they had found mistakes in Genesis 1, felt it necessary to throw the entire Bible overboard and abandon the faith altogether, while others sought a solution in which the

Bible and science could be harmonized.

One of the most obvious ways of harmonizing was to equate the days of Genesis 1 with long epochs or ages, immense periods of time within which astronomers and geologists could fit their findings. Or have there perhaps been others who thought to themselves, "The days of Genesis 1 were ordinary twenty-four hour days, and those geologists and folks like them are selling us a bill of goods?" But sticking one's head in the sand does not solve anything, of course, to say nothing yet about the stubbornness it displays toward the person who still desires to remain Christian as well.

Without pretending that we are above these debates about Genesis 1, we might well ask whether there really was a genuine conflict between Scripture and science, and whether the search for solutions to such questions has perhaps been superfluous. Was the creation story being properly understood? Or might we at this point properly apply an analogy that we once heard someone use in connection with a discussion of these matters?

Imagine a great industrialist, someone like Henry Ford, sitting in his old age among a group of his grandchildren, who are ten or twelve years old. They ask their grandfather how he managed to build up such an enormous industrial empire and make such a name for himself. What can the grandfather tell his grandchildren to give them some idea of how he laid the foundation for that industrial empire?

He begins to tell them stories, speaking to them not as his equals but as children. Limiting himself to their capacity to understand, he tells them a few things about his company with which they are also familiar, giving them some understanding of the company as an international automobile manufacturer.

But imagine now that two of these grandchildren later attend university and study economics and related sciences. Armed with this scientific background they plunge into their grandfather's enormous business archives. One of them might well come across material that gives him a different impression of the company's history from the stories his grandfather told him when he was ten or twelve, and he might then come to doubt his grandfather's word. The other grandchild might look for all sorts of explanations to make the whole picture fit together so that he can still protect his grandfather's honor. But is all this argument really necessary? Did the grandfather tell these stories—on a child's level—intending them to be subjected to the critique of economists later on?

It has pleased God our Father to tell us something about the origin of the great things that we see with our eyes, things that lead us to glorify his name. He was under no obligation to do so. But he could not speak to any human being about such matters as his equal. Yet because he wanted to be honored as the only almighty God (Rev. 4:11), it pleased him to tell us a few things about the creation.

We have no right to try to pick apart God's lesson about creation. Perhaps he wanted to protect Israel at the same time against the foolish idea that this world is somehow the result of some horrible struggle between primordial monsters or forces, or the idea that the things of this world together constitute a second god alongside him.

Therefore God let us know something about the origin of all things, namely, that they all owe their existence to his creating hand.

It was his prerogative to use whatever language, culture, and nation he chose as he communicated this information. Of course that had no small influence on the manner of presentation. The Lord did not use concepts common in our age in telling about the creation, for such concepts would not have been understood by ancient Israelites. Thus Scripture sometimes speaks of the earth as though it had four corners and rested on pillars (Job 9:6; Jer. 49:36; Rev. 7:1; 20:8), and at one point we get a hint of the idea that the land all floats on water (Ps. 24:2). Since we no longer think of the earth in such terms, are we now forced to shove such Scripture passages aside as though they are not true, or must we attempt, in some way or other, to bring them into agreement with the precise results of science?

Surely there is no need to adjust Scripture to science. There is no conflict whatsoever here. Whenever someone says something, he has certain purposes in mind and draws on the language of those he is addressing. How could Israel's prophets, poets, and singers have been understood in their own time if they had used the language of our century?

Those pillars and foundations of the earth are not controversial today. It would be foolish to argue about such things. But should we then criticize the story told in Genesis 1 on the basis of current scientific understanding of the structure and history of the universe and the earth, and are people then supposed to devote all their attention to harmonizing the simple story told in Genesis 1 with current scientific conception about the earth's beginnings?

Here again an example may be useful. In Genesis 1:6–8 we are told that God made the firmament. In Hebrew the word used for firmament is *raqia'*. We must not give this word *raqia'* the meaning of "atmosphere" or "stratosphere," for these are modern concepts. Scholars tell us that the Israelites thought of the *raqia'* as a dome or covering made of a blanket or plate metal. The dome contained some doors and windows, and above it was water. Today some will immediately argue that because there is no such dome above the earth, it could not have been created by God, which proves that the Bible is flatout wrong at this point. But have we thereby proved the falsity of what we are told in Genesis 1:6–8? Or should we struggle to rescue this passage of Scripture by arguing that the Hebrew word in question really means "atmosphere"? Both responses are illegitimate.

The person who wrote these verses in Genesis for his contemporaries wrote the truth. Who made all things we see around us—including the things we do not yet see? Who else but the LORD could have made this world that we describe in various ways at different times, depending on the progress of science? Our God is the Creator of heaven and earth. How else could the author of Genesis 1 make his hearers and readers understand that the full honor for all the created reality they saw around them was to be attributed to the one true God? Did he have any choice but to speak to them in their own language and make use of the images and concepts they were accustomed to? He therefore described the sky, which still looks like a dome when we try to focus on it today, as a *raqia'*, using a word that expresses an idea we no longer share today, although the distinction between waters above and waters beneath is still important for us today.

In this way we can easily understand the intention of the author of this passage perfectly well, just as we can understand his purpose with all of Genesis 1. This is especially true when we take note of the conclusion and the sequel of this chapter, for then we can discern the underlying plan.

From the very beginning, Genesis 1 was elegantly designed to lead the Israelites to sing the praises of the one who, since Horeb, had allowed his people to call him Yahweh. As they read or listened, they would have to come to the conclusion that the honor and glory for everything that existed was to be ascribed to the God of Israel. The entire story was structured in such a way that the believing Israelites could not help but shout the praises of Yahweh, who had spoken to his people at Horeb, where he told them (among other things) about how he had created the heavens and the earth. Even the formidable and fearsome sea was his creation. With his mighty hand and with playful delight he made all of this, and afterward he rested without anything or anyone disturbing him, even as now he favored—indeed, commanded—his people Israel with the gift of a day for undisturbed rest and for catching their breath.

Created after the Sixth Day

According to the author of Genesis, Adam was created on
the sixth day. What about Eve? It does not appear that the
author of Genesis wanted to view the sixth day of creation as
completely different from the ones that came before. He had
spoken of them essentially as ordinary days.

After the author of Genesis had dealt with the creation of
all things, he came to the creation of Eve. The fact that he follows such an order already gives us reason to suppose that the
creation of Eve took place after the six days. This impression
is strengthened in that various events are presented as taking
place between the creation of Adam and the creation of Eve.
There was simply too much for all of it to have happened in
one day. As we saw earlier, the readers of Genesis thought in
terms of ordinary days, days with an evening and a morning.

The author tells us, for example, that on the sixth day the
creation of cattle, wild animals, and reptiles took place. The
creation of the man was next. But there also had to be room
somewhere for the planting of the garden and for the animals
to parade in front of Adam. The latter event must have taken
place slowly. Adam must have looked the animals over very
carefully so that he could get to know them and give them
all suitable names. We are also told that Adam fell asleep and
that the LORD took a rib from his body, from which he made
a woman as a partner for Adam. Finally, we are told about
Adam's joyful cry in response to this, the most beautiful of
all God's gifts.

We find it hard to believe that all the events mentioned in
Genesis 1 and 2 are to be understood as taking place on one
day, the last of the six days of creation. Why? Because the
Bible teaches us to doubt God's power? Of course not! The
point to remember here is that the Bible describes Adam as a
mere creature, a person with limited capacities. The various
things we are told about in connection with Adam at the beginning of Genesis must have taken a good deal of his time.

The first people to hear and read the story about the creation of Eve could hardly have been left with the impression that her creation is to be understood as having occurred at almost the same time as Adam's creation; quite the contrary.

The conclusion that Genesis 1 and 2 depicts the creation of Eve as taking place not on the sixth day but later might meet with certain objections. Two of the conceivable objections will be dealt with here.

The first objection stems from Genesis 1:26, where we read that God said, "Let us make man [i.e., people, plural]." Verse 27 then says, "And God created man [i.e., a man, singular] in his own image." Although these are singular forms, we should not exclude the plural aspect here, since the word *man* is used in a collective sense. Thus it applies not to Adam alone but to both Adam and Eve and to the entire human race. The text goes on to say, "Male and female he created them." Like the animals, human beings were created with the capacity to reproduce themselves. This is important because God wanted to see his earth populated by this last sort of creature, the most beautiful one of all.

This explanation of Genesis 1:26–28 seems perfectly acceptable. But if people want to go on and conclude from this that Genesis depicts the creation of Eve as taking place on the sixth day, we must draw the line, for we would wish to add something to the explanation of these verses. The reference to Eve's creation in these verses must be understood proleptically, that is, as pointing ahead. In Genesis 1:26–28 the author reaches a climax. This is even apparent from his style. Earlier we pointed out what stylistic technique he uses. Why does he use such elevated language here? Because this final creature, man, rises above all the others, hence the use of the poetic devices of repetition and parallelism. And because the author wanted to report that God wished to see the entire earth populated with this last creature to be created, he adds that God created this creature, "man," both male and female. Here he is pointing ahead to the creation of woman, which was still to come, thereby bringing up something that happened somewhat later, according to his own account.

When we go on reading beyond Genesis 1:26–28, we can easily see that this explanation is correct. From the references to "the man," we can see that only Adam was on the scene at this point (see 2:7–8, for example). God created "the man" as a living soul. Then he planted a garden and placed "the man" in it. Only then do we get the story of the creation of Eve.

The second possible objection might be formulated as follows: If one were to deduce from Genesis 1 and 2 that Eve, according to the author, was not created at the same time as Adam on the sixth day, there is no one who would object to this conclusion more strenuously than the author of Genesis himself, for he modeled his entire creation story on the structure provided in Exodus 20, namely, that the LORD created the heavens and the earth in six days. Did he not also write that God rested at the end of his six days of creation and found that everything was very good?

Let's begin with the last sentence. The author did indeed conclude the creation story with the words "And God saw everything that he had made, and behold, it was very good" (Gen. 1:31). That is what the text says, thereby preparing the way for Genesis 3, where we read about the rise of sin and corruption. Death did not come into the world from God's hands. The creation was good, but in 2:18 we read that God said, "It is not good that the man should be alone." These are the words that introduce the story of the creation of Eve. Then how can anyone ask whether Adam was still alone?

As for the rest of this second objection, we do not have the right to restrict the verb *create* only to what God did during the six days of creation, any more than we may restrict the word to the very first moment. Scripture does not say anything about a special first moment, and although we can easily conceive of someone using the word *create* only in relation to God's work in Genesis 1, Scripture does not limit the word in this way, as we saw earlier. Nor would we be justified in thinking in terms of a distinction between "creating" in connection with Adam's coming into the world, and "building" in connection with Eve (2:22). In Genesis 1:1–2:3 the word *create* (*bara'*) is used six times, and the word *make* (*'asah*) eight times. Thus they seem to be used interchangeably. In some passages Scripture speaks in one breath of *creating* and *making* and *forming* (*'asah* and *yatsar*). Job 38, a chapter that also deals with creation, likewise shows us that the Israelites saw little difference between *creating* (*bara'*) and *building* (*banah*), for it freely borrows terms from building (e.g., measurements, stretching a line).

In these last two sections we again ended up talking about Genesis 1, ascribing some poetic features to this passage. We have also pointed out how this chapter, in a sensitive way, must have led the Israelites to glorify the LORD as Yahweh, their Deliverer, who led them out of Egypt. Therefore, without at all taking this in the direction of Karl Barth, we can say that the very first page in the Bible already proclaims gospel. This Creator, O Israel, is your God Yahweh!

Created as a Helper

It is striking that the first designation of Eve that we are given is *helper*. Just as the story about the creation of the man begins with certain thoughts on God's part ("Let me now make people in my image," see 1:26), the story about the creation of the woman also begins with God's thoughts. We read that God thought to himself, "Now I have created the *'adam*, the man, but he is still completely alone, without a helper suitable for him" (see 2:18).

The idea that comes to expression here in Hebrew is that the woman is the man's *complement*. This even comes through in some translations (e.g., the Luther Bible). The idea being expressed here is that God was giving Adam a counterpart in the form of a creature whom he immediately recognized as like himself, but with the difference that she was female, while he was male. Together they formed a unity; they were a pair, an exclusive pair, just as my right hand and my left hand form a unique pair, and yours as well. But note that my right hand and your left hand do not form such a pair. That's what the Hebrew text expresses here by speaking of the woman as the man's *complement*. God now gave Adam a counterpart who suited him in a unique way. But first God made it clear to Adam that there was something missing. When we miss something, we learn to appreciate it.

The writer who tells us this reminds us that God had formed all the animals of the field and the birds of the heavens out of the earth. Thus they were like Adam, but at the same time there was a tremendous difference between all those creatures on the one hand and the man on the other. God let Adam see this—or perhaps we could better say that he let him *feel* it.

He had all sorts of animals appear before Adam. The text actually says *all* animals, but we deliberately used the phrase "all sorts of animals." (The man gave names to "all the cattle," and so forth.)

This is perhaps a good place to emphasize that the Bible does not always use certain terms in the very same way we do. When we come across a word such as *all*, we should not treat it as an accountant would in preparing a financial statement. *All* can often mean "many" or "all sorts of." That is just what we find here. Thus we need not suppose that every last animal on earth paraded past Adam.

The scene can be pictured roughly as follows. From Genesis 3:8 we learn that the LORD used to walk with Adam through the garden. On one or more of those walks, he must have

noted with satisfaction how well Adam was able to characterize the various animals they encountered as they walked. To
each one he gave a name that expressed the animal's nature,
a name that really said something about the animal. Perhaps
the names he gave had something to do with their physical
features, just as we often name birds descriptively (e.g., the
spoonbill or the red-winged blackbird). They were reveal-
ing names. But there was no creature that Adam could name
woman. That name would not have suited any of the creatures in the garden, for there was no counterpart to Adam, no
helper to complement him.

God then judged that the time had come to create a wife
for. Adam. Thus we can hardly leave it an open question
whether Adam was alone in the garden at first.

Was the author of Genesis also using this story to combat
the pagan view that the animals received their names from
the gods? The express manner in which he tells us that it was
Adam who gave the animals their names suggests that he
was (2:19).

The LORD made Adam fall into a deep sleep. Here we cannot
help but think of the kind of sleep an anesthetic produces in
a person who is to undergo surgery. The LORD then took a rib
from Adam's body, and from it he made a woman whom he
brought to Adam.

We are not told when the LORD told Adam just what he
had done while Adam slept. This may well have occurred during one of the walks they took together. The LORD must have
told Adam and Eve a great deal during those walks, e.g., about
the creatures on the earth who were created before Adam, and
perhaps about many other things that have not been handed
down to us. We were not there to hear those things, for we are
a long way down the line of descent from Adam.

The expression in Adam's joyful cry, "bone of my bones
and flesh of my flesh," is used more often in Scripture (see
Gen. 29:14; Job 2:5). In today's language we would say, "My

own flesh and blood!" Adam's joyful cry is passed on to us in Scripture in the form of two lines of Hebrew verse. Of course we must not conclude from this that Adam was the first poet, or even that he was the first Hebrew poet. The Israelite narrator was simply making use of a right every storyteller enjoys, namely, to pass on Adam's words in the form that he knew would appeal most to his Israelite readers and hearers. Why did he do that? To make them understand how good everything was that came forth from God's hand, including the woman.

Adam received her with a passionate cry of joy as a perfect gift from God's hands. From God's side nothing had been neglected. She could be a rich blessing to Adam—or perhaps we should say: could have been.

Naked

We are now coming to the end of the two stories—one about the garden and the other about the creation of woman. The Israelite readers would need to know these stories in order to be able to properly understand what was to come. We feel a certain growing tension as we read through Genesis 1 and 2. How beautiful everything could have been for the human race!

Do we also feel the tension in the last verse (2:25)? "And the man and his wife were both naked and were not ashamed."

There are some scholars who translate the last phrase "they were not ashamed before each other." This is certainly a possible translation, but there is no need to read the passage this way. This reading does not represent an improvement. In fact, it sounds downright improbable. Is that really worth mentioning, that the man and his wife were not ashamed of their nakedness before each other? Is that the paradisiacal element of this story?

A much more obvious direction to take here is to think in terms of nakedness before God. After all, this passage is concerned mainly with the relationship between humanity and God; God is the leading figure in both stories. The LORD planted the garden (2:8), and the LORD brought the woman to Adam (2:22). Moreover, it is highly likely that God encountered the man and the woman from time to time. Where else would they have gotten their knowledge about the things that had happened before their birth?

The author of Genesis now concludes his account of the originally good and pure relationship between God and humanity by announcing that Adam and Eve still dared to appear naked before God. They walked right up to him unclothed. Soon this would change; they would hide from God (3:8). But now everything was good—very good—even after the creation of Adam's wife. Her presence did not change the picture in this respect. "The man and his wife were both naked and were not ashamed—before God" (2:25).

Words like this must have spoken to Eastern hearts and minds much more than to ours—and especially to the Israelites'. For the better part of the year, walking around naked is out of the question for us: it is too cold. Because the Near East is so much warmer, the other purpose behind clothing could come out much more in such a passage, namely, clothing as an indication of position, as a way of showing respect. Israel's priests enjoyed the privilege of being allowed to "approach" the LORD. They were even spoken of as "approachers": they were the ones who approached the LORD and stood before him. Still, they could never appear before the LORD without first having clothed themselves very carefully. The priest's breeches had to cover their "naked flesh" (lit., "flesh of shame"; Exod. 28:42–43). Israel knew the opposition between flesh and holiness as an opposition between death and life. (We will have more to say about this in connection with the garments worn by Israel's priests.)

If we say that Adam and Eve walked with the LORD as innocent children with their father and mother, this would still be too weak a comparison, for there are no more innocent children. No, there was nothing whatsoever in Adam and Eve that displeased God, nothing at all reminiscent of the corruption and death that God abhorred so thoroughly. Everything about Adam and Eve spoke of life and health. They were pure and holy in God's eyes. They felt that themselves and therefore they were not ashamed before him—not yet.

CHAPTER 6

Rebellion

There is nothing striking about the transition from Genesis 2 to Genesis 3 in the Hebrew Bible. As you know, the chapter number is not really part of the original Hebrew text. The first verse of chapter 3 originally continued the story with these words: "And the snake was more clever [ESV: crafty] than any other beast of the field." There seems to be nothing special about this sentence either.

But the Israelite ear picked up something here—a play on words. This was an indication that there was a transition to something different. That is simply how it was done.

The last verse of Genesis 2 reads, "And the man and his wife were both naked ['*arom*] and were not ashamed [before God]. The first verse in chapter 3 reads, "But the snake was more clever ['*arum*] than any of the beasts of the field which Yahweh Elohim had made." The Hebrew word used for "naked" in 2:25, then, is basically the same word that is used for "clever" in 3:1. Or rather, the consonants are identical; the only difference is one of the vowel sounds. In the first case, the word means "naked," and in the second case, it means "clever." What does this tell us?

This play on words is typical of the book of Genesis. The author apparently used them to capture the attention of his readers. "Pay attention!" he was telling them. "Now comes something very special that gives our story an entirely new turn."

The Background

Earlier we repeatedly asked, How did Israel understand this or that? What would the Israelites have made of such-and-such a statement?

Here we would like to begin with such a question again. The well-known story of Genesis 3 is seldom discussed by Christians or dealt with in sermons apart from the figure of Satan in the background. From the New Testament we learn that Satan was behind the snake's mission (John 8:44; 2 Cor. 11:3–4, 13–14; 1 John 3:8; Rev. 12:9; 20:2). The New Testament also tells us that Christ is the second or last Adam (Rom. 5; 1 Cor. 15) and informs us that even Christ was tempted by Satan (Matt. 4).

It is because of the New Testament that we enjoy this clear perspective. But we should not suppose that the Israelite church, the church before Christ's coming, saw and understood nothing of this. On this point, too, the rule is that the New Testament does not present us with anything brand new. This is already apparent from the way it deals with this subject. The apostles Peter and John write in their letters about the rebellion of the devils as a well-known matter. Apparently it was often discussed in early Christian preaching (2 Pet. 2:4; Jude 6). Our Savior had often spoken of Satan and his devils in a very similar way, without providing any further explanation.

From this we can conclude that even before Christ's coming, Israelites knew about Satan as the great figure in the background of Genesis 3. Christ and his apostles could simply presuppose this knowledge. This conclusion is explicitly confirmed by a passage in the apocryphal book known as the

Wisdom of Solomon, where we read, "Through the devil's envy [or jealousy] death entered the world" (2:24 NRSV). This is an indication of how Old Testament Israel understood the background to Genesis 3.

The question might well be raised why nothing whatsoever is said about the figure of Satan in Genesis 3. In dealing with this question, the following considerations should be borne in mind.

First of all, we should not allow ourselves to be misled by the way certain Bible translations have rendered 3:1. The snake is sometimes spoken of as "cunning" or "tricky," and the Hebrew word used can indeed have this meaning (see Job 5:12; 15:5). But in Proverbs the same word is repeatedly used to mean the opposite of gullible and simple-minded (e.g., Prov. 14:15, 18). Thus Proverbs used the word not in a derogatory sense but in a positive sense, that is, as meaning clever, wise, and sensible.

Why could such a translation not be used in connection with the snake in Genesis 3:1? Why must the snake be introduced there as an animal with which we are not likely to sympathize? Is that really the thrust of this verse? Just a few verses before we were told that everything God had made was very good. And even despite the events of Genesis 3, the snake is not always depicted in unfavorable terms in later Scripture passages. Snakes were worshiped in certain Canaanite circles, which may have some remote connection with the fact that the Aesculapian snake sometimes appears as a symbol on ambulances. As for Israel's own history, think of the story of the bronze snake in the wilderness. And when our Savior sent out his disciples, he told them to be wise as snakes (Matt. 10:16). He probably was thinking of certain snakes that were so wise—or were reputed to be—that they plugged their ears and refused to listen to the music of the snake charmers (Ps. 58:4–5). The disciples, likewise, were not supposed to allow any sorts of strange ideas to penetrate their minds but were to stick to his teaching.

When Israelite readers and hearers got to the story in Genesis 3, they must have understood immediately that the wicked language in which this "wise" animal expressed itself could not have come from the animal itself. And there would not have been any doubt as to whether Adam and Eve immediately understood this, for they were already well aware of the great differences between human beings and animals. They knew that humanity was God's image. Human beings listened to God's voice and responded to it. They ruled over all the other creatures on earth and received from God the garden with its tree of life and the tree of the choice between good and evil. The man also received the woman, and thereby marriage. But the animals did not share in any of this.

As soon as Adam and Eve heard an animal speak, they must have understood that something abnormal was going on. And this impression must have been strengthened by the content of the snake's words: they heard the snake ask whether God had forbidden them to eat of all the glorious fruits in the garden. That was a false accusation: Adam and Eve knew their good God better than that. Such a twisting of words had to have a deeper source than an ordinary animal, regardless of how clever that animal might be.

Now this source, this spiritual background, should have been mentioned explicitly—at least, if Genesis were written according to our tastes. But the author of Genesis seems to have had entirely different tastes: he did not want to "lay it on too thick." Shouldn't we allow him the right to tell about the events in such a way that those who were present would recognize his account as presenting the events just as they happened, while leaving the background for people to figure out for themselves? There must have been people in the world in which the Bible originated who could figure such things out. Revelation 12:9 later spoke simply, without further elaboration, of "the great dragon . . . , that ancient serpent, who is called the devil and Satan, the deceiver of the whole world." There seems to be little reason to fear misunderstanding here.

A few more comments on Adam and Eve are in order. We need not worry about their ability to see through what was really going on when the snake spoke to them. We can leave such worries to those who do not seem able to read Scripture without first putting on their evolutionist lenses. Such evolutionists tell us that the mental capacities amounted to very little or nothing in the case of our earliest ancestors. They increased among their descendants, slowly growing to the proportions they have reached today. But the apostle Paul indicates that if we were to draw a graph charting the change in human mental capacities since Adam and Eve, the line would go downward rather than upward (see Rom. 1). When we bear this in mind, we see that we must be careful about what we say regarding "the fall" in Paradise.

According to Paul, the fall was not something that took place by accident, but something deliberate; it was rebellion, wanton disobedience (see Rom. 5).

We should also bear in mind—and this applies to all Bible reading—that the Scriptures do not give us an exact transcript of everything that was said on this or that occasion, such as one might get from a tape recorder, but only a report—and sometimes nothing more than a short summary. But there must be no misunderstanding on this point, for we realize that this is a remark that can easily give rise to misconceptions. Yet such dangers should not keep anyone from saying what needs to be said. Even the best of words are open to misuse.

The point we wish to make here is that the world-shaking events of Genesis 3 could not possibly have taken place in such a short time as it takes us to read this chapter of twenty-four verses aloud. Yet we need not doubt for a moment whether what Genesis 3 tells us about the discussion between the snake and the woman and then between God and Adam is really true and represents a reliable report. That is not what is at issue here. The issue is how extensive or how condensed the report is.

We can be sure that we do not know everything there is to

know about this matter. We know enough, but surely we do not know everything. And this consideration should teach us to be cautious. We should not force meanings into words. To take one example, in Genesis 3:3 Eve says to the snake that God forbade them to touch the tree of the choice between good and evil, but earlier in Genesis we read nothing with regard to any such command about touching. May we deduce from this that Eve made that command up? Can we make the prejudicial assumption that through such a wanton, wicked lie she was already walking the path of sin, by presenting God's commandment to the snake as something harsh and hateful? Couldn't it just as well be the case that God, concerned as he was for life, at an early point gave Adam and Eve some fatherly advice to the effect that they should not even touch the tree of the choice between good and evil? And couldn't that part of the story even have been passed on to the descendants of Adam and Eve, only to be dropped from the story at some point when it was handed on? We simply don't know. There is so much we don't know. In fact, what we don't know may likely outweigh what we do know.

God's Disappointment and Anger

Revolutions generally produce the opposite of what they promise. This became clear right in connection with the very first rebellion on earth. The promise was that Adam and Eve would become God's equals. They themselves would know (that is to say, be able to decide between) good and evil. They would be as free as God himself. But nothing of that promise came true. The true freedom of a child over against his father was changed into the fear of an evildoer when he appears before the law-giver and judge. Adam and Eve crept away, afraid of their good God. Later Adam explained to God, "For I was naked."

We should not suppose that Adam was offering a flimsy

excuse here: it was a horrible reality. Why else would they be so quick to cover their nakedness with fig leaves? And let's not forget either that all of us have been hearing about sin all of our lives. Adam and Eve, on the other hand, first faced sin suddenly. And their first reaction was to be ashamed and creep away from God's presence. (Doesn't this also seem to indicate that our translation of Gen. 2:25 as "not ashamed before God" is correct?)

The LORD's response to their sin was closely tied in with their former intimacy with him. Nothing had changed from his side. He probably came into the garden again at his usual time.

In the Near East, when the sun has passed its peak in the sky and the afternoon shadows begin to lengthen and a breeze begins to blow, it is a very refreshing time of day. In Palestine that's the time to take a walk (see Song 2:17; 4:6). Therefore, when Genesis 3:8 tells us that the LORD walked in the garden "in the cool of the day," we should read this as an indication of the time of day, one that would have been familiar to the Israelites reading Genesis.

Bible translations are divided on whether Adam and Eve heard the "sound" of the LORD or his "voice." Either translation is possible, but the latter seems the more likely of the two, for we are then told what the "voice" said to them: "Where are you?" Was God's disappointment already to be heard in that question? What was going on?

In the subsequent questioning and discussion, God followed a certain order: he directed his attention first to Adam, then to Adam's wife, and then to the snake. He magnanimously let himself be led from the one to the other as each sought to evade the guilt. But when it came time for judgment, he took the lead and reversed the order. First he cursed the snake. Then he turned to Adam and Eve, but he did not curse them.

He did curse the earth because of Adam, but he did not curse Adam himself. We do not read that either Adam or Eve was cursed, although we do read later that Cain was cursed. Our original parents were indeed severely punished, but in such a way that God's goodness and willingness to forgive shone through, and in such a way that they would continue to feel his fatherly love and faithfulness.

The snake was cursed directly. Why did God curse this animal, which had served as an instrument of Satan, instead of cursing Satan himself?

To such a question we would answer: but isn't that really what God did? Here, too, we should remember that the author of Genesis tells us his story in his own way.

Perhaps a comparison would be helpful here. One day a king discovered among his most trusted and highly placed courtiers a plot against his life. The king himself found a dagger with which he was to be stabbed, or the poison that was to be poured into his cup. If the king in his wrath then threw that dagger or this cup of poison to the floor and stomped on it, would anyone be so foolish as to protest, "But the dagger or the cup, O king, couldn't help it"? The guilty ones watching the king would never be so foolish as to say such a thing. They would be trembling and would stand pale with fright, for what lay there on the floor was the proof of their treachery.

Questions have sometimes been raised about the existence of the snake before the events in the garden. It has been suggested that the snake had not always crawled on its belly but that it walked instead, or perhaps even flew. After all, the LORD decreed, "On your belly you shall go . . ." (3:14).

We should not quickly brush such a suggestion aside as pure fantasy, for it fits in with what we said earlier about the summary character of the reports we read in Genesis. On the other hand, we do not see any need for turning to such a hypothesis. We would prefer to remind you of the comparison above. We should view God's words to the snake as an expression of his great rage. As he looks at the contemptible murder weapon in the hands of his unmasked deadly enemy, the LORD cries out to the snake in deep indignation, as it were: "And just what did you have in mind? You, crawling on your belly over the ground with your mouth in the dirt—do you propose to elevate yourself? Forget it! Stay right where you are! What was earlier your natural existence and way of life will from now on be your punishment and shame."

As for the silence about Satan's name, we would remind you again of the commandment to Israel that the names of the idols were not to be mentioned (Exod. 23:13; Ps. 16:4). Wouldn't that commandment apply especially to the grand master behind the idolatry? (See Lev. 17:7; Deut. 32:17; 1 Cor. 10:20; see also Bar. 4:7.)

Friendship Forbidden

"I will put enmity between you and the woman" (Gen. 3:15). Throughout the ages this text has been given various different names. It has been referred to as the *protevangelion* (i.e., the first gospel) and the "mother promise" (i.e., the promise from which all subsequent promises have come forth). It is widely believed that this is the first passage in the Bible to speak of the Messiah. Is not the Messiah the one who is to "crush" the snake's head? There are Roman Catholic scholars who interpret this text not just christologically but "Mariologically," in which case the woman referred to is identified as Mary.

If we were to say a radical "no" to all of this, we would no doubt open ourselves to the wrath of many of our fellow believers. We would be asked whether we were familiar with the wide perspective Scripture itself opens in such passages as Isaiah 65:25 and Revelation 12. On the other hand, we would not be entirely alone in such a conviction either. Scholars today are somewhat more sober and straightforward in their approach to the Scriptures than some of the interpreters of earlier eras. Yet if we go back to the days of the church fathers,

the picture changes again: a Roman Catholic scholar tells us
that most of them, including the most important ones, did not
so much as mention the mother promise and the Messiah in
connection with Genesis 3:15—let alone mention Mary!

The text is translated in the future tense: "I will put enmity." But this is a poetic passage in the original Hebrew, and
therefore we may translate it in the present tense if we wish:
"I put enmity." God was telling the snake and the woman that
there would be enmity between them from then on.

It is important to remember that these words were addressed to the snake. A great many Bible readers believe that
the mother promise was addressed to Mother Eve, but this
is not so. The LORD addressed these words to the snake. The
deeply angered king was still addressing the contemptible
conspirator squirming before him with the proof of his guilt
out in the open. If we were to switch to a different comparison, we could say that a concerned father, who had just discovered that his son had become good friends with the worst
companion conceivable, was addressing the boy who was such
a bad influence on his son and telling him that there was to be
no more contact between the two of them.

Thus our good God turned first to the cause of the misery,
to the one who had deceived and misled his child. With his
strong hand he forcefully split them up. Then he proclaimed
that there would be war between the two former comrades;
he didn't just predict it but actually decreed it. From then on
the two would fight each other: the one with all his followers would do battle with the other with all his followers. He
was demanding an everlasting family feud between the two of
them and their descendants.

The LORD spoke here of seed: "between your seed and
her seed." The Hebrew word for seed (*zera'*) can also have the
broader meaning of "party" or "followers." Scripture speaks,
for example, of the *zera'* of the wicked (Isa. 1:4) and of the
zera' of the righteous (Prov. 11:21). If we take the latter meaning as the one intended in Genesis 3:15, we must read the

text as an order from the LORD calling for war between the
snake and the woman—and also between the snake's followers and the woman's followers. By "the woman's followers"
we would then mean all of mankind—not just a few here and
there, but all people. And when it comes to the snake's followers, we should not just think of vipers and boa constrictors
and rattlesnakes but should look to the spiritual background
mentioned earlier.

God told Eve that she and her "followers" (i.e., the entire
human race) were to make war on the snake and his followers
(i.e., Satan and all his devils). But just as God did not pay
Satan the honor of mentioning him by name, the author of
Genesis stuck to the prohibition given to Israel against taking the name of false gods on one's lips, to say nothing of the
name of the grand master of all the idols. Hence the war to
be conducted is described in words which, if taken literally,
would apply only to people and snakes: "It [the seed of the
woman] shall crush your head, and you shall crush its heel."

There are some scholars who prefer an even stronger translation that suggests that the seed of the woman is to aim at
the snake's head. If they are correct, we must interpret God's
statement to mean not just that the woman and her followers
are to defend themselves against Satan and company, including the devils and the idols, but that they are to actively make
war on them and attack them. They are always to be on the
lookout for them. Thus they must not just defend themselves
but must take the offensive.

Then what about the *protevangelion* or "mother promise"?
If one is determined to speak of "gospel" here, there is nothing wrong with that. But we would ask, Why here? Why not
already in Genesis 3:8, where the LORD asks, "Where are you?"

If we speak of gospel in this story, we must not overlook
the fact that the very first proclamation of the gospel in the
Bible takes the form of a call to battle as a universal duty.
According to God's will, the entire human race is originally
mobilized for the great war against Satan, idolatry, and un-

belief. After Adam and Eve took the foolish step of making friends with someone who led them toward nothing but death and corruption, God immediately pulled them away from their new friend and placed them at his own side—next to the God of life. In those first parents the entire human race was dragged back across that dangerous line and placed next to God. That's why all unbelief and godlessness on earth are to be strongly condemned as a sliding back, a renewed desertion, a repetition of that original refusal to serve God, our Creator and Redeemer. That's why the preaching of the gospel must go out to all people with a command to believe and to turn in repentance to the only true and gracious God.

That proclamation is not just something we *may* listen to; more than that, we *must* listen to it. Belief in the gospel proclaimed in the Scripture is not to be regarded as the hobby of some eccentric group; it is the solemn obligation of all people to take God's side in the holy war he announced in the garden of Eden. The question "May I really believe?" is thoroughly foolish, then, for reasons that are ages old.

Please understand that we have no objection to speaking of the Messiah in connection with Genesis 3:15. Everyone does so as a matter of course. We cannot keep him from our thoughts as we read such a passage: we think of the one who has come into the world with the command "to destroy the works of the devil" (1 John 3:8) and who carried out this command by rendering obedience unto death (Col. 2:15).

Yet we should abandon our custom of speaking of such passages as specifically messianic. Is there any part of the body through which no blood flows? Is there any page of Scripture that has nothing to do with Christ? By speaking of certain passages as specifically messianic, we run the risk of not doing justice to others. The term *messianic* can be used with reference to any passage in Scripture and should not be reserved for certain passages only. Various terms related to *messianic* are likewise unneeded. There is no point in going through all sorts of acrobatic stunts to haul Christ into the picture in Old Testament passages so that we can interpret those passages and preach on them "christocentrically." All we need to do is to indicate what place a given passage occupies in the larger whole of the Law, the Prophets, and the Psalms.

Condemned to Death

"When you eat of it, you will surely die." This was the warning God had given Adam and Eve. And he is faithful to his threats as well as his promises. Therefore Adam, after his transgression, had to be condemned to death. This followed naturally from what God had said earlier.

"The wages of sin is death" (Rom. 6:23). We often remind each other of this well-known text, and this is perfectly in order—provided we do not assume that for God, every sin leads to the punishment of death. The threat of death came to Adam, and the sin he was being warned against was eating from the tree of the choice between good and evil. We are not able to sin as Adam sinned (Rom. 5:14), for we are not Adam and do not have the same agreement with God that Adam had. Only our Lord Jesus Christ has since been able to occupy a place like that of Adam. When he did so, he won life for us—eternal life (Rom. 5:6; 1 Cor. 15). Through Adam's transgression death came into the world for all people (Rom. 5:12).

In Genesis 3 we read about other punishments in addition to death. Were these other punishments already mentioned beforehand as threats? Quite possibly. Here again we must bear in mind that there are many things that may have happened that are not reported to us in Scripture. God may indeed have warned Adam in advance in some way or other about the possibility of losing all the good things he possessed. He may have warned him that he would be sent away from the glorious garden with its exquisite fruits that grew there naturally, and that he would then have to live from what grew out in the fields, fields that he would have to subdue in the sweat of his brow because they were full of thorns and weeds. The Israelite readers for whom Genesis was written knew all about such fields (see Mark 4:7; Heb. 6:8).

Then there are also the other punishments of which Genesis 3 speaks. It is not necessary to maintain that Adam and Eve must have been surprised at those punishments; in fact, they probably realized better than we do what the consequences of their transgression would be. Never again on the earth were there two people of such wisdom.

The LORD, moreover, is not only almighty but also sovereign. He had the right to impose the punishment of death at any time that might please him. We are told that Adam lived to the age of 930. Thus he lived for a long, long time before the sentence was finally carried out. Moreover, the LORD paved Adam's path with the hard stones of heavy labor and the sweat of his brow. As for Eve, the route she had to follow was no less difficult. Ahead of her lay the pain of childbirth and oppression.

That, at least, would be the rule. "He shall rule over you," she was told. Note that these words came from the LORD's mouth as a prediction and not as a command. Therefore, in our wedding ceremonies we should not make too much of this text, as though it calls for blind submission of wives to husbands.

The LORD was not issuing a decree but was looking into the future, where he saw the daughters of Eve bent low under a burden of pain. The LORD let it be known that this was how it would be, but it was certainly not his wish or his command. Therefore a husband need not worry that there is anything wrong with manifesting his love and concern for his wife and making things easier for her. The apostle teaches us that this is God's express command: "Husbands, love your wives" (Eph. 5:25).

In Genesis 3, then, the death knell sounded. "You are dust, and to dust you shall return" (3:19). That is the conclusion of the beautiful story of Genesis 1, the story of the creation in which everything was originally good. We can now see that Genesis 2 was preparing us for this story by telling us about the planting of a garden full of wonderful trees and about the creation of woman. We needed to know about these things in order to follow the drama that unfolds in Genesis 3. Even so, we do not understand the story fully; no one will ever be able to fathom just what happened there in the garden. How was it possible for the devil, death, and corruption to break into this place of joy and life?

Perhaps we have already gone far enough with this complaint. The Bible does not ask and answer such questions; it simply tells us the truth. Adam was not an ignorant soul but a completely responsible creature placed in a unique position. That's why his deed had such ruinous consequences for all his descendants, as the New Testament shows us. Did Adam realize this? If so, this must have bothered him deeply all his long life. Imagine being condemned to death and being the cause of the death of all your children!

Comfort

Whenever the death knell of Genesis 3 rings in our ears, we cannot help but hear sounds of life intermingled with it. God offered comfort immediately.

The words he spoke to the snake and the woman mentioned punishment, but there was comfort even in that punishment. On the very day of the so-called mother promise, God dragged all of them (Adam and Eve and their seed) away from Satan and released them from Satan's clutches. He placed them by his own side again and called them to serve by participating in the holy war (3:14–15).

We hear more such sounds in the verses that follow. As we

listen to God's word of punishment to Eve—and, in her, to all women—we must not neglect to note that a merciful Father is speaking here. Even if Eve would have to follow a path of much pain and suffering, of indomitable desire for the man and of oppression by the brute force of the man, she would still become a mother (3:16). Once again we should try to imagine how such words must have sounded to Israelite ears, for Genesis was first of all written for the people who counted such women as Sarah and Rachel and Tamar as their ancestors—women who all yearned for children and descendants. Therefore they must have understood very well what Adam meant when he named his wife Eve after she gave birth (3:20). The Septuagint simply translates this name as *Zoē* (i.e., life): "Because she was the mother of all living."

We turn now to those garments that the LORD made for Adam and Eve. Here we must bear in mind that nakedness was already mentioned before that fall into sin. If we remember again that our story was written in the world of the ancient Near East, where the cold was not the sole reason for wearing clothing (clothing would be needed for protection against the cold only during the night; see Deut. 24:12–13), we will see that decorum, honor, and respect were important factors as well (see 1 Sam. 19:24; John 21:7).

The striking thing is that God gave Adam garments made of animal skins. Could this have something to do with the fact that he had not yet given the animals to man to eat their flesh (see Gen. 9:1–4)? Did God kill the animals himself because he wanted to spare his children the sight of death as long as possible? In any case, they received the garments from him. Perhaps he was thereby offering them comfort. Was it his way of showing them that they would still be able to approach him?

We can raise questions here, but definite answers cannot be given. We have received only a few short reports from this gray, distant past. We do get the impression that the Israelites must have understood these matters better than we do now. But we also get the impression that the Israelites together had the material needed for weaving together the two threads that make up the cord of God's concern with our first parents after their original transgression—the thread of God's fatherly wrath and the thread of his fatherly mercy.

Eternity and Life

The same mercy of God seems to manifest itself in the conclusion of Genesis 3 (vv. 22–24). The LORD did not want man's hand to reach out any more and pluck that fruit of the tree of life now that humanity had eaten of the tree of the choice between good and evil, for then they would live "forever."

"Behold, the man has become as one of us in knowing good and evil," we read. There are some who wish to read these words as an indication not of mercy but of mockery and divine irony.

Now, it is not to be denied that there is such a thing as divine irony and mockery mentioned in Scripture. Think of Psalm 2, which tells us of God's laughter and mockery. But is Genesis 3 the kind of chapter where we would expect joking, mockery, and biting sarcasm from God? As we see it, the passage as a whole draws our attention to God's fatherly sadness and anger and also to his fatherly mercy. Mockery is a weapon of last resort. Was there a place for mockery here, right after the mother promise, at the very beginning of the way of salvation?

In the first place, we would propose the following translation of God's words in 3:22, adding a few explanatory words and comments between brackets: "Behold, the man has become like me [he has become like a god] when it comes to choosing [for himself] between good and evil. Well then, let him not reach out. . . ." Then follows the statement that the LORD had the man driven out of the garden and had the way to the tree of life guarded by "cherubs with a shining sword."

There is not much that needs to be said about the cherubs. If we bear in mind that Genesis was written first of all for the Israelites, we see that the figure of the cherubs as God's watchmen was nothing strange. Israel knew about the cherubs from the tabernacle; the people had either seen such figures with their own eyes or had heard about them. They also had read or heard about cherubs in the chapter of the Torah that dealt with the construction of the tabernacle.

The tabernacle was God's dwelling place among humanity; it was a reminder of what had been lost and a prophecy pointing to paradise to come. That tabernacle, a place of light and life, of splendor and garlands and blossoms and flowers, also included some images of cherubs, figures that could symbolize more clearly than any verbal proclamation that God deeply hated death and sin but deeply loved holiness and life. (We will have more to say about this in connection with the book of Exodus.) For the present we would simply remind you that Genesis ought to be read against the background of the heart of the Pentateuch (i.e., Exodus, Leviticus, and Numbers).

Two words in this discussion need our attention—*eternity* ("forever") and *life*. As far as the word *eternity* is concerned, it is important to free this biblical word from the meaning it has taken on in the minds of many Christians, namely, unlimited, endless duration. For many, the word *eternal* means almost the same as "divine." Furthermore, we must remember that the Hebrew word for "eternal" used here ("live forever," Gen. 3:22) and in so many other passages means "long" or "very long" or perhaps even "of indefinite length," which in not the same thing as infinite duration. For example, the high priesthood was promised to Phinehas *eternally* (*'olam*, the same word that is used in Gen. 3), whereas in fact it lasted no more than a few hundred years (Num. 25:13).

When we turn to the meaning of God's words in 3:22

about Adam and the tree of life, we could say first that the
LORD did not shorten Adam's route toward death very much,
as we saw earlier. Adam lived some 930 years in all (5:5). But
neither did the LORD want Adam to live too long in the state
that had come over him after the fall into sin. Therefore he cut
off his access to the tree of life. That way Adam would not live
"forever," which would be too long.

In the second place, there is the word *life* as it occurs in the
phrase "tree of life." Here we must be careful not to slip into
the custom of spiritualizing the word *life* whenever we come
across it in the Scriptures. When Proverbs, for example, says
that wisdom is a "tree of life" (3:18), we are justified in not
taking the word *tree* literally, but we should not do the same
with the word *life*, for what Proverbs teaches in that verse is
that those who are faithful to the commandments of the LORD
can, as a rule, expect to live a long, healthy, and happy life on
earth. We should also think of life in the more familiar sense
when Genesis speaks of the "tree of life."

As for the meaning of God's words in Genesis 3:22 about
Adam and the tree of life, the most obvious explanation is to
assume that God had endowed the fruit of this tree with special powers for the lengthening and strengthening of human
life. The other trees also provided nourishing food to eat, but
the food of that one tree was especially nourishing, which is
why it came to be called the "tree of life."

The thought that the LORD had made such foods extraor-
dinarily nourishing so that people were strengthened by them
in a special way need not strike us as far-fetched or unbiblical.
The Bible tells us that God made Elijah capable of great physical achievements by providing special food for him (1 Kgs.
19:8), and it mentions trees bearing fruit with healing power,
as though there was nothing unusual about such a thing
(Prov. 13:12; Rev. 22:2). Are not such things known to us as
well? Think of all the human lives that have been saved and
prolonged greatly by medicines made wholly from plants, like
digitalis and penicillin. The LORD knows much better than we

do the medicinal properties of certain plants.

It appears, then, that the LORD was so merciful to Adam that he did not allow him to die right after he ate from the forbidden tree, but he did not let him live too long either. Genesis will tell us soon enough what it was that God wanted to spare Adam from by taking him away in death. Adam and Eve had to watch the sad consequences of their transgression, but for them there was an end. And Abel was probably the only child they had to surrender to death. There was much for them to cry about, but they were also spared much. They were spared the later degeneration because God did not allow them to eat any longer from the tree of life.

We now know that God had much better things in mind for them, including life on this earth—but then without sin, sickness, suffering, and death. They would live on the new earth with Jesus Christ, who would one day make all things new and restore human life completely.

A Covenant of Works?

Perhaps it has struck some readers that we have managed to discuss Genesis 2 and 3 without speaking of a "covenant of works." Is there a reason for avoiding this expression? On the other hand, one could also ask, Is there any reason to use it if Genesis 2 and 3 do not use it?

What do we mean by a covenant of works? During the 17th and 18th centuries, particularly in the Netherlands, there was a great deal of discussion about this doctrine, both for and against. Let us allow both sides to state their positions briefly.

In our view, no one is more qualified to explain what was meant at that time by such a covenant of works than Herman Witsius (1636–1708), a professor at Franeker, Utrecht, and Leiden. He wrote a significant book about the various dispensations of God's covenants with man. He tells us that in addition to the covenant of works, there is also a "covenant of law," since it was prescribed in the law. It was sometimes also called the "covenant of nature," since it was based upon nature and is just as old as nature. What about the covenant of works? Witsius defines it as follows: "This covenant is an agreement between God and Adam, formed after the image of God, as by which God promised eternal life and happiness to him, if he yielded obedience to all his commands; threatening him with death if he failed but in the least point: and Adam accepted this condition" (*The Economy of the Covenants between God and Man: Comprehending a Complete Body of Divinity*, book 1, ch. 2, p. 50).

Witsius clarifies this by referring to two texts that occur in the repetition of the law, namely, Leviticus 18:5 and Deuteronomy 27:26. In the first of these texts we are told that the man who keeps the statutes and ordinances will live. This, according to Witsius, indicates the condition for the covenant of works in Genesis 2. That condition is repeated for us in the laws. As for the threat, it is repeated for us in Deuteronomy 27:26: "Cursed be anyone who does not confirm the words of this law by doing them." Thus Witsius finds instruction about the covenant of works in the law, the law later given through Moses.

He manages to tell us all sorts of interesting things about that covenant of works. First, we learn about the parties to this agreement, namely, God and Adam. Witsius tells us all sorts of interesting things about Adam. He assures us that Adam knew that God was triune. The proof? Adam was a prophet and therefore he must have known that the Father had said to the Son, "Let us make people." In this context he appeals to the "church father" Epiphanius. He even writes about the various places where the Hebrew text speaks of God in the plural (i.e., Isa. 54:5; Ps. 149:2, Eccl. 12:1; Job 35:10). These plurals would be dangerous, he tells us, if they were not pointing to the doctrine of the Trinity.

In the second place, Witsius informs us about the condition in the covenant of works. It was a twofold condition. First of all there was the law of nature, which was built into Adam's own nature, the so-called conscience of the pagans. This law is identical in substance with the Ten Commandments. Secondly, there was the probationary command of Genesis 2:16–17. Actually, it was but a prohibition, intended as a loving warning.

In the third place, Witsius tells us about the promises of the covenant of works. God promised Adam eternal life. The proof? The apostle writes in Romans 8:3 that by sending his Son, God did what the law could not do because it had become powerless through the flesh. Therefore, if sin had not gotten in the way, the law would have led humanity to that eternal life that it now receives in Christ. When Witsius discusses these things, he jumps nimbly from the covenant of works to the later law and back again. It seems as though these are all the same to him! He believes, for example, that Adam was the heir to eternal life in accordance with the formula of Romans 10:5 (which deals with righteousness by way of the law).

In the fourth place, when it comes to the punishment threatened under the covenant of works, Witsius points first of all to Genesis 2:16–17, but then he expounds on the word *death* for a while. This word also refers to the misery of this life, especially spiritual death. This is rather typical of his approach. What Scripture states is for Witsius secondary, and what it does not state is primary.

By this point we have gone far enough in our discussion of Witsius and would add only for the sake of curiosity that he maintained that the covenant of works had four sacraments: paradise, the tree of life, the tree of the knowledge of good and evil, and the Sabbath. This may lead you to scratch your head. The Sabbath? Yes, indeed. The Dutch Reformed in the seventeenth century not only inherited a Sabbath dispute from England, but to make matters worse, this trouble was also coupled with the conflict occurring shortly thereafter regarding the covenant of works.

Now let's listen to someone from the other side of the debate. Balthasar Bekker (1632–98) has become famous—or perhaps infamous—because he was said to have denied the existence of angels and devils. This charge is not justified, but it is true that Bekker did not spare shrines and sacred cows. He put an end to belief in witches in the Netherlands and Germany and tried to calm people's fear of comets. He was a man who was both respected and feared. Interestingly, it was Bekker who first sought to explain the Belgic Confession on the basis of original sources.

Bekker maintained that God had not made a covenant of works with Adam. The tree of life was not a sacrament of spiritual and eternal life in heaven, but had only natural power with regard to natural life. These were the sorts of views Bekker held. His colleagues judged that these views savored "of unsoundness in the substance of the doctrine."

That is how things were in those days for a minister who did not believe the doctrine of the covenant of works. He was viewed as possibly more dangerous than someone who criticized the Dutch equivalent of the King James Version or the widely accepted authorized commentators on the Dutch Bible. Wilhelmus à Brakel was surely expressing a much more popular view when he opened his treatment of the covenant of works with the words "Much hinges on the knowledge of this covenant, for anyone who does not possess this knowledge or denies this covenant will not understand the covenant of grace." In one province of the Netherlands, preachers during the eighteenth century were required to subscribe to a doctrinal statement that included an affirmation that Adam is the head of all of us in the covenant of works.

Bekker's most serious offense was his denial of the covenant of works. It cost him his professorship. Eventually he was censured and deposed in a dictatorial manner that does not speak well of the Reformed churches of his time. We would need a separate volume for narrating and showing that in practice, Reformed churches have been governed for centuries in a manner more dictatorial than presbyterial.

Bekker had taken the same position as Johannes Vlak, another man with a name that made people tremble. A special set of doctrinal articles were formulated expressly to counteract his influence. Still, when we undertook to read Vlak, we were in for a pleasant surprise—which is not to say, of course, that we agree with everything he wrote.

Vlak's major publication purports to be a treatment of the "eternal gospel." Among the many good things that can be said about this little book is that it stressed that element of *gospel* in the law of Moses. On this point we would choose immediately for the side of Vlak rather than that of Witsius. The subtitle makes it clear that the author wishes to discuss the gospel as given by God to people first before the law (i.e., from Adam to Moses), then through the law, and finally without the law, when Christ fulfilled the shadows. This gives us an overview of the three parts into which this little book (published in 1684) is divided. It deals with the gospel under the promise, the gospel under the law, and the gospel under freedom.

On the back side of the title page we find 1 Corinthians 1:30, an appeal of the apostle Paul for unity in mind. We also find the admonition that the Synod of Dort directed to teachers to the effect that they should stay away from phrases that are not found in Holy Scripture. If only people understood what Vlak was getting at there!

In the preface Vlak declares that the Reformation has freed us from scholastic theology, the old leaven of papal thinking. We have now begun to teach our children the language of the Jews in place of that half-Ashdod language (an allusion to Neh. 13:23–24). But alas, the instruction given by the foremost teachers of the Reformation has been lost from sight so completely that if anyone dares to assert such things today, he may well be viewed as an importer of scandalous new ideas. This was Vlak's comment on the "lovelessness" of the times in which he and his contemporaries lived. What had become of the old freedom?

As for the Heidelberg Catechism, the Belgic Confession, and the Canons of Dort, they stipulated nothing regarding the doctrine of the covenant of works. Calvin, commenting on Jeremiah 31:31, declared that God never made any covenant other than the one he entered first with Abraham and subsequently established with Moses. Pareus wrote that as far as he knew, Scripture nowhere speaks of a covenant of nature. He mentioned still more names as well and took their side in maintaining that there is no covenant of works.

Theology, for Vlak, was simply "the doctrine of the truth and faith of the Scriptures concerning the salvation of sinners through Jesus Christ." If everyone stuck by this definition, he maintained, the theological disputes would soon be over.

Vlak raises the question why people worry so much about the purpose of the Sabbath before that fall into sin. And why all the speculation about what would have become of the human race if Adam had not fallen? Why wonder whether the Son of Man would then have come? Moses, he points out, ignores all such questions.

As for the covenant of works, Vlak writes,

> For my part I cannot understand why it is necessary to think of man before the fall as being related to God through a covenant of works, a covenant which is then alleged to be repeated in the Law of Moses, and whose conditions and commands are included in the Ten Words together with Leviticus 18:5 and Deuteronomy 27:26—if the covenant is obeyed, life, and if not, curse and death. Paul is said to be referring to this in Romans 10 and Galatians 3 and various other passages. I

must admit that I am not so enlightened as to be able
to find a covenant of works before the fall or a repetition of it afterwards. The Holy Spirit does not use such
an expression, neither there nor elsewhere.

Vlak promised to demonstrate that the texts usually referred
to do not speak of a covenant of works.

He kept his promise. In the course of a fairly short discussion, he managed to present a pertinent analysis not just of
such passages as Hosea 6:7, which seems to speak directly of
a covenant with Adam, but also Leviticus 18:5, Deuteronomy
27:26, and other such passages that seem to deal with such a
covenant indirectly.

What is of special interest for us, of course, is what Vlak
wrote about the Law. Did he view the Torah of Moses as a
writing that dealt mainly with the covenant of works made in
Paradise? Not at all! Consider this heading, which he placed
above one of his chapters: "The purpose and use of the Promises and the Law, not as a repetition of promises relating to a
covenant of works but as promises of the fathers in the covenant of grace under the dispensation of the Law of Moses."

In this chapter he dealt with Leviticus 18:1–5, the famous
passage where Moses tells the people to keep God's statutes
and promises: "If a person does them, he shall live by them."
Vlak comments on this passage as follows.

The promise is bound up with the entire law, just as those
who keep Christ's commandments and do them partake of the
tree of life (Rev. 22:2, 14). Life is the promise of the entire law.
But this promise must not be understood in a Jewish way (re-
ceiving life through one's own righteousness in the works of
the law), or in a Socinian way (making the law a new covenant
of works, as people sometimes do with Christ's commands),
or in a Roman Catholic way (where good works give one a
claim to life), but in an orthodox way. What Vlak means by
this is that those who are convinced of their sinfulness by the
law and the commandments must take refuge in those com-

mandments and statutes that speak of atonement, cleansing, forgiveness of sins, and repentance, which is to say that they must seek refuge in Christ, for all these things are shadows of Christ. That was the way of life back then.

It was not a question of perfection of one's virtues but of forgiveness and true uprightness. Thus, when Scripture says of certain persons that they walked according to God's commandments (e.g., Zechariah and Elizabeth), we must not understand this in Roman Catholic terms, as though such people were absolutely perfect. What would then be the purpose of all those commands about guilt and sin offerings, the great Day of Atonement, and so forth? And if the priest Zechariah was unblemished, why did he have to offer sacrifices for his own sins? What would then be the purpose of all those prayers for forgiveness? Just as Christ has commanded us to believe, repent, be baptized, and join in the Lord's Supper, so the commands given to the Israelites by Moses aimed at life.

In short, Vlak had a number of good things to say about the law of Moses, and anyone who does this is always worth listening to. But anyone who speaks of the law in negative terms deserves our resistance. That's why it was necessary to devote attention to the doctrine of the covenant of works.

It's not that we object to anyone speaking of the original relationship between God and man as a covenant; Augustine did so, and many Christians have followed his lead on this point. We would ask only whether it makes a great deal of sense to emphasize an alleged covenant relationship in Genesis 2 and 3 if these chapters themselves do not use the term *covenant*. Yet it is indeed possible for a chapter in the Bible to talk about a covenant without using the word: think of Leviticus 8, for example. (The Bible does speak of the "covenant with Levi" in various other places.)

When it comes to God's alleged covenant with Adam, there is little scriptural evidence to go by. The most likely text is Hosea 6:7, but there has been controversy about this text all through the ages. Some translate this text as "They have transgressed the covenant *like Adam*." There is also the possibility that the text is to be read, "They transgressed the covenant as though it were only a human covenant." As for Calvin, he read "like Adam" as "like people." Thus Calvin says nothing about Adam and certainly nothing about a divine covenant with Adam.

One might wish to use the term "covenant" in this sense: God immediately broke the covenant between Satan on the one hand, and Adam and Eve on the other, as we see from Genesis 3. If such a use of the term is legitimate, one could also say Adam broke the covenant God wished to make with him, as we see from Genesis 3. But then such a low-profile statement must remain just that, and a particular exegetical or theological opinion should not take on the features of an official confession which requires our subscription.

The absence of the word *covenant* in Genesis 2 is not the decisive point, then. Witsius rightly observed that Adam undoubtedly knew about more things than Moses touched on in his short report. Still, we must be exceedingly careful when we raise the question what sorts of things Adam knew about. Can we really draw conclusions about a complete covenant from the simple command listed in Genesis 2:17? To do so is to state the case quite strongly.

And if there was indeed such a covenant, why call it a covenant of works? Doesn't the Bible teach us that the desire to be justified on the basis of our own works is the sin of man? Why then would people adorn this sin with a crown of righteousness in the covenant before the fall? As for the expression "covenant of nature" (the theory behind this expression is that the moral law, which is the basis of this covenant, was known to man by nature, in his heart), Klaas Schilder has definitively shown in his commentary on the Heidelberg Catechism that it is unacceptable.

But that this covenant should be called the covenant of

law is the worst mistake of all. (The reasons for this name should be apparent from the quotations from Witsius above.) When we speak of a covenant of law, what does this do to our good Torah? Wouldn't that amount to falling into the trap of the Jewish opponents of Paul, who tore Christ out of the setting of the law?

That would truly be to use the law, that gospel of shadows, as a whip that drives sinners together and herds them toward Christ. But this is not the sense in which the law is a "disciplinarian" leading us to Christ (Gal. 3:24). The law is a "pedagogue." This word may make us think back to the stern discipline Israel had already received, but we must not forget the real meaning of the word *torah*—teaching. The LORD used the Torah to raise and nurture Israel. There's more to an upbringing than punishment, although there is indeed place for punishment. Moreover, we should not think of "discipline" in negative terms, for there is much more to it than restraint. Discipline covers all aspects of upbringing and is not to be identified with punishment.

To everything that smacks of identifying the good law of Moses with the so-called covenant of works, wherein the whole matter resembles the speculative analysis of Witsius—to all of this we are definitely averse. If that title "covenant of law" really were correct, we would not take much pleasure in writing about that glorious law of Moses as we find it in our Bible.

Chapter 7

Cain and Abel

We have almost reached the end of the second division in the book of Genesis. No doubt you recall that the first section is comprised of 1:1–2:3 (the creation story), while the second one covers 2:4–4:26, in which we are told first about the planting of the garden, the creation of woman, and the first disobedience with some of its consequences.

All there is left to deal with now is the story of Cain's misdeed and the splitting of humanity into two lines: the line of Cain and the line of Seth. But this divergence between the two lines really began with a divergence between two individuals.

The Contrast between Cain and Abel

The greatest contrast between Cain and Abel was not the work they did. The one tilled the soil and the other kept livestock, but this is mentioned to us only to explain the material they used for their respective offerings. The contrast is this: the one simply gave God something without thinking much about it, while the other made a careful choice. Abel selected animals for sacrifices "of the firstborn of his flock and of their fat portions" (4:4). The word *fat* is often used in Scripture to indicate the best, the choicest, the most important (see Gen. 45:18; Deut. 32:14; Pss. 22:29; 65:11–12; 81:16).

Abel's choice of material for sacrifice was determined by faith. Therefore what he offered to God was a more acceptable sacrifice than what Cain offered (Heb. 11:4). The apostle John says that Cain was of the devil and murdered his brother. Why did he murder him? Because his own works were evil, while his brother's works were righteous (1 John 3:12). The word *works* can be applied to a person's entire life, but the unbelief that characterized Cain's entire life was manifested most strongly in his choice of material for sacrifice. What a glaring contrast between his unbelieving stinginess and the pious generosity of Abel! The evil one, of whom the apostle John writes in 1 John 3, saw his chance to drag the very first seed (*zera'*) of Eve, her oldest son, back over the line God had drawn between the woman and the snake, although Cain is not entirely a passive participant, a victim to be pitied.

Genesis does not mention Satan, the figure in the background. Only Cain is declared guilty of the hatred—religious hatred—that filled his soul. Like the people of whom John was speaking, he hated his brother because of his brother's faith and religion. He even forsook the communion of the first pious ones (1 John 2:19) and went over to the evil one, with whom God had just forbidden Eve and all her children friendship of any kind. But Cain could no longer put up with the piety of Abel. Genesis 4 does not tell us much about this, but the apostle John found enough material there to be able to sketch Cain as the first one to hate believers and forsake the church. The two lines in Genesis 4 begin to diverge at the point where Cain turns his back.

The question is often asked how Cain and Abel could have known that God accepted the sacrifice of the one but not the sacrifice of the other. Remarkably, Genesis does not give us the answer to this question, just as there are many other questions it does not answer for us, questions like how God spoke to Cain, and how the first people came by the custom of offering sacrifices to God.

Here again we would remind Bible readers that Genesis was not written in the first place for us but for the Israelites. For these first readers Genesis apparently discussed the issues in question in a manner that raised no problems whatsoever. How often did they see no sacrifices being offered? We never see sacrifices, normally. Moreover, they were taught from their youth by parents, teachers, and priests how much the lawfulness of worship to the LORD, the God of Cain and Abel, involved the heart. Therefore it must have been obvious to the writer and first readers of Genesis 4 that the practice of offering sacrifices was not a human invention but a divine command, a revelation, an express decree from above. The fact that a passage of Scripture is silent on this or that point can mean either that the matter is unknown or that it was too well-known to the original readers to be worth mentioning.

The writer of Genesis must have accepted it as obvious that God the LORD still spoke to the first people after sin came into the picture, just as he had spoken with them in Paradise. There is some basis for this conjecture, for we read later that Cain went away from the countenance of the LORD.

We should not understand this to mean that the LORD wished to be served only in the vicinity of the garden of Eden. The statement means only that after his encounter with God described in Genesis 4:9–15, Cain left the LORD's presence. Ecclesiastes 8:3 speaks in a similar way of leaving the king's presence.

Thus it does not seem at all unlikely that God continued to speak with Cain and his contemporaries in a way that resembled his contact with Adam and Eve in the garden of Eden. If this supposition is correct, why would the LORD not have spoken in those conversations to someone or other about sacrifices in general, and to Cain about his sacrifices in particular? In such a conversation the LORD could well have made his displeasure with Cain's sacrifices known. "Is this all you have for me, Cain?"

Moreover, God had a surprising amount of patience with Cain. Or do we get that impression only because his conversations with Cain are reported to us at such length? This gives us something to think about. Is the Bible already telling us about God's great patience with mankind from the time of Cain to the flood?

In any event, Cain did not lack for warnings. Why are you angry, Cain, and why that scowl on your face? Are you not allowed to raise that face of yours if you do what is right, if your "works" become different, namely, your entire attitude toward life, your relationship to God, as it comes through in your sacrifices? But if you refuse to do what is right, sin is lying in wait for you at your door. Sin's desire is for you, but you must rule over him. You must not let that hellhound be your boss (see Gen. 4:6–7).

Unfortunately, these warnings did little good. How this must have disappointed God! He is the one who later revealed himself to Israel as Yahweh, the God who abhors sin, violence, and death and who loves the life of his creatures, especially the lives of human beings. We know that he sent no one less than his Son to bring about the deliverance of human life.

This God cursed Cain. We do not read that he cursed Adam, but we do read that he cursed Cain. "What have you done? Listen, the blood of your brother cries out to me from the earth. And now, cursed are you."

Even so, God's attitude toward Cain was strikingly mild and patient. When Cain protested boldly against the punishment, which he claimed was too severe, God gave him a sign. Note carefully: he did not place a sign on him, in the sense of a distinguishing characteristic, but he placed a sign *before* him.

What was that sign? Did God perhaps perform a miracle by which everyone would know how expressly he forbade the shedding of blood, especially vengeance for Abel's blood on Cain by one of his brothers or sisters? God abhorred death, including the death of Cain and his line. Cain, too, had been created by God himself!

The Contrast between Cain's Line and Seth's Line

The second section of the book of Genesis ends with a characterization of the sharp opposition between two lines of descendants. One of those lines carried on in the style of Cain, and the other in the style of Abel. It was the Cainites versus the Sethites—flesh against Spirit.

First a tiresome question—or rather, a question often raised by tiresome people. Young Christians like to ask their elders, "Where did Cain find himself a wife?"

Cain chose a wife from among his sisters, of course. He must have had a number of sisters, for Adam fathered "sons and daughters" (5:4). There were no genetic problems involved in such interbreeding, for every child of Adam and Eve contained all the necessary genetic material for bringing forth healthy descendants. Furthermore, at that point the human race had not yet degenerated because of sin and its consequences as much as it has by now. The process of sin and corruption was not yet as greatly diminished as in later centuries. This we gather from the long lives that many people were able to live in these earliest times, according to Scripture. Could this longevity have been an aftereffect of Adam and Eve eating from the tree of life before being expelled from the Garden?

We should also note that Cain very well may have been married before he murdered Abel. This misdeed seems to have been committed when he was a grown man—somewhere in the neighborhood of 20–30 years of age. Wouldn't Eve already have borne a number of other children after the birth of Cain and Abel? And if Cain was married, his wife certainly might have borne him children by then. Thus he may have had a family of his own. And we should not forget that it is in connection with Cain's line that we first hear talk of building cities. To build and populate cities, you need people. The building of cities that we encounter in Genesis 4, of course, should be viewed as the expression of a desire for safety, power, and might.

In any event, the report about the building of cities and such events is typical of Cain and his line. The Cainites are probably also the ones who first began taking two wives. If we remember that Genesis was written first of all for Israel, we can read this passage (along with 2:24) as a sensitive warning against Eastern polygamy. Such warnings come up more often in Genesis (think of the story of Jacob). Genesis never sounds warnings in a heavy-handed way. The pastoral statements on the Sabbath (2:3) and marriage (2:24) stand alone. The author of Genesis is careful not to lay it on too thick.

The names Adah and Zillah, the wives of Lamech, might be taken to mean "show" and "shadow." If so, the first name speaks for itself. The significance of the second would be clearer to people who endured the heat of the ancient Near East than it is to those who live in cooler climates.

Among the Cainites we also come across extensive property holdings. Then begins the life of nomads with their great herds. This would have been of great interest to a people like Israel.

Among the Cainites life was soon made more pleasant through joyful music. They also knew how to make sad music. There are people who enjoy sorrow—at least for a while.

The people of Cain's line also made things easier for themselves by learning to work with metal. Just think how different the world would be without metal! Today we have gone a long way in the direction of the Cainites. We have learned to tremble at such words as security, power, property, capital, industry, luxury, technology, beauty, and enjoyment. "And the sister of Tubal-cain [perhaps this name means "Tubal the Smith"] was Naamah." Again a remarkable name. Genesis 4 is swimming in plays on words. The Hebrew word *qayin* means "smith." When Cain was born, Eve said, "*Qanethi* a man," that is, "I have received a son." *Abel* means "frailty," *Adah* means "ornament," *Zillah* means "shadow," and *Naamah* means "loveliness, beauty."

Suggestions have been made that the name Cain has something to do with the gypsylike existence of the smiths among peoples like the Israelites and their neighbors. Did the name of Eve's son remind the Israelites in some way or other of a life of wandering? We cannot be sure about these things, but it is generally assumed that the names as they come to us in these early chapters of Genesis are not the original names but a Hebrew version of them, for the first people on earth did not speak Hebrew. The author of Genesis, or perhaps some earlier storyteller, presented Hebrew versions of various words and names that had been passed down to him in the tradition of previous generations. This was done for the sake of his hearers and readers. He tried to do it in such a way that there were often additional nuances and shades of meaning in the terms and names. This phenomenon of plays on words involving names appears quite often in the Old Testament. Most good commentaries take the trouble to point them out. Earlier we mentioned Naamah. She was probably given this name in her younger years because of her great beauty. But the author of Genesis, writing at a much later time and in a different language, must have chosen to mention her name in his narrative because it was a striking way to characterize the entire Cainite line. What came first for the Cainites was property (in modern terms, money), second was women, and the trio is only complete when we add murder: money, murder, and women.

When it came to murder and violence, Lamech was right there. We sense the contempt as the author of Genesis looks at this man from various angles. We hear the Spirit of the prophetic Word teaching the covenant people Israel to abhor such a lifestyle. Lamech was not just a murderer of his neighbor; he was first and foremost a hater of God. He even dared to heap scorn on Yahweh. He made light of God's promise to protect

Cain's life by saying that he, Lamech, would see to his own protection. Moreover, he would avenge not just seven times but seventy-seven times. Not just for deep wounds would he demand blood vengeance, but even for blows and scratches.

How horrible such language must have sounded in God's ears as it rose from the earth on which everything had once been so good and had breathed of peace and spoken of life. Out of an atmosphere of life that seemed to be full of joy rose a raucous cry of death, the death that the LORD later taught Israel to abhor, just as he abhorred it himself. (We will have more to say about this in connection with Exodus and Leviticus.)

Over against the Cainite line Genesis places the line of Seth. Pay careful attention to the quiet comparison that Genesis makes here. The men of might and women of show that we read about in connection with Cain's line are not found here. Accommodating yourself to others is also an art.

There does not seem to be much room for doubt that Eve brought other children into the world between Abel and Seth (Gen. 5:4). Yet Seth is expressly mentioned as the one to take Abel's place.

We would propose the following explanation. One day the mother of a number of children lost one of them in death. It was a boy. Not long afterward she brought her tenth or eleventh child into the world. It was also a boy. Years later, looking back, she says, "When I lost that boy in death, God gave me this one to take his place." This must have been how Eve, the mother of all of us, looked upon the birth of the son who was named Seth: in him she took comfort after the death of Abel. We are told expressly that Eve named him Seth, which means "replacement": "For God has given me another son in place of Abel, who was killed by Cain." The text itself does not directly indicate it, but it seems obvious to assume that the last few words were also spoken by Eve. Here we hear a mother speak of her pain and sorrow, but at the same time of her faith. God was her Comforter, even though he was much more upset than any human being about how death had forced its way into the world of humanity. Was there anyone who understood Eve better than he did? Every human being must be something special and beautiful to God, especially such a pious person as Abel.

"To Seth also a son was born" (4:26). When we read this simple text quickly, we do not get the impression that the author of Genesis wants to draw our attention to anything special here. We almost read right over it, as if it were a routine birth announcement in some church paper. But that's not what the author of Genesis wants us to do.

In Hebrew this text reads roughly as follows: "And to Seth, also to him, was a son born." Pay careful attention! Seth received seed too. Did you get the message? Seth, in turn, also became the father of a house, a line. Cain was not the only one, then.

This is what the author of Genesis wishes to emphasize here. Indeed, Seth's line is *the* line. Yet, at this point the author does not feel obliged to give us a long series of names—and certainly not a series of proud names like the ones he provided in connection with Cain's line. No, for the present he mentions only two names. The first name is Seth, which we have already discussed, and the second name is Enosh.

Let's pause for a moment by this name. Originally it must have been a somewhat different name, but for the sake of Israelite hearers and readers, no doubt, a Hebrew form of the name is used. But the author probably still wanted to express something of the original meaning of the name. Well then, that meaning was "weakness, perishability"—at least, that's the meaning of the closest Hebrew word. The Hebrew word *'enosh* must mean something like "weak humanity." In Psalm 144:3 the son of *'enosh* is the weak son of man whom God still deigns to look at. The days of *'enosh* are like grass (Ps. 103:15).

Imagine what an impression the name Enosh must have made on Hebrew hearers and readers. What a contrast with those stirring names in Cain's line, that sick glorification of human might, that delight in progress (toward death).

With Seth begins a different line, a different group, a different seed. How is this line characterized? "Then they began to call on the name of Yahweh."

Again we must remind ourselves that the book of Genesis was written first and foremost for the Israelites, for the people who confessed that Elohim, the God of heaven and earth who was not completely unknown to other peoples, is Yahweh, the God of life, who had delivered Israel from her miserable, deathly state in Egypt. Since that time he liked to be known among the Israelites as Yahweh. (We will come back to this name in connection with the book of Exodus.)

This verse in Genesis does not intend to go into the name Yahweh as such. Still, we should note the contrast between violence and death among the Cainites on the one hand, and Yahweh, the God of life, among the Sethites on the other. In the days of Enosh, a beginning was made among the Sethites in calling on the name of the God who later wanted Israel to call him by the special name Yahweh.

What does the expression "call on the name of Yahweh" mean? Judging by Genesis 12:8; 13:4; 21:33; and 26:25, the author of Genesis was referring to public worship services, a cultus in honor of the true God. What we learn in 4:26 is that such worship first began among the Sethites during the days of Enosh.

Why during the days of Enosh? We raise this question because of the presence of the word *then* in the text. It was probably not long after the entry of sin into the world and Cain's misdeed and the rise of his line to power and glory that the contrasts began to grow sharper and sharper. Those who wished to live by the command recorded in Genesis 3:15 saw themselves more and more as confronting a unified front of those who did not wish to be faithful to that command.

Among the Cainites the communion of the unholy unfolded in all its deathly splendor, as the runaways, those who
had deserted God's army and refused to fight for him in the
war (3:15), stuck together. What did the Sethites do in response? Exactly what sheep do when a dog appears in their
pasture. The sheep do not fight with the dog, but they crowd
together as much as possible, preferably with their shepherd
in the center. And that's also the style of the church.

The Sethites sought refuge together. In their fear because
of the threat posed by the Canaanites, they began to seek
God's protection together. The Israelite readers would understand that this meant seeking protection from Elohim, who
revealed himself to Israel in later ages as Yahweh, the God
with the mighty name and mighty deeds, as Egypt found out
to her great loss and the Gibeonites found out in great relief.
When the representatives of the Gibeonites came home, they
could say to the people waiting for them anxiously, "Don't be
afraid. We are now under the protection of Yahweh. His name
is above our heads" (Josh. 9). Don't you suppose they thought
of the name of Yahweh when they saw the sun stand still and
the stars join in the battle?

Calling on a name means asking for protection. The
weak appeal to the strong. We Christians will never be able
to accomplish much when we face the powerful name of the
"Cainites," even though we are often eager to reach for the
weapons of force and might. But the church must seek solace
and protection in calling on the name of the LORD.

David, the king with a humble heart before the LORD, understood this. He did not rest until he had brought the ark to
its place in Jerusalem, and he commanded his Levitical singers
to call on the name of Yahweh, that is to say, to call out that
God's mighty redemptive deeds were continuing among his
people now that his ark again had a place of honor in their
midst. This was important to heaven and earth, to nations,
seas, and fields. Now the world rested again on its pillars
(1 Chr. 16:8, 30). David saw the connection between God's

name, which was bound up with the ark, and the *toledoth* and heaven and earth (see Gen. 2:4).

We, too, the church gathered from among the Gentiles, are encouraged to call on the name of the LORD so that we may be saved (Joel 2:32; Acts 2:21). If things are well, our help is in the name of the LORD, who has made the heavens and the earth (Ps. 124:8).

CHAPTER 8

Continuing Corruption and Repeated Restoration

We have now worked our way through the second section of Genesis. This section began, "These are the *toledoth* of the heavens and the earth" (2:4). This section ran from 2:4 through 4:26 and showed us how sin broke into the life of peace and joy that God had given his people. That was quite something, for the consequences of that event are still working themselves out, just as the poisoning of a tree's roots has its effects on the entire tree. Thus the "*toledoth* of the heavens and the earth" do not form a closed period that has nothing to do with us today. We still live in that *toledoth* of heaven and earth. People sometimes throw up their hands in despair and ask, "Where will it all end?" We must still see what eventually becomes of heaven and earth. Christ has not returned yet, and the earth has not been renewed. There is still a great deal to be done.

That was section 2 of Genesis, then. As you will recall, Genesis has a number of other sections still to come, but they are not all as important as the one we have just dealt with. Genesis is a bit like a tree. You see one or two main branches go up, and a number of side branches that are not as important. Some of the "shoots" that Genesis mentions have already disappeared. For example, is there anyone who still speaks of the line of Esau (36:1)? But the other shoots are still in the picture today. Let's not forget that we who are Gentiles have been engrafted into the people that sprouted from Jacob (37:2).

The Triumph of Cain's Spirit

After Cain murdered Abel, the LORD expressly sent him away from the believers. There was to be no fellowship between this unrepentant persecutor of the church and the other descendants of Adam and Eve. Prominent among those descendants was Seth, whom we discussed previously. Just as we read that Adam was created in God's image and likeness so that he could become God's regent and rule in God's place, so Seth is said to be the image and likeness of his father (5:3). We do not read such a thing of any of the other sons of Adam who must have been born between the birth of Abel and his death as a grown man. Such a statement is made only about Seth. Why? We don't know. Later, in the discussion of the genealogies, there will be more occasions for admitting ignorance on various points.

Seth appears on the scene as Adam's successor. We could almost say that he is the crown prince, except that such a word does not seem fitting in a discussion of the church. And it is indeed the church that we are talking about here. Cain was censured and put out of the church. Adam was already growing older when his son Seth was born. (Seth received his name from his mother.) Tradition tells us that Seth succeeded his father as the leader of the segment of humanity that wanted to remain on the LORD's side, on the side of life, over against the front formed by Satan, Cain, sin, flesh, violence, oppression, and death.

Apparently people were willing to follow Seth as leader— at first, if not later. The Sethites seem to have grown considerably in number. But eventually they joined with the godless people on the other side and started going downhill.

Their decline started in a much different way than the people of Enosh's day originally feared. They were not flattened by the Cainite fist. We read nothing about any such development. What we read about instead is laxness: "The sons of God [i.e., the Sethites, the people of Seth, who was the son of Adam, the son of God—Luke 3:38] saw that the daughters of man [the Cainites] were attractive. And they took as their wives any they chose [without bearing in mind the will of God and of their parents]" (Gen. 6:2).

Some people believe that this text in Genesis is talking about marriages between supra-earthly creatures (e.g., angels, gods) and women. Even certain pious church fathers defended such an interpretation. The term *sons of God* can indeed mean "angels" (see Job 1:6; 38:7), but that does not appear to be what it means here.

If this were indeed what the text said (but then somewhat more expressly), it would have won enthusiastic approval as it circulated among the nations around Israel. Heathen antiquity was not at all put off by such stories of crossbreeding between different sorts of beings. The hearts of men have long been full not just of the deification of the sun, moon, and stars, of animals, trees, and rivers, but also the deification of human beings.

The special subject we are discussing here (i.e., religious marriage) is the subject of a famous book, *The Golden Bough*, by J. G. Frazer. This book appeared in 1906, which was before the enormous stream of modern archeological reports, and it drew heavily on the writings of ancient Greek and Latin authors. But what we find among the pagans and what our text (Gen. 6:2) may even be alluding to in a play on words should not be imposed on Israel. We then surrender our joy at the uniqueness of Israel's sacred writings. If there is one thing the Old Testament steers clear of completely, it is the crossing of the boundary between God and the creature. In the heart of the Torah we will hear more about this.

Were the people supposed to read this introduction to the Torah of Moses as something in direct conflict with the word it introduced? Were they supposed to find in Genesis some foolish pagan stories—that is indeed what they were—about gods or (wicked) angels seeking sexual delight in the arms of beautiful women? If so, why does Genesis 6 speak only of the punishment of people, saying nothing about the punishment of the wicked gods or angels who took the initiative?

There are other passages in Scripture where people are called sons of God (Exod. 4:22; Deut. 14:1; Isa. 1:2). No, it appears that the author of Genesis was simply picking up the thread of Genesis 4, regarding the Cainite city-princes with their polygamous and violent practices. The idea is that those with authority, like judges, kings, and potentates, resemble God himself (you will find this allusion in Exod. 21:6; 22:8, 9, 28; Ps. 82:1, 6; John 10:34–35). Genesis 6 is telling Israel that at an earlier time, very early in its history, the church declined due to the corruption of marriage. The Israelite readers and hearers could probably understand this story and what it meant for them very well. It was for them that Genesis was written first of all, for people to whom Moses said, "You are the sons of the LORD your God" (Deut. 14:1). They had to learn the lesson of Genesis 6 well.

The battle lines drawn in Genesis 3:15 had disappeared from view! The line God had drawn so firmly in Paradise had been crossed. The actual state of affairs, namely, that the two sides were at war, was no longer understood. And there is nothing as bad as when the very best spoils become the very worst. The people who were born of the mingling of the lines of Seth and Cain were ultimately so wicked and corrupt that our Lord Jesus Christ once compared them to the people who would be on earth during the time when he returned in judgment, "eating and drinking, marrying and giving in marriage" (Matt. 24:38–39). In our time we already see some elements of the situation Jesus was describing. Christianity is shot through with apostasy. Well, that's what the world before the flood looked like.

The LORD then made a decision, and he announced it via Noah: his Spirit, the source on which all of life was dependent, would be taken away from humanity (Gen. 6:3). Then sinful humanity would find out who it really was—nothing more than weak flesh. This statement on God's part is all the more remarkable because there were such strong people on earth in those days—giants. This is the meaning the Septuagint gave to the Hebrew word *nephilim*, and it was confirmed when the same Hebrew word appeared in Numbers 13:33. The spies who went into the land of Canaan felt like grasshoppers when they got near those giants.

The word makes us think of great strength, then. "These were the mighty men who were of old, the men of renown" (Gen. 6:4). There giants were probably much discussed in their time and afterward. It may be that we have echoes of these discussions in later stories about legendary beings among ancient peoples, such as the Titans among the Greeks. Could it be that the names of such gods as Zeus (or Jupiter) and Hera (or Juno) also go back to these stories? Those giants must have had giant wives. Could it be that these giants became gods for many ancient peoples? And could this in turn have something to do with that early view that the "sons of God" referred to in Genesis 6:2 were angels of some sort?

In the eyes of the LORD, all of them—parents and children alike—were weak, mortal creatures. They were flesh. He placed a limit on the length of their lives. If the situation did not improve within 120 years, God's patience would be at an end (6:3). Then they would all find out what they were—frail, mortal flesh.

The ultimatum did no good. Because God still showed so much patience—120 years is a long time—the warning was no doubt forgotten, just as we forget so easily in our day. An event like a terrorist attack gives us a bad scare, but soon we learn to live with the new situation.

In Genesis 6 we sense that the narrator is coming closer and closer to the story of "Noah, a herald of righteousness" (2 Pet. 2:5). The preaching of Noah and all his other work as well is to be placed in that 120-year period between verses 4 and 5 of Genesis 6. In 6:5 the judgment strikes. The people had simply ignored God as he spoke to them through the mouth of his prophet. Then God's patience ran out. Remember, nothing could be more untrue than to say that God's patience is inexhaustible. That's simply a lie: God's patience does come to an end. God does not let people make light of his threats (see Gal. 6:7).

It caused God deep sorrow that people conducted themselves toward him in such a manner. Finally he said, "I will blot out man whom I have created from the face of the land, man and animals and creeping things and birds of the heavens, for I am sorry that I have made them." But Noah found favor in the eyes of the LORD (Gen. 6:7–8).

The Sorrow of God

In Genesis 6:7 we find the LORD saying, "I am sorry that I have made them." This is the first place in the Bible where we read a statement to the effect that God was sorry he had done something. There are others, as you can easily see for yourself with the help of a good concordance. If you look under the verb *repent* (Hebrew *nakham*), you will find more passages in which we are told that it "repented" the LORD that he had done a thing.

Some Bible readers have difficulties with such passages. They also have problems with passages in which we read that the LORD was planning to do something, whereas later he said he would not do it. After the sin of worshiping the golden calf, for example, he said he would not go along with Israel to Canaan, but later, in response to Moses's prayer, he relented (Exod. 32–33). This may not have been problematic for such

Bible readers at first, but when they heard so much about God as the Unchangeable One in the sense that he never goes back on any of his intentions, it didn't seem right to them any longer, especially when they were reminded of 1 Samuel 15:29, where we read, "The Glory of Israel will not lie or repent; for he is not a man, that he should repent" (RSV). In some translations of this verse, the LORD is spoken of not as the "Glory" of Israel but as the "Unchangeable One."

This verse seems to suggest, then, that God never changes or repents of what he has done or was planning to do. But there are also passages in which it is said that God did change or repent of something. His angel had delivered Israel and carried her in the days of Egypt and Horeb. But when the Israelites were very disobedient toward the LORD, "he turned to be their enemy, and himself fought against them" (Isa. 63:10). And in the same chapter in which we read that God is the Unchangeable One of Israel, we also read, "Then the word of the LORD came to Samuel: 'I regret that I have made Saul king'" (1 Sam. 15:10–11).

What are we to do with such verses? Is there any way they can be reconciled?

A solution along the following lines was proposed. All the passages that spoke of change or repentance in connection with God were characterized as "anthropomorphic." But when 1 Samuel 15:29 says that God is unchangeable, it is not speaking anthropomorphically. Any appearance of contradiction would then fall away.

What does the word *anthropomorphism* mean? It does not appear in the Bible but was put together from two Greek words to deal with the difficulty we are discussing: *anthropos*, which means "man," and *morphē*, which means "form" or "appearance." An anthropomorphic passage, then, would be one in which things are cast into human terms.

How is the term used in the context of our discussion? Sometimes it is applied to the entire Bible. The Dutch Reformed theologian Herman Bavinck declared not just that the Bible contains anthropomorphic passages here and there, but that the entire Bible is anthropomorphic (*Reformed Dogmatics*, 2:99). What Bavinck meant by this is that God spoke to us in human language and human words. With this we can easily agree, but we hardly need such an imposing term as *anthropomorphic* to express the point. All we need to say is that the LORD wished to speak to people in a simple manner they could understand. Scripture testifies that God's Word is a light for us.

Bavinck would agree, but he wished to carry anthropomorphism in Scripture much further. When he discussed the creation of humanity in God's image, we see how far he wants to go. Scripture could not and would not speak in a human way of God, and attribute all sorts of human characteristics to him, unless God had first created humanity entirely in his image. There you have the far-reaching anthropomorphic character of Scripture, according to Bavinck. When Scripture speaks of God's hands and feet and heart and so forth, and also of God's repenting of this or that, it is all anthropomorphic language. Human characteristics were being attributed to God.

Does the term *anthropomorphic* help us or give us a solution to our problem? What is really going on in this discussion?

The talk about anthropomorphism is mere assertion. The introduction of a new term here is only a secondary issue. It has been claimed that the appearance of contradiction that we noted earlier disappears completely when we recognize that the Bible speaks of the LORD in human terms from time to time, that is, that it attributes human characteristics to him.

The intent of this approach is obvious. When there are two series of Scripture passages that seem to contradict each other, the contradiction is easily resolved by declaring one of the series anthropomorphic. The conflict suddenly vanishes. But may we operate in such a manner? May we use a term like *anthropomorphic* in this way? Is it correct to say that the Bible is only speaking anthropomorphically when it tells us that God changed his mind or that he was sorry he had done a thing? Is it really true that the Bible sometimes transfers human attributes to God? Are we showing the proper respect for the Bible when we say such things? Are we being humble enough? Or are we really being proud, placing ourselves above the Bible and judging it? ("This text is anthropomorphic, and this one isn't.")

Is it really true that the Bible gives us the impression here and there that God the LORD is a man? And does the Bible tell us that if God were a man, he would repent of this or that? We then think to ourselves, "But because he is not a man, he did not repent. Thus what the Bible says here is not true, strictly speaking."

Such an approach finally leaves us feeling a little dizzy and nauseous. We feel the only firm ground we have to stand on in this world (i.e., the Word of our God) slipping away from us. God, in reality, is not a human being, and what the Bible says about him in human terms cannot be accepted at face value. God did not really feel repentance or sorrow, even though the Bible said he did. God does not feel actual pain or actual affection, even if the Bible says he does.

Such reasoning cannot help but make us uneasy! The anthropomorphic solution to our problem seems to leave us feeling unsure about all sorts of things. If the talk about anthropomorphism is indeed correct, what is there in the Bible that we can accept as true? Don't we wind up dangerously close to what our fathers warned us against, namely, the view that the Bible is not God's Word but that God's Word is in the Bible? Where is the boundary? What yardstick are we using here?

Prof Benne Holwerda took an entirely different approach to this question in his lectures, which were published in Dutch in the form of notes after his death. According to Holwerda, we must not assume that Scripture speaks of God in anthropomorphic terms. Rather, it's just the other way around: humanity, according to the Scriptures is "theomorphic." In other words, humanity is created in the image of God.

The Bible tells us that God has a *temunah*. This Hebrew word is usually translated as "form" or "appearance." Among the features that make up God's appearance are his countenance, his hands, his feet, his bowels, and so forth. Immediately we must add that what is meant is not creaturely hands, feet, and so forth, but divine ones. We cannot form any conception of God's appearance, nor may we make images of him. The second commandment forbids it.

It pleased God to accuse Aaron and Miriam of a serious lack of respect for his servant Moses because he spoke to him "mouth to mouth" and had let him see the "form [*temunah*] of the LORD" (Num. 12:8). But we may not deduce from this that Moses saw God's "countenance," for we are told in Exodus 33:20 that he had not. On the other hand, we may not deny that God has a *temunah* and that it pleased God to make it visible to Moses in some manner or other. Perhaps he did so in the way he had shown himself to Adam and Eve in the garden of Eden. We read that they heard God's voice and used to take walks with him.

～◌

There is another misconception that comes into the picture here, namely, the view that a human being is made up of a body plus a soul. This misconception is not easily dislodged, for it is deeply rooted in Christian circles by now and permeates our language, especially the kind of language we use in church, which has its roots in conceptions current in medieval Christendom. But the Greek notion of the soul must be eliminated from our thinking. For the present we will not even deal with the accompanying error to the effect that for many Christians, the soul is a much more elevated creation than the body, which is an error from which not even Calvin freed himself.

The view that everything that constitutes a human being

is to be subsumed under either of the two headings known as the human body (matter) or the human soul (spirit) cannot be defended on scriptural grounds. As the Bible presents this reality, there is much more to a human being than matter and spirit. What are we supposed to do with the soul when the soul is spoken of in the sense of life? What about the soul in the sense of a desire to eat? (See Prov. 6:30 and Isa. 29:8 in the KJV.) What about a human being's talents and powers? They belong neither to the world of matter nor to the world of spirit.

The Bible speaks of a human being in a much more differentiated way than this basic separation into body and soul allows for. (The separation comes at death, when the body dies while the "Greek" soul remains alive.) Scripture speaks of a human being's heart, soul, spirit, understanding, powers, his outer side, his inner side, his flesh, his limbs, and so forth.

The Bible does not speak of a human being's body as something of lesser importance in comparison with the elevated soul. Rather, the body assumes the more prominent place. Thus, if we were to speak of a biblical psychology, that psychology would have to orient itself clearly to the body. What we find in the Bible is not a view of the human being as a unified organism under the centralized control of the brain. Rather, a human being is presented as consisting of all sorts of organs that each possess a relative independence. Not only the heart and the mind have their own thoughts and plans, but also the eye and the hand and the tongue and the foot carry out their functions as independent entities. Thus we might say that when Scripture speaks about a human being with heart and hand and head and bowels and so forth, the Israelites thought in terms of a system of government like the one in effect in the United States rather than a monarchical or dictatorial system.

The Israelite could say that his soul thirsted, his flesh

yearned, his mind instructed him, his eye saw, his ear heard, his hand rose, and so forth. We, by contrast, would be inclined to speak of the self as performing these actions: I (myself) thirsted, yearned, saw, heard, and so forth. We do not say, "We will call the damsel, and enquire at her mouth" (Gen. 24:57 KJV). Instead we say simply, "Let us ask the damsel."

Older translations such as the King James Version tended to translate more literally and therefore retained many of these Hebraisms. New translations usually do not; they pride themselves on staying close to the speech patterns of modern English. That's all the more reason why we should be sure to have a King James Version around the house. If we do not look in the more literal translations from time to time, we will lose sight of how the Bible uses the term *soul*. (*Soul* often is rendered as "life" in newer translations.)

Because humanity is created in the image and likeness of God, the Bible's way of speaking about humanity also has implications for how it speaks about God. When the prophets wanted to declare that the LORD had said something, they proclaimed that the "mouth" of the LORD had said it. When we explain such a text, we are entirely justified in saying that what is meant is simply that the LORD said it. But it serves no good purpose to erase the word *mouth* from our text. When the Bible talks about the "countenance" of God, we may not say simply that this is figurative language that means something else, for this would be to contradict Scripture.

Because humanity is created in God's image, such talk is not figurative language but reality. The Bible does not speak about God in human terms: it's just the other way around. The human being's form and thoughts and deeds are discussed in terms modeled on God. Because God has a *temunah* (form) and therefore a countenance, the human being, who is created in his image, has a countenance as well.

From this perspective we now come back to the question of

the sorrow of God. Because God can repent of something he has done or decided, a human being, who is created in his image, can do so as well. Therefore we need not be perplexed by Bible passages that tell us that God was sorry he had done this or that, and we need not "explain" such passages in a way that substitutes a different meaning for what the text actually says. When we read in Genesis 6, for example, that something "pained" God in his heart, we must show enough respect for the text to let it stand.

God was deeply disappointed and saddened when he saw what had become of his world. He was not indifferent to events on earth; rather, the developments caused him great pain, even if it was not the pain of one who has been defeated. God continued to cling to his plan for his creation.

Later, God was sorry he had made Saul king and he was very sad when he saw what Saul had made of the kingship in Israel. (There was nothing wrong with the kingship in itself, of course.) Then, too, God was not discouraged and defeated in spirit but clung to his plans for the kingship in Israel.

We need not be perplexed either about 1 Samuel 15:29, where we read, "The Glory of Israel will not lie or repent; for he is not a man, that he should repent" (RSV; see also Num. 23:19–20). Here any thought of a connection between sin and repentance in God is cast aside. With us as human beings, of course, there is often such a connection, for we are sorry for sinful deeds and repent of them. But Israel's God does not lie and does not have to repent of what he has said.

There are also times when we repent of a good deed or intention. Sometimes we wish we could take a certain promise back: we have given our word, but we would rather not keep it. Yes, we are unfaithful at times; that's the sort of thing one has to expect of human beings. They may say they will do this or that, but when the time comes they do not follow through. People lie and fail to keep their word. What 1 Samuel 15:29 wants to tell us is that there is none of this to be feared from God. God keeps his words; we can rely on his promises. We can always count on him.

Thus we can speak of sorrow and pain in connection with God. We can even say that he repented of this or that, but we can never speak of repentance from sin in connection with God.

A New Humanity from Noah's Family

The Bible's account of the flood is rather lengthy. What is the reason for this? One reason, of course, is the importance of the subject. Another reason must have been to introduce some corrections in the face of all the other flood stories that were circulating in the ancient Near Eastern environment in which Israel lived. Through the work of archaeologists we now possess a considerable number of these flood stories. At the same time, remnants of flood stories have been found among people who have migrated a long way away from Israel's habitat, from which we see what a deep impression this event must have left behind.

When we turn to the Mesopotamian flood stories, we are dealing with very ancient literature that manifests striking similarities with the biblical story of the flood. The similarities are so striking that we cannot deny that there is some sort of relationship.

We need not make a problem of this—not at all. The entire human race springs from a common ancestry. Therefore it should not surprise us that stories about Paradise and the ark are to be found among all sorts of people; in fact, this only confirms the scriptural account. We should also remember that when it comes to the knowledge of God and his works and commandments, the process of apostasy and corruption does not proceed with equal rapidity in all segments of humanity. If Israel spoke of "Elohim," she could be understood by many of the neighboring people because of what they had in common in the way of language and stories passed on from earlier generations. And Israel was related especially to the

Mesopotamian world through the patriarch Abraham. Therefore it should come as no surprise that Israelite literature bears a definite resemblance to Babylonian literature.

When it comes to flood stories, however, there are differences as well as similarities to be noted when we compare the Israelite account with the Babylonian one (see the eleventh tablet of the Epic of Gilgamesh). A believer who compares the two will soon be calmed by what he finds, for the biblical account also won the trust of the Lord Jesus Christ and his apostles, as we see from their words in the New Testament.

What are the major differences between the two accounts? In the Bible we read nothing about a gathering of gods who quarrel and bicker with each other but also decide on the destruction of humanity. The Bible does not say anything either about one god secretly sabotaging the whole plan by warning a special favorite of his among the people on earth about the coming catastrophe. And we certainly do not read anything in the Bible about trembling gods who are frightened afterward at the force of the waves they have unleashed and who creep away like frightened dogs. The Babylonian account even includes a happy ending in which the hero of the story is finally brought to the domain of the gods with his wife, his daughter, and his boatman.

These elements are all absent from the Genesis account. And the Chaldean account in turn lacks the undergirding presence of a divine promise, to say nothing of the covenant of faithfulness bestowed upon Noah by God. The flood story in the Bible is gospel, and its theme is "Noah found grace in the eyes of the LORD."

From these words we hear what a clearly Israelite theme is given to this international flood story as recorded in Genesis. The Elohim who delivered Noah and his family from a suffocating world full of godlessness and violence through the great flood was the same Elohim who, since Egypt, had permitted the Israelites to call him Yahweh.

It is an old question whether Genesis speaks of a complete flood or a partial flood, that is, whether the flood covered the entire surface of the earth or only a part of it. The impression we get from the Bible's flood story is that all living creatures on earth, that is, on land, were affected, except Noah and those who went into the ark with him. But here, as in the case of Genesis 1, we must remember that such Hebrew words as *'erets* and *'adamah*, "land" and "field," are not to be equated with the modern concept of the earth as a globe, and that the word *all* is often used in the Bible in the sense of "many." For our part, we see no other option but to believe in a complete flood.

For the rest, may we look to the biblical story of the flood for answers to geological and other scientific questions about possibilities and impossibilities in God's incomprehensibly rich creation? The story was not given to Israel for any such purpose. What was important was for the people to hear and remember what happened to humanity earlier at one point when it had turned its back on God. It is in such terms that the apostle Peter discusses the flood: "By the word of God heavens existed long ago, and an earth formed out of water and by means of water, through which the world that then existed was deluged with water and perished" (2 Pet. 3:5–6 RSV). Both the land and its inhabitants disappeared.

It is noteworthy that Noah took more clean animals than unclean ones into the ark. The Israelite readers must have understood right away that this had something to do with providing for his family. The clean animals were milk producers. It must have been a comfort to Noah and his family to also be allowed to keep unclean animals, for it showed them that the LORD still had a good future and a full life on earth in mind for them.

Early in Genesis, then, we already hear talk of clean and unclean animals. Such talk does not begin with Leviticus 11, which is in the middle of the Torah of Moses. Genesis lets us know that the distinction between clean and unclean animals goes back to before the time of the Israelites. We also come across it among some of the people who lived around the Israelites. The Lord made this distinction part of his service. As we will see later, he did so in a beautiful and meaningful way that pointed in the same direction as the great flood, that is, toward deliverance and life. Noah found grace in the eyes of the Lord.

There are two aspects to the flood, then. The Lord did indeed manifest his wrath and punish humanity, but he also showed mercy and spared Noah and his family. God provided food and drink for them in a wonderful way. It still remains beyond our understanding how it was all possible. The Lord watched over the life of humanity in a fatherly way as it hung by a single thread. He spoke comforting words about the future, took measures against the power of wicked people, of wild animals, and of the elements of nature, and promised a regular succession of the seasons. Finally, he confirmed his faithfulness to these benevolent promises through the sign of the rainbow.

Noah and his family were already familiar with this natural phenomenon. They had already noticed that the rainbow seemed to embrace the entire would with its enormous arms. Just as truly as the rainbow could be seen in the sky, the Lord would always keep his covenant with Noah and all living souls. He promised that he would never let something like the flood happen again.

The chapters about the flood preach to us the gospel of the God who takes pleasure in the preservation of human life. We should not read these chapters in search of answers to questions that come up in biology and geology and natural history. The purpose for Israel and for us that God's Spirit intended these chapters to serve becomes apparent when we focus on his sadness at the degeneration and wickedness of the people on earth.

The spirit of Cain seemed to have penetrated everywhere—
the spirit of hatred of all that is good, of mockery, of the quest
for pleasure, of the glorification and deification of power, of
polygamy, and of violence. In short, the spirit of death was
triumphant. In such a world, Noah's family, a little church of
eight souls, would have drowned if God had not protected
them by drowning the world. Such are the terms in which the
apostle Peter describes this event. Just as we who were once
pagans were saved by baptism from perishing in the paganism
of our forefathers, so the waters of the flood saved Noah and
his family from the godlessness of their contemporaries (see
1 Pet. 3:19–21).

Cursed Be Canaan!

There is an appendix to the flood story. If we may indeed
conclude that the international flood story has a special Israelite stamp on it as we find it in Genesis (think of the many
references to Yahweh), we can surely expect something of special interest to Israel in this appendix. We learn that Noah
pronounced a blessing over two of his sons (Shem and Japheth) but that he cursed one of the sons of Ham, his third
son. Cursed be Canaan! To punish the evil Ham had done,
not all his descendants were cursed, but only his son Canaan.
"Cursed be Canaan; a servant of servants shall he be to his
brothers" (Gen. 9:25).

Who were these brothers of Canaan? We find out from
the Table of Nations in Genesis 10: Cush, Mizraim, and Put.
These three names refer to the inhabitants of the great areas
that have come to be known as Egypt and Arabia. We know
that the inhabitants of Canaan did in fact live for centuries
under the domination of the pharaohs, the kings of Mizraim
(i.e., Egypt).

The name of Canaan also comes up in connection with
Shem's blessing: "Blessed be the LORD, the God of Shem;

and let Canaan be his servant" (9:26). What does this signify?

Again we must bear in mind that Genesis was written first and foremost for the Israelites. We must be careful not to make Noah an Israelite, of course. Neither may we argue that the author of Genesis simply put some words in Noah's mouth to please the Israelites. That would be to deny the truth of Scripture, for we would then be making the prophecy in 9:18–29 the product of historical hindsight.

On the other hand, we have good reason to suppose that certain elements were focused on within the stories handed down from generation to generation and translated into the language of the Israelites with a certain purpose in mind. Hebrew was not yet spoken in Noah's days. Not only was translation needed; there must have been a certain reworking of the material that took place as well. This can hardly be denied when we remember that Yahweh is purely an Israelite name, a Hebrew name. Noah himself would not have known this name or used it. But we do find the name being used in 9:18–29.

Thus Noah's blessing is passed on by the Israelite storyteller in words that were understandable to his hearers and readers. Only because he did so could they understand what Noah was getting at. The purpose must have been this: never will the knowledge of the true God be completely missing among the descendants of Shem. The statement that comes right after this is that Canaan would have to serve privileged Shem. The thrust of Noah's words must have come through at once. Who could help but think of the subjection of Canaan by Israel? What we are told about Canaan in Genesis 9 fits right in with the impurity and immorality of the Canaanites as the Israelites had come to know them.

We also think that to properly understand Noah as he blesses Shem and Japheth and curses Canaan, we should try to listen with an Israelite ear. The repeated mention of Canaan in Genesis 9 must have impressed the Israelites and gratified them. They must have reacted by thinking, "There you have it! Those Canaanites have been up to no good from the very beginning. Their founding father was already guilty of impurity, and therefore of horrible disobedience and rebellion. That's why Yahweh decreed the proper punishment for the Canaanites, his descendants—subjection. Canaan was subjected to the brothers Shem and Japheth."

It was indeed the proper punishment, the fitting punishment. Israel was often shown how Yahweh used this method: a given sin would bring punishment to fit the crime. And God used the same method in blessing. When the midwives Shiphrah and Puah spared the newly born Israelite males, they were blessed with children themselves (Exod. 1:15–21). But when David took Uriah's wife and then his life, the LORD put David's wives to shame in public and said to him, "The sword will never depart from your house" (2 Sam. 12:10–11). That's how Yahweh went about things. That's how Israel already got to know him from the book of Genesis, from the story of Canaan's disobedience, which was punished with a life of subjection.

The name Canaan also comes up in Noah's blessing for Japheth, functioning again as a dark contrast. Japheth received a beautiful blessing. In Hebrew this blessing is reported in a particularly joyous way with a play on words: *yapht 'Elohim le-Yepheth*. This means "May Elohim [the ancient Semitic name for God] grant expansion to Japheth." A wish is expressed that the descendants of Shem and Japheth will live in peace with each other. "And may he (Japheth) dwell in the tents of Shem." But for Ham—or more specifically, the son of Ham, who bore the name Canaan, a name that meant a great deal to Israel—evil and degradation is predicted. "And let Canaan be a servant to him (Japheth)." By now we should see just how much this chapter must have spoken to the Israelites.

This chapter does not contain just history. Here we already have proclamation in the genre of the prophetic books Joshua, Judges, and so forth. We see ancient Israel (the first readers and hearers of Genesis) embroiled in the great struggle of that day—Israel was supposed to oppose Canaan and keep her distance from him. That's why this story was appended to the story of the flood and why it was put in language that would speak eloquently to the Israelites.

We must view this passage of Scripture as an extension of the history of Seth's line. It was important for Israel to realize why Seth's line had declined—mingling with the ungodly, which was the same danger that later threatened Israel from the side of the Canaanites. In fact, Israel was not merely threatened by this danger but was actually infected with Canaanite pollution, even though she had promised to remember her descent from Shem by way of Abraham.

Heading toward Abraham

Abraham is the figure we must keep in mind as we read the early chapters of Genesis. The line that Genesis traces leads to Abraham. We see this especially in chapters 10 and 11. Those two chapters are made up of three parts: (1) the Table of Nations in chapter 10, (2) the story of the city of Babel and the building of the tower in 11:1–9, and (3) the genealogy that leads from Shem to Abraham in 11:10–26.

There is a good deal of material in these chapters, then. It would not be difficult to lose sight of the goal while reading them, if only because of all the names we are confronted with in chapter 10. It could be quite discouraging. But there is no need to fear all those names. To begin with, let's note a couple of things about them.

The first point is not of overwhelming importance, but it may be of interest to note that there are seventy-one names in all—according to the Hebrew Bible. But the Septuagint, the ancient Greek translation, has seventy names. The reason is that in 10:26–30, the Septuagint does not have thirteen peoples coming forth from Joktan but only twelve (Obal is omitted). On this small point the Septuagint may well be correct.

This gets us thinking about the way the Bible uses numbers. Here we seem to have the number seventy, while in many other places we come upon the number twelve, and so forth. The question is often raised concerning what we are to make of the number of names in a genealogy. Is there a tendency to impose a certain style on the genealogies?

Think, for example, of the three lists of fourteen names each in Matthew 1. Could the number fourteen as used there have something to do with the fact that the Hebrew letters in the name "David" have a numerical value of fourteen when added together? It is clear, in any event, that if Matthew had gone about his work with the mathematical accuracy of a modern accountant, he would have had to mention more ancestors of our Savior. He calmly left some out—and that in a book addressed to the Jewish nation and intended to prove that Jesus is indeed the true Messiah. This is certainly an indication that he didn't expect any criticism of his method of grouping names together and arguing on the basis of those groupings. Some who have made an intensive study of this matter point out that ancient history was sometimes divided into periods of equal length (e.g., Shem to Abraham, Abraham to the entry into Canaan, the entry to the time of Saul, and Saul to Zedekiah).

If the discovery of such stylistic devices tends to throw us off stride, it should not. We should ask ourselves whether perhaps we are bringing mistaken expectations to Bible reading. Do we sometimes demand that the Bible live up to our standards for a history book, a law book, a song book, and so forth?

The second point we would make here is that the author of Genesis is apparently in a hurry to get to Abraham. This we can already detect from a quick survey of the Table of Nations in chapter 10. The table does not employ the usual order in which the names of Noah's sons are mentioned (i.e., Shem, Ham, and Japheth). Verse 2 begins with the sons of Japheth. By verse 6 attention switches to the sons of Ham. Shem comes last, starting at verse 21, instead of first.

Why is Shem last? To show that he is not important? Not at all. He is last because he is the most important of the three. Moreover, by ending with Shem, the author of Genesis can also show that we are on the way to the genealogy recorded in 11:10–32. In other words, we are heading toward Abraham!

Abraham, the man who rises from Shem's line, is the author's real concern here. Abraham is Israel's founding father. Thus the line leads to Abraham and his descendants. That's the subject on the Israelite storyteller's mind as he mentions all those nations. This is an important point that should never be forgotten. But before we turn to the Table of Nations in Genesis 10, there is something to be said about angels.

Nations and Angels

Earlier we mentioned the number seventy. Another text comes to mind when we think of this number—a line in Moses's song in Deuteronomy 32: "When the Most High divided to the nations their inheritance, when he separated the sons of Adam, he set the bounds of the people according to the number of the children of Israel" (v. 8).

That's how this text reads in the familiar words of the King James Version. Is that the best way to translate this text? We will return to this question later. First there is another point to be taken up.

Because the text mentions a splitting up and separating of peoples or nations, it seems natural to think of the Table of Nations in Genesis 10 and the building of the city and tower of Babel in Genesis 11, which lead to the confusion of languages and a subsequent dispersion. But this is not to say that Moses was thinking of a dispersion of the people that took place all at once. Scripture does not give us any reason to suppose that the dispersion occurred suddenly and was completed quickly.

What exactly did Moses mean by this line in his song? It would be especially helpful to know what Moses meant by the "children [Heb. *bene*, "sons"] of Israel." One commentator suggests that those "sons of Israel" are the seventy descendants who accompanied father Jacob when he went to Egypt. Moses would then be making a connection between the seventy nations in the Table of Nations and the seventy descendants of father Jacob (Gen. 46:27, Exod. 1:5).

This interpretation is not acceptable, however, for it is artificial, forced, and speculative. If there are indeed seventy nations mentioned in Genesis 10, what reason does the text supply for thinking that this has anything to do with the fact that father Jacob had seventy descendants with him when he went to Egypt?

But if this approach is mistaken, what does the text mean? The expression "sons of Israel" could refer simply to the twelve sons of father Jacob, that is, to the Israelites. In that case Moses would be saying that God so guided the dispersion of mankind and the separation into nations that the children of Israel or the twelve tribes could at a certain point receive their designated place in the land of Canaan. The land was at their disposal.

But this interpretation is not acceptable either. Has God indeed arranged the boundaries of the peoples in such a way that a place was left open for Israel in Canaan? It doesn't look that way, for the Israelites found the land inhabited by Canaanites and had to go through an intense struggle to inherit a place for themselves. There was simply no vacancy in Canaan. Therefore we should not interpret the expression "sons of Israel" to mean the Israelites or the twelve tribes.

It seems rather difficult, then, to attach the proper meaning to the phrase "sons of Israel" in Deuteronomy 32:8. But the difficulty quickly disappears if we read "sons of Israel" as "sons of God," which is what the English Standard Version does. There are good reasons for accepting such a reading: it appears that a copyist somewhere down the line—perhaps in nationalistic fervor—inserted the name Israel. The reading "sons of God" is supported by the Septuagint, and Augustine seems to have accepted it as well.

What Moses was saying, then, was that God set the boundaries of the people in accordance with the number of the sons of God, by which he means angels. The angels are often referred to in Scripture as the "sons of God" (see Job 1:6; 2:1; 38:7; Pss. 29:1; 89:6). So convinced were the men of the Septuagint of this reading that they freely translated, "in accordance with the number of God's angels." This was actually more of an interpretation than a translation.

It appears that what Moses wanted to say in his song was that when God scattered the people across the earth as nations, he did two things—one general and one particular. In general he assigned the nations to angels, but in the particular case of Israel he did not do so. He reserved Israel for himself. Thus we would translate Deuteronomy 32:8–9 as follows:

> When the Most High assigned the people their inheritance, when he made the children of Adam split up, he set boundaries to the people in accordance with the number of the sons of God. But his own people remained Yahweh's own portion; Jacob remained a possession that he kept for himself.

This fits right in with the glorious words with which Moses continues his song. Israel was the apple of God's eye!

As we read through the Old Testament, we repeatedly come across the figure of the Angel of Yahweh. This figure appears for the first time in the chapters about Abraham, the founding father of Israel, the "rock from which you [i.e., Israel] were hewn" (Isa. 51:1). We must bear in mind that God apparently chooses to make use of angels in ruling the nations—not just good angels but also evil ones. This becomes apparent from certain passages of Scripture. When in Ahab's day the prophet Micah saw the Lord sitting on his throne with the whole host of heaven of his right hand and at his left hand, a spirit came forth as a lying spirit to mislead Ahab (1 Kgs. 22:20–22). Isaiah saw the day coming when the LORD would not only judge "the kings of the earth, on the earth" but also "the host of heaven, in heaven" because they, too, shared in the guilt for the evil done by the kings and peoples on earth (Isa. 24:21). Daniel saw a Man appear in great glory (a glory very much like that of our glorified Savior as described in Rev. 1:13–15). This Man said to Daniel that he was indeed late in coming and explained that the delay was caused by "the prince of the kingdom of Persia" (Dan. 10:13). Clearly he was referring to an evil angel who was scheming against the Jews at the Persian court. Another such evil angel was referred to as the "prince of Greece." Daniel was told that the good angel, Michael, who is called a prince of the Jews or "your [plural] prince," had joined the Man in doing battle with the prince of Persia (Dan. 10:20–21).

That's how the Bible speaks of people and angels. Among the angels are not only good ones and evil ones, but also higher ones and lower ones. Michael is referred to in Daniel 10 as a "prince" and in verse 9 of Jude's letter as an "archangel." Revelation 12:7 speaks not just of "Michael and his angels" but also of "the dragon and his angels."

Yet not one of these angels is as high as the Angel of Yahweh. The first word that the Hebrew text uses to refer to him (*mal'ak*) can indeed be used for others, including both human emissaries (Josh. 6:17, 25) and angels (Gen. 19:1). But when the Bible speaks of the Messenger or Angel (*mal'ak*) of Yahweh, it is referring to a figure who is more than a mere creature. When he appears, it is the LORD himself who appears. Sometimes a story begins by speaking of the Angel of Yahweh but then switches to speaking simply of "Yahweh" (see Josh. 5–6, for example). The Angel who appeared to Joshua near Jericho was first referred to as the "commander of the army of Yahweh," but then he demands divine honors and is referred to a little later simply as Yahweh (Josh. 5:14–15; 6:2).

How about the New Testament? Does the Angel of Yahweh appear in the New Testament? There is no direct reference to the Angel of Yahweh in the New Testament—at least, not in such terms. But we would be making a serious mistake if we said that the New Testament was completely silent about him, for the opposite is the case: the New Testament is overflowing with reports about him. The Angel of the covenant, who was to be announced by John the Baptist, according to Malachi 3:1, is our Lord Jesus Christ (Luke 1:76; 7:27).

And what is it that especially impresses us about the New Testament Angel of Yahweh, the Lord Jesus Christ? That he is far superior to all the angels, even in his humiliation. But when Christ is taken up to heaven, he is praised by the many angels who stand around the throne of God. (See Revelation 5, a chapter that describes what we might call the "view from above" of the ascension of our Lord.) God now allows the glorified Christ to unlock the future (Rev. 5:5). The rest of Revelation shows us how angels appear in the picture constantly. They leave the assembly around God's throne and release their plagues on the nations. It is through them that Christ controls international political affairs—as the ruler of the angels and of the kings of the earth (Rev. 1:5).

When it comes to the church, however, Christ appears in a more personal way, which is understandable. The church is his body. Its members are parts of his body—his arms and legs, as it were. He is her Head. Therefore he also puts many ministering spirits to work serving her (Heb. 1:14). But when it comes to his church, those ministering spirits are not enough. Therefore he gets involved himself, and not just by interceding for the church daily with the Father. When men on earth dared to lay hands on Stephen, for example, Christ stood up indignantly from his throne, which God had prepared for him (Acts 7:56). And what did he say to Saul on the way to Damascus? "Why are you persecuting me?"

The book of Revelation shows us that by means of angels Christ exercises his rule over his church, a people who have a special place in his heart. Who could help but think of Genesis 32 here? True, God did look out for ancient Israel by sending angels, but he had already drawn very near to the patriarchs by having his Angel, the Angel of the LORD, appear to them. And later the children of those patriarchs were repeatedly visited by the Angel of the LORD, who led the way for them and preceded them in the pillar of cloud. They were also admonished by the Angel at times, and even severely punished by the Angel (as with pestilence, in David's days).

God dealt with his new covenant people in the same way. He dwelled with them, the church of the new dispensation, more intimately than ever before. His Word became flesh—a human being just like us, a man! Even after his exaltation, when he was given all power in heaven and on earth, Christ continued to walk before his church as he went about his busy work with nations and angels.

Just as God never let ancient Israel out of his own hands but kept her as his personal possession and jewel, so God's Son dealt with the church gathered from among the Gentiles. For centuries he has carried our interests in his high priestly heart. He knows our loves and sorrows. One day he will allow us to judge with him as kings and judges over peoples and angels. "Do you not know that we are to judge angels?" (1 Cor. 6:3).

We will encounter the Angel of the LORD repeatedly in the Old Testament, and we will observe God's special dealings with his favorite people, Israel, which he expresses through this Angel, and we then think again of the song of Moses. Moses sings of Israel as the portion God has set aside for himself as his special possession. Then we will also look ahead to the Man whom Daniel and John saw as the Lord of all nations and angels, but whom we will behold especially as Zion's faithful Priest-King in heavenly glory.

This is a good way to look at Israel's privileged place among the nations. Into that Israel we have been engrafted!

The Table of Nations in Genesis 10

Earlier we mentioned Genesis 10, which lists the descendants first of Japheth, then of Ham, and finally of Shem—in that noteworthy order. We would do well to divide this table of nations into three parts as we discuss it.

Part 1 of the Table of Nations

Earlier we commented that it is not at all surprising that many Bible readers find nothing attractive about Genesis 10. It is a chapter that is often passed over when the Bible is read at the table after meals. It does not seem to be a chapter that lends itself to discussion in the family circle.

To begin with, there seems to be no way to survey the host of names to see what they mean. That people should find it confusing is understandable. But what if part 1 of our Table of Nations (10:2–4) were printed in our Bibles as follows? First:

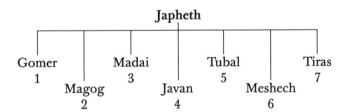

Then:

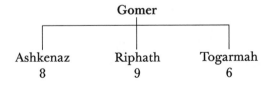

And then:

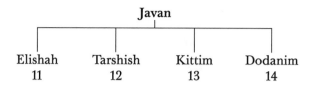

Javan

| Elishah | Tarshish | Kittim | Dodanim |
| 11 | 12 | 13 | 14 |

Such a list or table could at least be surveyed easily. And we would immediately learn something from it, namely, that Genesis 10 does not intend to give us a complete genealogy of Japheth. That it is not complete quickly becomes apparent from the fact that nothing more is said about the descendants of most of the children of Japheth. We are given further details only about two of them—Gomer and Javan.

From this we see that Genesis 10 is not really a genealogy in the usual sense of the word. We do not have the usual list that runs from father to son, to grandson, to great-grandson, and so forth. We are dealing here not with individuals but with nations. We hear this at once in such names as Kittim and Dodanim, which are plural forms. The other names are also to be read as referring to nations.

But if we are indeed dealing with nations, Bible readers might well be interested to know where all those nations lived. Unfortunately, we cannot satisfy their curiosity completely. We simply cannot be sure where the peoples mentioned in Genesis 10 lived. Let's review the names, which are numbered in the chart.

(1) It is generally assumed that the land inhabited by Gomer lay to the north of the Black Sea. The name of the Russian peninsula known as the Crimea comes to mind, for the consonants *g-m-r* or *k-m-r* may well have been transposed as *k-r-m*. Gomer is then said to have been chased by the Syrians into Asia Minor and Armenia.

(2) Although there seems to be some trace of Gomer outside the Scriptures, this is not the case with Magog, a name that Bible readers will recognize as occurring in Ezekiel 38–39

and Revelation 20:8. It is conceivable, however, that Magog is Mat-Gag or Mat-Gagasia, of which we read in writings found in Egypt. The name might then refer to the land of Carchemish, a Hittite kingdom in North Syria.

(3) We are better off when it comes to Madai. We know that this name refers to the Medes. They appear in history very early under the name Manda and are best known to us as the destroyers of the city of Nineveh, the mighty city of the Assyrians, which lay to the west.

(4) Javan was the Hebrew name for the Ionians. The name referred to the Greeks who lived on the western coast of Asia Minor. The name was also used by Israel in a broader sense to refer to everything Greek.

(5–7) Tubal must have lived to the south of the Black Sea as a neighbor to the Cilicians, Meshech and Togarmah. As for Meshech, his dwelling place is thought to be the northwestern part of Armenia, Caucasia, and the eastern coast of the Black Sea. Tiras is generally identified as the Etruscans, sea bandits who originally had their eyes on Egypt but later settled along the coasts of the "Tyrrhenian" Sea and in Etruria. They called themselves the Rasenna, but the Romans called them Etrusci or Tusci (hence Toscane) and the Greeks called them the Tyrrhenians. If this identification is correct, Tiras has exercised an enormous influence on Europe and thereby on the whole world.

Earlier we saw that of the seven Japhethite peoples mentioned above, only two are mentioned as descending from them. First a word about these two groups.

(8–10) The first group stems from Gomer. Ashkenaz is the Scythians, who inhabited Armenia. Riphath is unknown, but his likely dwelling place was somewhere in Asia Minor. Finally, Togarmah, famous for trade in horses and mules, was a neighbor of Gomer, Meshech, and Tubal, according to Ezekiel and some extrabiblical sources as well. His dwelling place is also Asia Minor.

(11–14) The second group falls under Javan, that is, the

Ionians or Greeks. Among these Greeks Genesis 10 first of all reserves a special place for Elishah, which people today place in the neighborhood of Phoenicia. Some scholars think of the Alasia of antiquity, which today is called Cyprus. Tarshish is known in the Old Testament as a port city in Spain at the mouth of the Guadalaviar. It was famous for its trade in tin and silver. It was originally founded by the Phoenicians as a manufacturing center and later developed close relations with the Greeks. This is probably the reason why we do not encounter Tarshish in 10:15 under Sidon and thus under Canaan, but rather under Javan (the Ionians, the Greeks). Thus we must be very careful in applying our ethnological knowledge to Genesis 10.

In the third place, under the heading of Javan came the Kittim or Kittites, whose name is derived from the city of Kition, on Cyprus. This is another name that directs us to Cyprus, then, just as Elishah did above. Later, Kittim takes on a much broader meaning and comes to refer to all the Greeks. Finally, Dodanim is a copying error and should be read as Rodanim (1 Chr. 1:7), which is the name of the inhabitants of the island of Rhodes.

These are the Japhethites, then. They make up only part 1 of the Table of Nations in Genesis 10. The table told Israel that Japheth lived in the area from the Medes in the east, south of the Caspian Sea, as well as in Armenia and northern Asia Minor, and finally in the Greek islands in the direction of Tarshish. Today we would speak of Europe or, to be still more modern, the West!

Part 2 of the Table of Nations

Next come the Hamites mentioned in 10:6–20. There are a great many names in all these verses. We should try to get an overview of all these peoples. Therefore one could lay out 10:6 as follows:

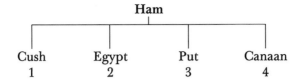

(1) The name Cush was already discussed in connection with Genesis 2 and the garden of Eden. Here the name probably does not refer exclusively to the people who lived to the south of Egypt, the Ethiopians, but also includes the peoples beyond the Red Sea in Arabia. Cush covers the great area of Arabia and southern Egypt.

(2) The Hebrew text then speaks of Mizraim, but we have translated this name "Egypt." If it were left untranslated, the impression might be created that we are dealing here with individuals rather than nations, but we saw in part 1 of the table that nations are meant. Kittim and Rodanim were clearly plural forms. Mizraim also looks like a plural form, but it is in fact a dual form, because of the -aim ending. (In English we have only singular and plural, such as "eyes," "hands," and "shoes.") Israel probably used Mizraim in the dual form because Egypt was a double kingdom consisting of Upper and Lower Egypt. The pharaohs wore double crowns.

(3) The name Put is sometimes encountered in extrabiblical literature, but no one has been able to pin this nation down to a location. It is conceivable that it is another name for Somaliland.

(4) The name Canaan is well-known: it covers the inhabitants of the area the Mediterranean Sea and the Jordan.

When we get past the first four names, which represent the sons of Ham, we encounter the same phenomenon as in part 1 of the Table of Nations: we are given a whole series of nations that spring from the first set of names, although nothing more is said about Put. Thus the Bible tells us about three groups of Hamites.

(1) The first group is mentioned in 10:7. It can be pictured as follows:

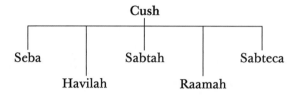

The Cushites, then, were made up of five nations: Seba (which may have lived along the African coast of the Red Sea), Havilah (Arabia), Sabtah (which can perhaps be identified with Sabota, the capital city of Hardamaut), Raamah (southern Arabia), and Sabteca (which is unknown but may also have been located in Arabia). Raamah is the only one of whom we are told more:

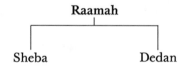

Sheba is well-known to us from 1 Kings 10, where we are told about the Queen of Sheba, who came to visit King Solomon. Sheba's capital city was Marib, in southern Arabia. But Dedan is probably a nation that spread out across Arabia.

(2) The second group of Hamites is mentioned in 10:13–14. We can trace them as follows:

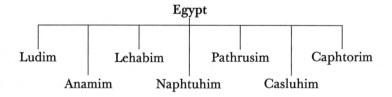

Here again we do not have the certainty we would like to have. It is generally believed that the Ludim, the Anamim, and the Lehabim all were Libyans. The Naphtuhim seem to have been inhabitants of the Delta. The Pathrusim lived well to the south of them, for *Pathros* means "land of the south" and thus refers to Upper Egypt. The Casluhim are completely unknown to us, and the Caphtorim are the Cretans.

After the name Casluhim we read the parenthetical remark "from whom the Philistines came" (Gen. 10:14). This seems to be a copyist error, for this parenthetical remark was originally behind the name Caphtorim. According to Amos 9:7, the Philistines were descendants of the Caphtorim.

(3) The third group of Hamites are the descendants of Canaan. We get the impression that the author of Genesis felt he had to "honor" this branch of the Hamites with rather extensive coverage. What we read in 10:15–19 can be traced as follows:

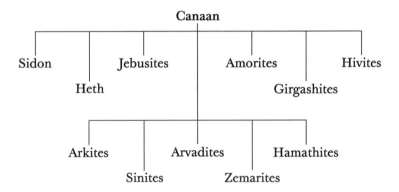

Sidon is mentioned as the "firstborn," that is, the most important. Sidon was an important city of trade that was later overshadowed by the neighboring city of Tyre. Then follows Heth (the Hittites). The reference here is not to the Hittites of Asia Minor but to a very ancient Canaanite people. The Jebusites lived in Jerusalem and the area around it. The Amorites mentioned here were the remnant of a once-mighty people and lived around Hebron. The Girgashites are unknown to us. The name Hivites may mean "tent dwellers." The Arkites, the Sinites, the Arvadites, and the Zemarites were the inhabitants of four cities in the territory associated with the Philistines. The Hamathites lived at the extreme northern boundary of the land that Israel came to occupy.

Part 3 of the Table of Nations

We have now discussed the first two groups in the Table of Nations. To sum up, we could say that Genesis 10 viewed the Japhethites as living especially to the north and west, while the Hamites lived to the south. The S(h)emites found their dwelling place in between them.

In Genesis 10 the Semites are dealt with last. By now this should not strike us as strange, for we saw earlier that the author of Genesis reversed the usual order (Shem, Ham, and Japheth) with an eye to what was coming, that is, in order to prepare for the genealogy of Abraham in 11:20–26.

Yet we get the impression that the author of Genesis feared that his Israelite readers and hearers would not be pleased with his reversal of the usual order, leaving Shem until the end. Why else would he make an excuse right at the beginning, in 10:21? In fact, he offers a double excuse—or perhaps a triple excuse.

First of all, through this verse he begins listing the remainder of the table of nations in an enthusiastic way that is often obscured in our English translations: "Shem received descendants too! He, the father of all the sons of Heber, he, the older brother of Japheth!" Here the similarity with Genesis 4:21 comes to mind: "But Seth received descendants too!" At once we sense what the writer is getting at: he is asking for attention. He wants his readers and hearers to be acutely conscious of the direction they will now be going, the direction they all want to follow. Are you still awake? A little further and we'll get to Abraham!

The first characterization of Shem also points in this direction: "the father of all the children of Eber." Note that the text does not say "father of the Hebrews." That would not have been a title of honor. The name Hebrew, which already appears in Genesis 14:13, has taken on the same meaning for us as Israelite. The language that the Israelites spoke for a long time is known as Hebrew. Yet Hebrew was originally not the name of a tribe or nation, but of a certain kind of people among the nations and tribes. Originally the word seems to have had a social meaning rather than an ethnological meaning, and not such a fond one at that.

That social meaning did not involve honor and respect: a Hebrew was a homeless wanderer, a stranger, and could therefore easily slip into a situation of poverty, oppression, and slavery. A Hebrew might well be made to serve others (see Exod. 21:2; Deut. 15:12). Still, a Hebrew was not always a weak figure: think of "Abram the Hebrew" (Gen. 14:13). Yet Abram was a true Hebrew in that he lived in Canaan without being a ruler or king and without owning any land. Thus he was essentially "homeless."

But the term *Hebrew* did not only make people think of a stranger and of slaves. It also had a military ring to it, as we see from various passages in 1 Samuel (e.g., 13:19; 29:3). In this sense the term *Hebrew* can be compared to the term *Chabiroe* or *Chabiri*, which we are acquainted with from extrabiblical sources and which likewise had a threefold meaning of stranger, or slave, but also a bandit who could join with his comrades to be either a powerful support or a dreaded enemy. When we think of the raid that Simeon and Levi organized against the men of Shechem (Gen. 34), we can easily understand why the name "Abram the Hebrew" in Genesis 14:13 had a military ring to it. Didn't this "Hebrew" demonstrate his military powers in a battle against a whole coalition of kings?

In ancient times, the name Hebrew was employed too often to express scorn and contempt for us to regard it as an honorable appellation for Shem in 10:21. The original text does not point in such a direction either. Therefore we must not identify the "Hebrews" with the "sons of Eber." No, when

Shem is spoken of as "the father of all the children of Eber," this is an enthusiastic indication of the direction that is now to be followed. It is as if the author wanted to say, "Now we are finally getting to our destination." From 10:25 and 11:15 we learn that Eber was not the ancestor of all the Semites, but certainly of many Semites, including the line from which Abraham was born. And that's the important thing. We are now getting close to Abraham, for now we hear mention of Shem, and then of Eber.

The second characterization of Shem that we are given is that he is the "elder brother of Japheth." Nothing is said about Shem being the brother of Ham. Israel would not regard it as an honor to be related to Ham and thereby to Canaan and the Canaanites. Such feelings ran deep.

What people are descended from Shem? Just as we did with the two earlier parts of the Table of Nations, we can trace Shem's descendants in the chart on the next page.

Let's begin our discussion of all these names with the "Big Five." Obviously we should read these names, too, as referring not to individuals but to nations. They are peoples who lived in the area that stretched from the Persian Gulf (the territory of the Elamites) to the well-known land of Syria in the west. (In Genesis 10 Syria is referred to as Aram.) In between lived the Assyrians (Asshur), and also Arpachshad and Lud. Just as we are certain about the territory of the Assyrians, a nation as cruel as it was famous, we are uncertain about Arpachshad and Lud. In the case of Arpachshad this is a real shame, for we must come back to him later. For the present we can only say that the name Arpachshad is listed among the names of various peoples and therefore must also be read as the name of a nation.

There are only two reports of further descendants of Shem's sons. We are told more about Aram, and then about Arpachshad. Note the order. When the "Big Five" are first mentioned,

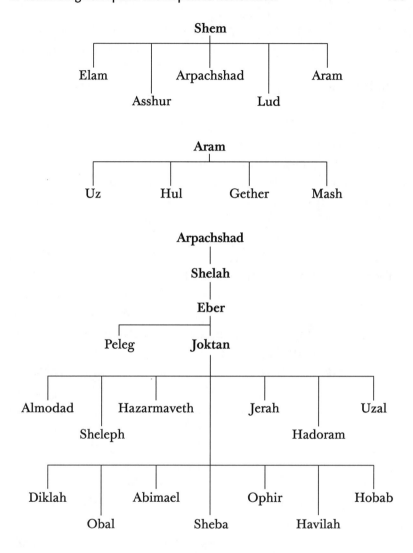

it is the other way around—first Arpachshad and then Aram. That order was probably chosen for aesthetic reasons. It was considered good form to begin with the east and end with the west. The list of peoples in Acts 2 does the same thing.

The author of Genesis goes contrary to that tradition when he tells us first about Aram and then about Arpachshad. This is probably to be explained on the basis of the same consid-

eration already mentioned earlier, that is, the desire to emphasize the connection with the later genealogy from which
Abraham would spring, namely, that of Heber, and more particularly that of Peleg, of whom we are told in a play on words
that in his days "the earth was divided" (10:25).

The word *earth* (*'erets*) as used here surely cannot be a reference to the entire globe. Just as in Genesis 1, here too the word
has a limited meaning and applies only to the area known as
Mesopotamia, or more particularly, to the population of this
area, of which we read more in Genesis 11, which tells us about
the building of the city and tower of Babel and the subsequent
confusion of the languages.

When we turn to the descendants of Aram, we can offer no
information about them. We really know nothing about Uz,
Hul, Gether, and Mash. All we can say is that many scholars
believe that Uz is the land in which Job lived (see Job 1:1).
Here we see again that these names of nations often function also as the names of regions and lands. We turn now to
Arpachshad. We first come across this name among the "Big
Five." Clearly it is included there as the name of a people.
But in Genesis 10:24–25 we read that Arpachshad became the
father of Shelah, and Shelah the father of Eber. Eber became
the father of two sons. The name of the one was Peleg, and the
name of the other was Joktan. In this setting, Arpachshad is
to be read as a personal name. In later ages, the descendants
of Arpachshad must have adopted the name of their founding
father as their national name.

Unfortunately, we must also confess our ignorance with
respect to many of the names of the descendants of Joktan.
We know nothing about these nations and regions. The only
exception is Hazarmaveth. This name refers to the present-day
Hadramaut on the southern coast of Arabia. But beyond this
we cannot say anything with certainty about the Joktanites.

This is a shame especially because of Ophir, for this land
is mentioned a number of times in Scripture. We know, for
example, that the ships of Solomon and Hiram used to fetch

gold, silver, and precious stones form Ophir. Yet no one knows exactly where Ophir is to be found. The Joktanites are generally placed in Arabia. The fact that Ophir, apparently a distant land, was counted as belonging to Joktan need not cause any problems. After all, isn't faraway Tarshish reckoned with the Greeks? Thus Ophir, which was a long sea journey from Israel, could still be reckoned with Arabia.

We now have surveyed what the author of Genesis wanted to say to his Israelite readers about the world of the nations before proceeding to speak of Abraham, their forefather. Out of that great multitude of nations God had chosen Israel to be the people to whom he showed his love in a special way. What mighty nations lived all around Israel! Japheth had expanded tremendously—to the north to Caucasia and the Crimea, and to the west to the Greek islands, and even all the way to Spain.

Ham was even more powerful in Israel's eyes, as he had expanded across Mesopotamia and toward the south, to Egypt. His influence in Canaan was great. Several of the nations who were later Israel's archenemies and oppressors (see 10:15ff.) were descendants of Ham, such as the Sidonians, the Hittites, and the Amorites.

Genesis 10 is not giving us lessons in ethnology in the modern sense, but it is preaching the gospel to us. It shows us the development of power in a world that was hostile to Israel in many respects. Japheth was to the north and west, while Ham was to the east and south—and was even present right in Canaan itself. A frightening prospect. Even so, Shem received his descendants and his place.

The people must have whispered assurances to each other about this in the days of oppression, when Ham was swallowing up Israel's strength and children in Egypt, or when the people were being pressed hard in Canaan by all the Hamites there. Here was the comfort: "To Shem also, the father of all the children of Eber, the elder brother of Japheth, children were born" (10:21). In Israel he could be recognized and honored as the father of that small line, that little sprout from which Abraham came forth.

Even today, Japheth, living in the West, dominates the many Hamite peoples with powerful technology and scientific knowledge. But he found his greatest treasure in the tents of Shem, from which Abraham's greatest Son emerged—Jesus Christ, the Redeemer of the world.

The City and Tower of Babel

We already heard a prelude to Genesis 11:1–9 when we discussed a bit of family history in connection with Arpachshad and his descendants. We read that in the days of Peleg, "the earth" was divided. Actually, there is also a prelude to 11:1–9 in 10:8–12, which tells us about Nimrod, who was the first "mighty man" or power holder on earth. This great hunter, Nimrod, appears in the midst of the Hamites. We said nothing about him earlier, intending to discuss him instead in connection with 11:1–9, which tells us about the city and tower of Babel. Some of the things that come up in this passage can be explained on the basis of the preceding chapter, but there are also a couple of matters that need a separate word of explanation.

It is important to keep the context in mind. Genesis again wishes to show us God's complete abhorrence of the vain boasts that issue from people's hearts. He despises people's proud feelings and vain actions. All this has the smell of death about it.

This is a lesson for Israel, teaching her that her life and happiness are to be sought in Yahweh alone. It is also a lesson for the church of later times, which has also been mesmerized repeatedly by numbers, money, great buildings, beautiful garments, sparkling addresses, humility intended to impress people, thrilling self-denial, key positions, influence, and so forth. Over here shrewd, intelligent leaders, and over there deep religiosity with or without the diversion of pleasure and enjoyment. But our Savior condemned all of this when he said, "What is exalted among men is an abomination in the sight of God" (Luke 16:15).

In ancient Israel the children were not taught to despise everything that was not Israelite, unlike the Greeks, who looked down on anything that was not Greek and declared it to be "barbaric." Through the story of the flood and the Table of Nations in Genesis 10, Israel was reminded of the unity of the entire human race. The Israelites knew that all men are of one blood (Acts 17:26). And this awareness naturally bore fruit in certain ways. It led the Israelites to be sober when they talked about the nations of the world, for the Israelites knew they were really only a small drop in the bucket. Still, all those other nations were made up of people of like nature with themselves, even the most powerful nations, the ones that ruled over many others. There was awesome Assyria, for example, whose very name instantly made people tremble.

And then there was Babylon. Babylon was the "great city" (Gen. 10:8–12). That was where the kingdom of mighty Nimrod had begun. In the Mesopotamian world the name of Nimrod was still famous as the name of the war god Ninurta. From 1 Chronicles 1:10 we gather that he was a unique historical figure, for "he was the first on earth to be a mighty man." Still, there were many who imitated him, and he seems to have left a following behind, men who followed in his dictatorial footsteps. Perhaps by way of comparison we should think of the term *caesar*. It was originally the name of a certain person, Caesar, but eventually it became a name for the office he held. In time the holder of that office was revered as a god. Thus in the ancient world, of which we are told a few things in Genesis 10:8–12, the name and fame of Nimrod left traces behind. Originally the name was associated with one man only, but later it came to be applied to a series of men of a certain type. The first of these men came forth from the Cushites, Genesis tells us. Thus he came from Arabia, the cradle of the nations. From there great swarms of people apparently spread out across Mesopotamia.

To Nimrod's fame is added the following comment: "a mighty hunter before the LORD" (10:9). This comment calls for some explanation, but as we examine it we must be careful not to lose sight of the main lines. There are two things to be noted here. First there is the expression, literally, "before the face of Yahweh," and secondly the words "a mighty hunter."

"Before the face of Yahweh." Naturally, such an expression would be used only in Israel, for it was only in Israel that God was called Yahweh, since the time that he had said to Moses at Horeb that he wanted to be called especially by this name among the Israelites. (We will come back to this matter when we deal with the book of Exodus.) Before that time people would have said "before the face of Elohim" (or "El"). Those were the usual names for God, which Israel had in common with the other peoples. In Israel, then, the older, more general expression "before the face of God" had been replaced by the specifically Israelite expression "before the face of Yahweh."

So now the question becomes, What meaning are we to assign to the original expression "before the face of God"? It seems to be fairly simple: it expresses superiority, a higher degree of something. The "thunder of God" was an especially severe thunderstorm (see Exod. 9:28). A "cedar of God" was a very high cedar (see Ps. 80:10). A "city of God" was an enormous city (see Jonah 3:3), and an "army of God" was a huge army (1 Chr. 12:22). In the Mesopotamian world ("on the earth," i.e., in the land), Nimrod was a "hunter before God," that is to say, a hunter of fantastic capabilities.

What about the word *hunter*? It appears that there was a direct connection in the Mesopotamian world between hunting and being king. Hunting was one of the royal pastimes, and one might almost think that the term *hunter* was one of the king's titles. A picture of King Assurbanipal that has come down to us depicts him hunting. Assyrian kings often had their courage and skill depicted in the course of hunting lions. This pride in hunting went back a long, long way, as we see from the Epic of Gilgamesh: the legendary Gilgamesh is also depicted as a lion killer.

In 10:8 the figure of Nimrod appears in the middle of the Table of Nations. The text points to this dictator as the one who laid the foundation for such dominions as the ones we know by the names Babel, Erech (the Sumerian Uruk, to the south), Accad (to the north, which is the reason why the language of Mesopotamia was long known as Akkadian), and Calneh, which is unknown but might conceivably be a reference to Nippur. Note that we speak here only of the foundation, the beginning. Later rulers followed the example Babel had set.

Thus Genesis 10 had already spoken of the rise of these oppressive powers. What was one to think about all this? How did the LORD regard it? Genesis 11:1–9 gives us the answer to this question.

At the very beginning of the rise of this oppressive power, the LORD already let his disapproval be felt. Right from the outset he was displeased by the concentration of people in one place and the consolidation of power, condemning it as foolishness. One day he finally said, "Well then, let me go down and confuse their language."

What the text literally says is, "Let us go down" (11:7). Some translations reflect this. But here we must think back to what was said above about Genesis 1:26 and 3:22. The use of the plural in such passages goes back to the use of the divine name Elohim, which is a plural form. Therefore it seemed natural to use plural verbs and pronouns when speaking of "Elohim." This practice became so well entrenched that when later Israelites used the name Yahweh in place of Elohim or combined it with Elohim, they often retained the plural verb form.

That's how things often go when forms of expression work their way into our language, especially religious language. Apparently people did not sense any need for a change, and so the expression stuck. We need not seek anything more behind this sentence. If Bible translations always rendered it, "Let me go down," the Bible reader could calmly keep reading and there would have been no need for this paragraph.

In Genesis 11 God's Spirit tells us how much the LORD despised the first attempt to form a mighty kingdom. Indeed, he made it a laughing stock. If we read 11:1–9 carefully, we sense that those grandiose deeds and the desire to make a name for oneself—*name*, in the Bible, carries connotations of power, security, and so forth—are turned into a joke. The LORD, with his great knowledge of his creatures and power over them, so arranged things that the builders could no longer understand each other. Soon the whole project collapsed in confusion.

Genesis uses a play on words as it tells us this amusing story, thereby bringing the story to a spiritual conclusion. No one really knows what the word *Babel* originally meant. But the language in general use in Mesopotamia had given this word an explanation that suggested heartfelt piety: Babel meant *Bab-ili*, that is, the gate of god. The plural was also suggestive: *Bab-ilāni*, that is, gate of the gods. That's why the city was known by two different names throughout the ages: Babel and Babylon.

Naturally, our Israelite narrator in Genesis 11 had no respect whatsoever for this Babylonian popular piety. Being as disrespectful as he can, he observes, "Therefore Babel [Heb. *b-b-l*] is just the right name for that city, for there the LORD confused their language [Heb. *b-l-l*]." We hear undisguised mockery here, behind which lies deep earnestness. The Mesopotamian quest for power, which oppressed so many people in all ages, is thoroughly condemned. The principle of pride underlying it is being turned upside down. That's the reason for including this story about this particular beginning.

The author of Genesis must have been aware, just as

scholars in our time have learned after extensive, tiresome excavations, that the "land of Shinar" (10:10 and 11:2), or Mesopotamia, later came to be covered with many ziggurats. There were so many of them that a single city might even have more than one. These ziggurats were terraced towers that reached a great height. Their height made a tremendous impression on the people; in an ancient song the top of Nippur's ziggurat is said to reach all the way to the heavens, while its foundation is in the shining depths.

It is in this light that we must read the words of 11:4: "a tower with its top in the heavens." Even today, when we look at the enormous ruins of the ziggurats, we can see what huge masses of stone were involved in their construction. That the builders of those colossal structures were aware of the enormity of what they were planning is apparent from the measurements of a certain ziggurat as we find them in a cuneiform document that seems to have come from the builder himself. The square occupied by the ziggurat was some one hundred yards on each side. There were seven levels above the ground level, reaching a total height of some one hundred yards. It was apparently this ziggurat that the Greek world traveler and historian Herodotus (fifth century BC) saw with his own eyes. He was told that on top of this structure there was a temple without any image in it. But the temple did include a large, richly ornamented bed on which the god slept whenever he honored the temple with a visit. Next to the bed stood a golden table. The only one who could spend the night there was a Babylonian woman designated by the god himself.

The author of Genesis must have known about such things. Yet he remains completely silent about them. He does not want to focus our attention exclusively on the place the tower assumed in the religion of the people at Babel. It would not be right if we were to talk only about the tower, for we read that the people wanted to build both a city and a tower, that the LORD came down to look at both the city and the tower (11:4–5).

This reminds us of 10:8–12, where we read about Nimrod, the mighty hunter who ruled on his own, and about the "great city." This is explained further here, and our attention is expressly directed to the recurring warning against human pride and violence in the book of Genesis. By way of some typical examples, this book shows us how the spirit of Cain also gained the upper hand after the great flood. The spirit of Lamech, the bruiser and sensualist of Genesis 4, and of the violent giants of Genesis 6, flared up again. This miserable spirit of bravado that God so deeply loathes, according to the Scriptures, got the people in its grip again, even though that which is exalted among men is an abomination in the sight of God (Luke 16:15), something he laughs at (Ps. 2:4).

God deals sternly with this spirit and wipes it out. But especially at the beginning, he takes a more gentle approach, mocking humanity's claim to greatness as he takes the wind out of its sails with a mere turn of his hand. Thus the author of Genesis 11:1–9 shows us that even after the flood, God punished the foolish spirit of self-glorification and glorification of violence, thereby making an example of it. He did so in an ironic way, for he simply changed a few things in the way people used their tongues and lips, their brains and palates, their voices and vocal cords. We do not know for sure just how he did it. But the result was that the great building project ground to a halt.

Genesis 11:1–9 represents an intermezzo. Therefore we must be careful not to overestimate its importance. For example, we should not make a great deal of the Pentecost event recorded in Acts 2 as a counterpart to the tower of Babel story. The only possible later allusion to this event in Scripture is Deuteronomy 32:8. Genesis 10, which demonstrates the multiplicity of the nations, taught Israel to remember that all human beings are of one blood and that all human beings owe the breath of their nostrils to God.

Genesis 11 shows us the weakness of the mightiest of these people over against God, who was later known to Israel as Yahweh. This was the God who came down to be Israel's Helper in Egypt. The same Hebrew word for "came down" is used in Exodus 3:8 (at the burning bush) as here in Genesis 11:5.

There must have been many, many generations of Israelites who trembled whenever they heard the names of Assyria and Babylon. It was for such people that the story of the confusion of the languages at the tower of Babel was written. Many a heart that quaked in fear at the horrible reports coming from the land of Nimrod must have derived quiet comfort from this story. Yahweh, the one and only God, was exalted high above the hubbub of the nations, languages, and tongues, and was able to ward off the most deadly threats to the lives of his people with a mere turn of the hand.

But the Spirit surely intended also to comfort the church of later ages with this passage by showing her that, despite all that had happened, God continued to take pleasure in the children of men. To save the nations he bowed low to seek out Abraham, hoping to use this one man to bring about the salvation of many.

From Shem to Abraham

The usual order, as you will recall, is Shem, Ham, and Japheth. But in Genesis 10, which presents the Table of Nations, the order is reversed: first Japheth, then Ham, and finally Shem. Why? So that we can better keep in mind the direction we are traveling, for we are heading toward Abraham. We already noted the direction presented in the section that comes before Genesis 10 (i.e., 9:18–29), where we read how Noah cursed Canaan. There the LORD was praised as "the God of Shem" (9:26). This was an allusion to the great privilege the Israelites enjoyed by being descendants of Shem and by being permitted to serve the God of Shem, who is the only true God. They did so as children of Abraham. And Abraham was a son of Shem.

That's almost how the author of Genesis presents Abraham. Look at what he has done in 11:10–26: he has placed only eight names between Shem and Abraham. Of all the fathers, sons, and grandsons between Shem and Abraham over a period of thousands of years, he listed only eight. So he must have omitted a great many. If we try to view the list in 11:10–26 as a complete genealogy, we face a riddle. Fortunately, there is no need to do so.

How are we to understand the fact that the list is so short? Again, the direction is the important thing: we are heading for Abraham!

We should not make the mistake of thinking that the genealogies in the Bible are intended to provide us with enough information to construct a biblical chronology enabling us to compute the exact number of years between Adam and us. The genealogies are not complete enough to make this possible. Unfortunately, this has not always been recognized in Christian circles. There have been scholars who developed a complete chronology on the basis of the biblical givens and immediately grew very defensive when anyone dared to criticize their work or called it into question.

The most famous example of such a chronology is the one constructed by James Ussher, a seventeenth-century Irish bishop. Ussher calculated that Adam was created in the year 4004 BC; unfortunately, this contention was even included in some marginal notes to the King James Version and was not dropped until the revision of 1885. Such unsubstantiated assertions have caused Christians a great deal of needless difficulty. Serious investigators need not fear any conflict between the results of their study and the givens of Scripture.

When we read Genesis 11 in the King James Version, we repeatedly come across the word *begat*. This usually makes us think of the male activity in the reproductive process: to beget is to father a child. And the Hebrew word used in Genesis 11

(*yalad*) does indeed have such a meaning in various passages. Yet it can also be used in a slightly different sense. In 10:13 we read that Mizraim *begat* the Ludim. We saw earlier that "Mizraim" simply means Egypt. Could we say that Egypt *begat* the Ludim? Somehow that doesn't sound right. A man begets children, but we do not apply such language to a land or a nation. The Hebrew word in question (*yalad*) can mean, in addition to "beget" (the male role), "to bring forth" (the female role). The latter meaning is the one that applies in 10:21: "To Shem also . . . children were born [i.e., brought forth]." Going back to Egypt and the Ludim, then, we could say Egypt brought forth the Ludim.

Thus we must be very careful when we encounter the Hebrew word *yalad*. In 11:10–26, we must understand this word in a bit different sense again. If we had to choose between "begetting" (the male role) and "bringing forth" (the female role), we would choose the former, for all the figures mentioned between Shem and Abraham were men. There are no women or lands or nations among them—not even Arpachshad, as we saw earlier.

Yet the word *yalad* cannot be understood here in the restricted sexual sense of begetting or fathering a child, for as we saw earlier, entire generations are omitted from this list. Thus the word must be understood here in a broader sense as meaning that "among the descendants of the man in question was a certain person named so and so." Of all the generations between Shem and Abraham—and there must have been a great many of them—only eight are mentioned. Thus, for some reason or other, many sons and grandsons and so forth are left unmentioned. When it comes to the list of Shem's descendants, not all the questions are answered.

Now it remains possible that several of the names in the generations that are not mentioned were not known to the author of Genesis. But since his goal was to proceed quickly to Abraham to tell his readers about their founding father, it may well be that he didn't mind skipping some names. He may have been just as happy leaving the list short.

It is also possible, of course, that the man knew many more names than he included, but that he thought it sufficient to include only eight names between Shem and Abraham. Perhaps he feared that the attention of his readers would wander if he made the list too long, and that they would be distracted from his goal, which was to teach the Israelite people about God's deeds in the life of Abraham, who was "the rock from which you [i.e., Israel] were hewn" (Isa. 51:1).

Abraham the Idol Worshiper

How did you feel when you first heard someone refer to Abraham as an "idol worshiper"? Did that not almost seem like a curse? But then you discovered from Scripture that this was not sacrilege but the sober truth.

Abraham lived in dark times. But it was not as if all knowledge of God had vanished from human circles. Polytheism was indeed dominant, but some memory of the true God continued to live on.

That memory could not die out altogether. The tradition with regard to God's deeds at the creation of heaven and earth, and of man and woman and the human race, his speaking to man, his instruction about good and evil—to mention only these few things—was too strong for that. This recollection of the one true God, in opposition to the gods devised by human beings, comes through in the human need to make one god the supreme deity elevated above the lesser gods. That one god would be called the "Most High."

In Phoenician literature recovered by excavators we find the divine name Elyon. Scripture uses this term too, but applies it to the LORD. We read often in Scripture of pagans who refer to the "Most High" or who are told something about the "Most High" as if this were the most natural thing in the world. Pagans understood such language. Such talk appeared to be possible because of the continuing movements of the currents of that sea of the knowledge of God that had originally surrounded our human race. Abraham spoke to the king of Sodom about "the LORD, God Most High, Possessor of heaven and earth" (Gen. 14:22). Melchizedek, the king of Salem, wished Israel the blessing "of God Most High" (v. 18). Balaam also took this name upon his lips (Num. 24:16), as did King Nebuchadnezzar (Dan. 3:26; 4:2). And Daniel in turn spoke to him about the LORD as the Most High (Dan. 4:24), as he later did to Belshazzar (5:18, 23).

That's simply how it was done. The LORD, after all, was the Most High, about whom even the pagans still said true things from time to time. Centuries later the apostle Paul appealed to this knowledge of God that still had not entirely disappeared in pagan circles, this knowledge of his words, deeds, and commands, when he spoke in Athens about "the God who made the world and everything in it, being Lord of heaven and earth, [and] does not live in temples made by man" (Acts 17:24). The Athenians did not laugh about his use of the singular here.

Yet the truth about the only true God was intensely suppressed through fantasy, through lies, through idolatry. That was even the case in the family of Terah, the home in which Abraham grew up. Idols were worshiped there, as we learn from Joshua 24:2, 15. In verse 2 Joshua says to the people of Israel, "Thus says the LORD, the God of Israel, 'Long ago, your fathers lived beyond the Euphrates, Terah, the father of Abraham and of Nahor; and they served other gods.'" What gods? The Bible does not tell us.

Thanks to the work of archeologists, we know that in the city of Haran, where Abraham used to live, there stood a temple of the moon god Sin. Were idols also worshiped in the home of Laban, the great-grandson of Terah? In the life of Laban we do hear talk about God (talk in which Jacob naturally joins), but we also find Laban bowing before "teraphim," which may have been household idols (Gen. 31:30, 34).

Thus there is not much that we know for sure with regard to Abraham's idolatry, but Joshua 24:2 leaves no doubt that it was indeed idolatry. This far-from-flattering Scripture passage was likely the source of the digression in the apocryphal book of Judith regarding the Jews, who were descendants of the Chaldeans and had earlier lived in Mesopotamia, and who went from there to Canaan "because they did not wish to follow the gods of their ancestors who were in Chaldea" (Jud. 5:6–7 NRSV). No less dubious, perhaps, is the historical value of the assertion that we find in chapter 12 of the book of Jubilees, a late Jewish writing, to the effect that the Chaldeans hated the Jews because Abraham had once set fire to one of their temples devoted to idols.

We have drawn attention to these extrabiblical stories handed down not because they should be regarded as of great historical value—although the New Testament does draw from an extrabiblical Jewish source at least once, in 2 Timothy 3:8—but because they make it apparent that the Israelites did have some interest in the religious ties between Abraham and the land and people of his birth. Jewish tradition has naturally turned Abraham into a pure believer in the one true God. Yet the Jews themselves seemed to be aware that there was a connection between Abraham and idolatry, though they could have stated it more briefly, like Joshua 24:2 does.

Isaiah speaks of the God who delivered Abraham (Isa. 29:22). How did the LORD do this? God had saved Noah and the seven other people who made up his family by way of the flood (1 Pet. 3:21). He could not deliver Abraham in the same way because of the promise he had made in Noah's days (Gen. 9:15).

He delivered Abraham by isolating him first of all from his land and his family. He called him away from the home of his father Terah and his closest relatives (12:1). And after he led Abraham to the land of Canaan, which was completely foreign to him, he revealed himself to this displaced person in a unique way.

Abraham must have had a great deal to learn from his heavenly Teacher, and we can be sure that he did learn much, with the proper result. He had to. At one point the LORD even said,

> Shall I hide from Abraham what I am about to do, seeing that Abraham shall surely become a great and mighty nation, and all the nations of the earth shall be blessed in him? For I have chosen him, that he may command his children and his household after him to keep the way of the LORD by doing righteousness and justice, so that the LORD may bring to Abraham what he has promised him. (18:17–19)

With Abraham, the son of Terah, God made another new beginning, although he was making use of what was already there. Genesis 11:26 speaks of the *toledoth* of Terah. Then began the period with which the Bible chiefly deals and in which we still live today—the time between God's special concern with Abraham the idol worshiper and the return of Abraham's great Son to inherit the promised world (Rom. 4:13).

We must not form any misconceptions of the time before Abraham, the period from the flood to Abraham. It was likely a very long period of time—about as long as the time that separates us from Abraham. In this period the people of the ancient Near East developed in all sorts of areas—agriculture, craftsmanship, trade, travel, building, education, science, music, art, weaponry, warfare, and so forth. Thus we should not think of those peoples as primitive. Excavations near the Nile and the Euphrates, in Crete and in Asia Minor, have shown what astounding achievements people were capable of after the flood. People were both clever and strong.

Yet of these people we can say what Paul said of the deca-

dent Greeks and Romans of his day, namely, that their foolish hearts were darkened (Rom. 1:21) and that they groped
around in the dark to find God (Acts 17:27). In that beautiful
ancient world, by whose ruins people today are still deeply
moved, the lamp of the knowledge of God and his works and
will and promises and commands was almost extinguished.

It was from this dark world that Abraham was "delivered."
Thus there must have been a great deal he had to learn about
his heavenly Teacher. Things that had been half forgotten or
even completely forgotten had to be learned anew.

When the LORD revealed himself to Abraham in the midst
of this dark world, he must have done so in such a way that
Abraham would immediately realize with whom he was in
contact—not with some idol or other but with the Most High,
the only true God. He must have been convinced of this in a
powerful way, for we read not only that the LORD repeatedly
let Abraham hear his voice and word but also that he came to
him in visible form a number of times. Thus God came very
close to Abraham.

Earlier we saw that it was in Abraham's days that God began to make appearances to which we attach the name "Angel
of the LORD." This figure is the one whom we may now know
as Christ. During the time of the author of Genesis—and perhaps even earlier—the Angel of the LORD must have been discussed among the Israelites; otherwise the author would not
have mentioned him suddenly in his story the way he did,
without a single word of introduction. The first appearance
of the Angel of the LORD is in the story of Hagar's first flight.
Here the Angel reveals himself as the one who has mercy on
the sufferer in Abraham's household (Gen. 16). That was also
how Israel knew him from her own history, beginning with
the Angel of the LORD who appeared to Moses at the burning bush. God had descended to be close to the Israelites as
Yahweh, as the God who promised to be with them (Exod. 3).

Let us read the chapters about Abraham in this light, pay-
ing careful attention as God, full of mercy, descends to hu-

manity, to Abraham. Here we start to move down the path that leads to the Word becoming flesh.

Through the intimacy of his contact with Abraham, God must have convinced him in a powerful way that he was dealing with the only true God as his Creator and Redeemer. Abraham's contact with God makes us think again of the Garden of Eden, where the LORD walked with Adam and Eve. God also walked and talked with Abraham—he even ate at Abraham's table. And he discussed his intentions with regard to Sodom with his friend Abraham.

Through all of this, Abraham must have been deeply convinced that he was in contact with the Most High and not with some lying spirit. He was dealing with the God of heaven and earth, the One in whom he could calmly place all his trust. God's word and works left no room for doubt.

It was by this route that the LORD became known to the Israelites. They were children of idol worshipers, just as we are, but they became children of Abraham long before we did. They were a people who were favored with grace early, in the midst of a sea of nations in the darkness. For centuries the Israelites could sing, "He declares his word to Jacob, his statutes and rules to Israel. He has not dealt thus with any other nation; they do not know his rules. Praise the LORD!" (Ps. 147:19–20).

CHAPTER 9

A Promise with Worldwide Scope

We are not to assume that once God had isolated Abraham from his milieu, he wrote off the other peoples of the world. The others were his creatures too. He continued to be good to them, day in and day out, year in and year out. He did not leave them without testimony about him, and he continued to fill them with food and gladness (Acts 14:17). He also gave them glittering gifts, including the capability for building rich cultures, the traces of which are still with us today. Many of our weights and measures, for example, are of Babylonian origin, such as of the notion of the zodiac, which is used in astronomy.

We know from Scripture itself—and this is even more important—that in Abraham's time, God was already planning to put an end to the sad ignorance of the nations.

God's Promise to Abraham

It was a worldwide promise that God gave to Abraham when he told him he would have land and family. This becomes apparent if we read carefully:

> Now the Lord said to Abram, "Go from your country
> and your kindred and your father's house to the land
> that I will show you. And I will make of you a great na-
> tion, and I will bless you and make your name great, so
> that you will be a blessing. I will bless those who bless
> you, and him who dishonors you I will curse, and in
> you all the families of the earth shall be blessed."(Gen.
> 12:1–3)

Here we see it. In this promise God already included
a blessing for the people who were not Abraham's descendants by blood. We can now understand what blessing God
was referring to. From Abraham's line of descent came Jesus
Christ, whom the Bible speaks of as "a light for revelation to
the Gentiles" (Luke 2:32). We could just as well translate, "a
light for the nations." Paul referred to people like the Gala-
tian Christians, who did not have a drop of Jewish blood in
their veins, as children of Abraham, simply because they had
come to believe in Christ (Gal. 3:8, 29). Thus God's promise
to Abraham recorded in Genesis 12:1–3 was very extensive in
its scope—worldwide, embracing the entire earth. We see this
when we look back, keeping the fulfillment in mind.

All of this still lay in the future in Abraham's time. When he
left his fatherland and his father's house and family and arrived in Canaan, the Lord appeared to him in the strange
new land and gave him the promise that he would give this
land to Abraham and his descendants (Gen. 12:7). For a man
like Abraham the Hebrew, the wanderer without a fatherland,
this must have been music to his ears. How this must have im-
printed itself in his memory forever—all the more so because
it appeared to be a completely reliable promise. God had not
thrown out those words simply to be done with the matter; he

remained faithful and watched over his promise.

This became apparent when selfish Lot looked out for himself at the time he and Abraham parted company. Lot chose for himself the fruitful fields of Sodom and Gomorrah. The LORD then comforted Abraham by repeating his promise and assuring him again that the land would be given to him and to his seed. Therefore he invited Abraham to travel around throughout the land and take a good look at it (13:15, 17).

Abraham trusted so firmly in this promise of God that he said to the king of Sodom, who wanted to present him with part of the booty taken in the battle described in Genesis 14, "[No,] lest you should say, 'I have made Abram rich'" (14:23). Doubtless this conduct was very pleasing to God. In the chapter that follows (ch. 15), we are told that God promised Abraham an even greater area—the land that stretched from the Euphrates to Egypt (v. 18). And centuries later, David and Solomon did indeed rule over approximately this area.

Later Paul went so far as to say that God had promised Abraham the whole world (Rom. 4:13). This apostle then saw God's promise to Abraham, spoken of in Genesis 12:1–15:6, as embracing a great multitude of peoples—all nations. Thus the nations were not rejected for good by God in Abraham's days. On the contrary, despite his bitter experiences with the world both before and after the flood, God began to extend his arms anew toward the nations that were falling away from him. His eyes rested on Abraham the idol worshiper, to whom he gave not only the promise of blessed seed but also the promise that he would be a blessing to all the nations of the earth. Thanks to the New Testament, we now understand that the seed through which Abraham became a blessing for all the nations was the Jewish people—especially its greatest Son, Jesus Christ, our Savior.

A Divine Mystery

From the New Testament we get some insight into God's way of dealing with Abraham. Paul tells us that he and his fellow apostles have been allowed some insight into God's way of dealing with the Gentiles, and into the entire plan of his treatment of them—deeper insight than anyone before. Before their time this had been a "mystery," something hidden.

The prophets had predicted that Israel would one day receive an enormous influx of Gentiles. The children of the desolate one (the church after the exile) would be more numerous than the children of the one who was married (the church before the exile) (Isa. 54:1; Rom. 9:30; 15:9–12; Gal. 4:27). In the one great church, there would be just as much place for pure Gentiles as for genuine Jews, pure descendants of Abraham. They would all enjoy the same rights. How was that possible? This was made clear to Paul and his fellow workers by the Spirit of God (Eph. 3:4–5). The mystery has been explained. And because the light of the New Testament now shines upon us, we can read Genesis 12–15 and understand these chapters as Paul did.

In Paul's day, when God sent the light of fulfillment to shine on these hidden things of the prophets, which were indeed known but not understood, he allowed this true Israelite and great lover of his people to see the solution to a riddle that had bothered him greatly and made him anxious. For before his own eyes Paul saw how the addition of the Gentiles to the church of Abraham and all the other saints of old occurred through the terrible disobedience and stubborn resistance against Jesus Christ that occurred among most of the Jews. He watched the inheritance of many of Abraham's children by blood slip away because of their unbelief. Now it went to strangers instead. Paul was greatly disturbed as he watched these events unfold. In his letters he mentions it as something that was never far from his thoughts and prayers.

But he also tells us how God comforted him. Paul was

allowed to learn to see and believe that this amazing course of events did not result from any mistake or any arbitrariness on God's part, but stemmed from deep divine wisdom (Rom. 11:33). When the LORD let these things happen, he was not acting in accordance with any whim or fancy or momentary inspiration, but in accordance with his plan. Behind it was an established plan, a wise intention that went back to the time before the foundation of the world (Eph. 1:4), an eternal intention (Eph. 3:10), an intention from all eternity (2 Tim. 1:9), a plan that God already framed in the time of Abraham.

Abraham's Amen and the LORD's Response

Did Abraham always believe in God's promises? This question can be answered with both a yes and a no.

We human beings certainly are not perfect, not in our faith either. The only perfect believer here on earth was our Lord Jesus Christ, "the perfecter of our faith" (Heb. 12:2). But Abraham complained to the LORD that he still didn't have a son to become his legal heir in accordance with the prevalent conceptions in his time and surroundings. Apparently in accordance with the legal patterns then in effect, his possessions would pass at the time of his death to Eliezer of Damascus, his most trusted slave, who was already placed over his entire household (Gen. 15:2–3).

Abraham was getting discouraged. He was already old, and so was Sarah, although she was ten years younger than he. But women of 60 or 70 simply do not bear children.

The LORD then comforted Abraham anew by assuring him expressly that his own son by blood would be his heir (15:4). The LORD even took Abraham outside, showed him the night sky with all its stars, and said, "So shall your offspring be" (15:5). By this word *offspring* (lit., *seed*), the LORD was referring to all of Abraham's posterity—not just our Lord Jesus Christ but all of Abraham's numerous descendants.

Even if Abraham was not a perfect believer, as a rule he trusted in God's promises. In many respects Abraham's life resembled that of David centuries later, who we know transgressed God's commandments. But after David died and was succeeded by Solomon and then by Jeroboam, the LORD appealed to the example of David as he put kings to shame (1 Kgs. 11:12, 34; 14:8). David's sins were not repeatedly called to mind (1 Kgs. 15:5). Sometimes the testimony God gave about David contained nothing but praise. Genesis 15:6 also tells us that Abraham believed in the LORD. The way the sentence is formulated suggests that believing in the LORD was an ordinary thing for him to do. Despite the weaknesses Abraham manifested as he walked along his path, he still stayed on the right road. Abraham never abandoned the route, even if he did stumble from time to time.

The Hebrew word translated in Genesis 15:6 as "believed" includes the word *'amen*. What the text literally says is that Abraham said amen to God's promise. The Hebrew verb in question was not reserved for religious contexts but could also be used to refer to relationships between people. This Hebrew word is used, for example, when we are told that King Achish trusted David (1 Sam. 27:12). Thus we could also translate 15:6 as follows: "And Abraham trusted Yahweh."

Scripture comes back to this verse frequently (see Rom. 4:3, 9, 18, 22; Gal. 3:6; James 2:23). What is discussed is not just the first half of this verse but also the second half, which reads, "And he [Yahweh] counted it to him as righteousness [*tsedaqah*]."

This is the first time this word *tsedaqah* is used in Scripture. We do, however, find earlier occurrences of the word *righteous*: Noah, we are told, was a "righteous [*tsaddiq*] man" (Gen. 6:9). This word *tsaddiq* is often used for those who hold on to the LORD and his word in faith. A righteous (*tsaddiq*) man was one to whom righteousness (*tsedaqah*) could be attributed. This word was used to describe Abraham.

The latter word came to be commonly used. In all ages there have been people who did not want to forsake the LORD but clung to him. Regarding the *righteousness* of people like Abraham, see Deuteronomy 6:25; 16:20; 24:13; Psalms 15:2; 18:20; 106:31, which speaks of Phinehas, who put a drastic end to idolatrous harlotry in Israel, which was "counted to him as righteousness from generation to generation forever"; Isaiah 1:27; and Matthew 5:20.

The LORD greatly valued Abraham's trust in him. That trust was pleasing to him; he regarded it as righteousness. The LORD delighted in Abraham's attitude toward him. Just think about it. Abraham trusted in God, in God's promise that his seed would be numerous, even though the natural course of things would seem to leave a man of his age little room for hope of seed. Nevertheless, he continued to place his trust in God. In God's eyes, this was what he appreciated so much in his friend Abraham.

We need to pause a moment to discuss the meaning of the LORD's action toward Abraham here.

Recently a Reformed biblical scholar (H. J. Jager) has observed that the meaning of Genesis 15:6 (and also of Rom. 4:3, where Paul cites Gen. 15:6, though according to the Septuagint, which transposes the active voice into the passive voice) "has not been understood for a long time in Reformed circles. People have thought only of a reckoning of the righteousness of Christ. And they wanted to read that into this text." As examples of this exegesis he mentions H. Bavinck, J. van Andel, G. C. Aalders, and S. Greijdanus, with counterexamples found in J. Ridderbos and J. G. Woelderink.

Indeed, we find two beautiful pages about the meaning of Genesis 15:6b in the book by J. Ridderbos, *Abraham, the Friend of God*. We would like to quote the following material from those pages:

No less penetrating than the testimony regarding Abraham's faith is what follows in Genesis 15:6b: "And he reckoned it to him for righteousness."

Now the word "it" naturally refers to Abraham's exercise of faith that has just been mentioned in Genesis 15:6a. The question might arise as to how this could be reckoned to Abraham for righteousness. After all, we are accustomed to say on the basis of Scripture that we possess no other righteousness than the righteousness of Christ, which is reckoned to us by God as though it were our own. And naturally this occurs in the way of faith, but then it is still not faith or believing in the proper sense that is our righteousness, but through faith we share in the righteousness that is in Christ, hence, in a righteousness that lies outside of us.

In order to find the answer to the question that has been raised, we need to proceed on the basis of Old Testament linguistic usage. In the Old Testament, especially in the Psalms, the psalmists speak very often of a righteousness that the believer possesses and on the basis of which the believer appeals to God. Should someone ask what is meant by this righteousness, then one immediately discerns that fearing God and hoping in him and walking according to the requirement of his commandment all play an important role in connection with this righteousness. This helps explain why this pleading of the psalmists on the basis of their own righteousness can give rise to our question as to whether they might be guilty of a certain kind of works righteousness.

In truth, however, it is not their intention that their good works should be the basis upon which they might appeal for God's favor and help. This appears already from the fact that these same people, whose righteousness is mentioned with emphasis, are identified time and again in the same context as being sinners.

The righteousness of the godly hardly signifies, then, their sinlessness. Therefore it is incorrect for people to interpret words like "just" and "righteous" as "that which corresponds to the established norm." Far rather it must be said that these Hebrew words proceed from the idea of a particular association and of the requirements that accompany this association. That person is "righteous" as he lives among others while satisfying the requirements which are placed upon him in association with his neighbor. Consequently, someone is righteous with respect to God who satisfies the requirements placed upon him by the association in which he is placed toward God.

In this connection we must continually proceed on the basis of the association of grace in which God appears to Israel in the covenant that he established with this people. . . .

Again, in this connection what is involved is not an earning of God's favor by their works. God had promised that favor and help in his covenant, and its essential character is grace. But only that person shares in this grace who holds fast to that covenant of God and to the God of that covenant. Precisely this is the reason why the psalmists plead so often on the basis of their righteousness, that is to say, on the basis of their holding fast to the covenant.

This righteousness is what we must understand when the text says that Abraham believed in the LORD and he reckoned it to him for righteousness. Abraham's faith is sufficient reason for God to respond to him as a "righteous" person, i.e., as someone who satisfies the requirement of that special friendship association in which God had entered with him. God had granted to Abraham his promise and his friendship; soon thereafter this would receive the special form of a covenant, but essentially the LORD had already revealed himself to Abraham as the God of the covenant and of grace. And were you now to ask what was the decisive thing whereby Abraham was accepted by God as friend and covenant partner, that is, as being righteous, and whereby Abraham could abide in that association of grace with God, then we are told here short and to the point: that all-decisive thing is faith.

The LORD valued Abraham's faith as righteousness. But how did Abraham find this out? How could he tell that the LORD valued his trust in God so highly?

We will find out the answer to this question later. But we can surely say at this point that Abraham received the same thing Phinehas received, whom we mentioned above. The LORD gave Phinehas a beautiful reward. For a long time the office of high priest was held by Phinehas and his descendants. In Psalm 106:31 the Hebrew text uses the word *eternal* to describe this promise, but earlier we saw that this word must be understood as meaning "from generation to generation forever." That was how the LORD manifested his good pleasure in the righteousness of Phinehas. So then, he dealt with Abraham in the same way: when Abraham hoped against hope as he continued to trust in God, the LORD valued this as righteousness by entering into a covenant with him that would last for many generations.

CHAPTER 10

God's Covenant with Abraham

There was nothing unique about the LORD's making a covenant with Abraham. The Bible tells us about other covenants the LORD made: he made a covenant with Noah; with Israel at Horeb and again in the plains of Moab; with the entire tribe of Levi, especially Aaron and his sons; and with David. Different elements were central to the arrangement of these various covenants. The way the covenant was made also differed from one time to the next: in some cases we read of an extensive ceremony, and in other cases we do not.

The LORD Makes a Covenant

When the LORD made a covenant with Abraham, he did use a ceremony. In doing this, he was following certain customs that seem to have been observed those days whenever people made a covenant with each other (see Jer. 34:18–19). What was normally done, as far as we can determine, is that a couple of animals were slaughtered and cut in half, with the two parts arranged on the ground facing each other. The parties entering the covenant would then walk between the pieces together. The idea symbolized by this ceremony was that the two people now joined in the covenant would from then on belong as closely together as the two halves of the slaughtered animal. Perhaps another idea was being expressed as well: "May God put us to death just like these animals if we break this covenant."

The Hebrew Old Testament speaks literally of "cutting" a covenant (see Gen. 15:18; Deut. 4:23; 5:3; Josh. 6:9). Greek also uses such an expression. We learn about the covenant God made with Abraham in Genesis 15:7–21. When the LORD said to Abraham that he was the same God who had chosen him while he was in the land of the Chaldeans and had brought him here to give him the land of Canaan, Abraham asked reverently how he could know this, that is, by what sign he could know it was true. God then gave Abraham the command to prepare for a formal ceremony in which they would make a covenant. On this occasion Abraham went through a tense night. He had made all the preparations. The animals lay there dead—slaughtered and cut in half. By then it was evening and the sun had gone down. Darkness descended, but the LORD did not come. He delayed so long that Abraham finally fell asleep. "And behold, dreadful and great darkness fell upon him" (15:12).

Then the LORD came and spoke. He talked about the old subject again—the promise he had already given. Now he added that Abraham would not be buried until he reached a great age. Thus for the present there was no reason for Abraham to be uneasy, so long as he continued to rely on what God told him.

The LORD also repeated his promise that Abraham would have a great many descendants. He gave him more details this time: Abraham's descendants would come to live in a foreign land, where they would be treated as slaves. But the LORD would deliver them from that land. They would even leave that land laden with plunder. Only then would they inherit the land where Abraham slept that night: the land of Canaan.

Why did all these things have to happen? Because the

LORD wanted to be patient and generous to the Canaanites a while longer. An ancient collective name is used here to refer to all the peoples that lived in Canaan at the time: they are spoken of as "the Amorites." The LORD said of these people, "for the iniquity of the Amorites is not yet complete" (15:16).

Some scholars have pointed out that the LORD probably chose to utilize the practice of making covenants prevalent at that time, but that he departed from it in one respect, namely, that the two parties did not pass between the two halves of the slaughtered animal together. Only the LORD passed between them. It is possible that the LORD was going directly contrary to the customs dominant at that time in the making of covenants, but we really cannot be sure. A few sentences back we used the word *probably*. It does not seem wise to attach far-reaching implications to this one fact. That the LORD should go between the slaughtered animals alone by himself seems obvious enough: Abraham was asleep.

Yet the fact that Abraham was asleep did not prevent him from becoming aware of what the LORD did. In the form of a frightening flame from a glowing oven, the LORD passed along this pathway of blood and death. Could this perhaps mean that the LORD was giving Abraham an assurance that when Abraham was dead and even more powerless than when he was an old man, the LORD would look after his descendants, that he would look after the children of his friend and covenant partner, and would use all his might in doing so? In any event, that's what happened.

The foreign land referred to in 15:13 is Egypt, of course. When the children of Israel were oppressed there later, God heard their cry and remembered his covenant with Abraham (Exod. 2:23). He delivered them with a manifestation of his awesome power and might. "With an outstretched arm and with great acts of judgment" (Exod. 6:6). How intensely the Israelites must have listened to such a story!

The Hagar Solution

The LORD our God is not just powerful; he is omnipotent. He did not choose to make an immediate beginning with the fulfillment of his promise after he had sworn his oath to Abram. Again the LORD delayed acting. Abram was eighty-five years old by then and had no child, no son (Gen. 16:16).

This time it was Sarai who got discouraged. She made a suggestion to Abram, a suggestion that strikes us as very strange but would hardly cause any puzzlement for the people of the land from which Abram and Sarai had come. Sarai asked her husband to take one of her slaves as his wife. When the slave bore Abraham a child, it could be regarded as Sarai's child. Such a thing was provided for in the laws of Abram's homeland. We would say today that the boy was registered as a child of Abram and Sarai.

Abram accepted this proposal on Sarai's part. We should not be too quick to condemn Abram and Sarai for their conduct here. Let's bear in mind that they were only the first generation of a church that had just been placed again in the light of God's address to humanity, whereas we have enjoyed the instruction of our Lord Jesus Christ and his apostles concerning marriage for centuries. Behind this deed of Abram and Sarai there was surely something we can sympathize with if we measure it by the standard of the flesh. In good faith, apparently, they believed that God's objectives could not be reached without their intervention. How often don't we make the same mistake? And let's not forget either that at this point the LORD had not yet said in so many words that Abraham would receive a son as his heir and as a child of Sarai. There was no mention of this before Genesis 16.

The slave woman's name was Hagar. She was an Egyptian. Sarai surely did not choose her for her beauty; in fact, the dark Egyptian women were not considered very attractive at all when compared with much lighter-skinned women like Sarai. Nor was the relationship between Hagar and Sarai ideal. When Hagar "saw that she had conceived, she looked with contempt on her mistress" (16:4). Neither do we read that the relationship between Abram and Hagar was ideal, or that Hagar meant much to Abram. When Sarai complained to Abram about how Hagar was offending her, Abram was not upset but simply reminded Sarai that she was still Hagar's mistress. Hagar was only a slave. Here Abram was acting in accordance with the law of his own time and his land, as we know it through the Code of Hammurabi, a Babylonian king. According to section 146 of this code, a priestess or a woman of distinction who had given her husband a slave who then bore him children could not get rid of the slave by selling her, but she could put some sort of sign on her so that she would be treated like a slave as before. Sarai made use of this right. But then Hagar ran away from her. The woman who carried Abram's son in her womb fled to the wilderness toward the land from which she had come—Egypt.

What a sorry story! The only one who was good to her was the Angel of the LORD. He could not bear the sight of Hagar's condition. Of the three people involved, she was by no means the guiltiest. In fact, she had been forced to put up with a great deal. The LORD promised her a son—a son who would be well-known. The boy would be named Ishmael, "because the LORD has listened to your affliction" (16:11) Here we surely get to know God! He had mercy on the suffering ones of Abraham's household.

Even then it pleased the LORD to wait thirteen more years. By this time Abram was ninety-nine years old, and Sarai was ninety. People do not have children at those ages. Sarai seemed to have one foot in the grave, and so did Abram.

Then the LORD came. He came when it would finally be clear to everyone who heard the story (and the story of Isaac's birth has become a chapter of history know all over the world) that the God of our deliverance and salvation does not need to make use of anything that comes from a human being. He does not even need Abram and Sarai with their Hagar solution to the problem. Hadn't he already shown his revulsion for reliance on the flesh in the cases of Cain, Lamech, the violent men of the period before the flood, and the Nimrod figures dwelling in the city and land of Babel? What is great among people is an abomination to God (Luke 16:15). In God's kingdom we find an entirely different style than in the kingdom of this world. God's kingdom is not interested in the greatness of human beings, their fruitfulness or understanding or numbers, and so forth. Quite the contrary (see 1 Cor. 1:17–31). Pagans and unbelievers do not see this, and even those who believe forget it all too easily.

Abram and Sarai were at least agreed that they had to do something to help God's plans reach fulfillment. They organized themselves and joined hands, even though their hearts were probably closed to each other at the time. They thought they had to do something together "for the LORD." What foolishness those who confess the LORD can sometimes engage in—aping the world and the flesh!

Finally, after those thirteen years, the LORD proceeded with the fulfillment of his original promise to Abram. And what did he say of that "marriage" of Abram to Sarai's slave? He was silent about it, and he was even so generous as to say something favorable to Abram about Ishmael (Gen. 17:20). After all, he was Abram's son. But to this day, Christianity has a painful reminder of this dark page in Abram's life through the eternal puzzle of the Arabic world with its religion of Islam.

The Covenant Confirmed

When the LORD finally proceeded with the fulfillment of his promise after another thirteen years, he first had a rather extensive conversation with Abraham. Let's look at the beginning of that conversation.

The LORD began with these words: "I am God Almighty" (17:1). That's what he placed first. This was God's business. That is what Abraham simply had to believe before everything else. And today that's still what we must believe—that our heavenly Father is almighty, that he is capable of taking care of his business.

As for Abraham's business, the LORD immediately proceeded to deal with that matter as well: "Walk with a perfect heart before my face." Do you sense the friendly admonition here? The LORD is telling Abraham, "Don't let your heart be divided between me and something else in which you place your trust."

The LORD apparently spoke these opening words to Abraham after he had manifested himself to Abraham in visible form, for later we read, "When he had finished talking with him, God went up from Abraham" (17:22). If we bear this in mind, the reason for Abraham's conduct after God's opening words becomes much clearer. When Abraham heard God speak these words, he fell down on his face before the LORD. That was how the people of the Near East fell down before their rulers in ancient times—with their foreheads and the palms of their hands against the ground. Thus Abraham had all the reason in the world to bow before the LORD who had just spoken and said, "I am God Almighty. Walk with a perfect heart before my face."

After this introduction the actual conversation began. What did the two talk about? As we might expect, they talked about the subject that had already filled the hearts of Abraham and Sarah for years, namely, God's promise that Abraham's seed would be numerous. They talked especially about the covenant the LORD had made with Abraham and through which he had bound himself even more firmly to the promise to give Abraham numerous descendants, the promise that he would uphold faithfully even after Abraham died at a blessed old age (17:7–21).

How did the LORD say this? He declared, "That I may make my covenant between me and you, and may multiply you greatly" (17:2). Unfortunately, at this point we must depart again from the major translations, which simply speak of "making" a covenant. Such a translation would be acceptable if the Hebrew text talked about "cutting" a covenant here, but it doesn't. What it literally says is "I will give my covenant between me and you." In plain English we would say, "I will keep my covenant; I will fulfill it." The New International Version (1984) therefore renders the text, "I will confirm my covenant."

The LORD would faithfully uphold and keep his covenant, the one he had made with Abraham on that memorable night described in Genesis 15. What he had promised, he would also "give." Later he said that he would maintain his covenant between himself and Abraham (17:7, 19, 21). In other words, he would make it stand. We should not translate that he would "establish" his covenant, for the covenant had already been established.

This was the subject of the conversation, then. The LORD would surely keep his covenant and make it stand. He would maintain it.

Three Assurances

Thereafter the LORD gave Abraham a threefold, actually a fourfold, assurance of his faithfulness to his covenant.

In the first place, he changed Abraham's name. Originally his name was a bit shorter—Abram. Abram is an ordinary name that we come across more often in Babylonian literature. But from then on God wanted him to be called Abraham, for this would testify that he would surely become the father of a great many people. Through this name, then, the LORD was repeating the content of the promise of Genesis 15. Not only would he see to it that Abraham had children, he also would watch over them and take care of them after Abraham was dead. The LORD would see to it that Abraham's descendants settled in Canaan.

In the second place, God imposed a covenant obligation on Abraham: from then on he and his descendants were to practice circumcision. "And it shall be a sign of the covenant between me and you [plural]" (17:11). In this way, too, the LORD was showing Abraham that the fulfillment of his promise of life and descendants was not dependent on what people could and could not do.

Circumcision was not something brand-new and unknown to Abraham. This is already clear from the fact that the institution of circumcision is communicated in only a few words. "You [plural] shall be circumcised in the flesh of your [plural] foreskins" (17:11). Abraham was expected to understand the meaning of these words readily.

Circumcision was already practiced by the Egyptians some two and three thousand years before the birth of Christ. This is clear from investigation of mummies and also from a bas-relief on a grave found in ancient Memphis. An operation is depicted: a man squats on his haunches before his patient, and he is busy cutting away his foreskin, that is, the skin at the very end of the penis, using a knife probably made of stone. According to Herodotus, this practice of circumcision was imported into Palestine from Egypt by the Phoenicians and the Syrians. No doubt Herodotus knew what he was talking about. He must have thought that the Jews also owed the practice of circumcision to the Egyptians. Apart from this issue, his comments do indicate that circumcision goes back a long, long way in history. And it is apparent that the Israelites indeed had circumcision in common with all the peoples around them, because only the Philistines were scorned as "the uncircumcised." The Philistines had come to Palestine much later than the other peoples and were of entirely different descent.

What circumcision meant for the peoples of the ancient

Near East seems fairly obvious. Success in marriage was deemed to be of great importance. The man who had many children (especially many sons) possessed a lot of power and security. Because the operation was performed on the young men as they were growing up, we can conclude that it was viewed as a preparation for marriage. Through circumcision, certain obstacles to fertility and marriage apparently were supposed to be removed.

The way the word *uncircumcised* is sometimes used in Scripture seems to fit in with this conception. When someone is not able to speak well, he is said to be "of uncircumcised lips" (Exod. 6:12). If he cannot hear, his ear is said to be "uncircumcised" (Jer. 6:10). And if the Israelites do not wish to listen to the Lord, it must be because of some obstacle: the foreskin of their hearts must be cut away (Deut. 10:16). Thus the word *circumcision* suggested opening, making ready, equipping, so that afterward the person concerned could take part in the great process of fruitfulness and life that filled the entire world.

The Lord now latched on to these generally accepted human conventions by imposing circumcision on Abraham as a commandment. But he did make one important change in the custom: he moved the time when circumcision was to take place. He made it much, much earlier. He moved the date of circumcision from the time a young man was about to marry to the earliest days of a baby's life. Circumcision was to be performed on the eighth day, when there could not yet be any thought of marriage on the boy's part.

Doesn't it look like God is poking a little fun at human power here? The connection in the minds of many people between circumcision and marriage is hereby denied. After all, the opening and continuation of life are in God's hand. In the language of that time and culture, God showed Abraham and Israel that fertility, life, numbers, power, strength, and security are all given simply by him alone.

The number of Abraham's children would be great. The

Lord stood ready to remove the obstacle to their coming into the world. That obstacle was death, the power of death as it already made itself felt in the lives of Abraham and Sarai. But at the same time he gave them a lesson that applies to all ages: "I am God Almighty." There is no need for us to do God's thinking for him or to organize his affairs or solve his problems. All we have to do is to walk uprightly before his face. He will then see to everything else. The source of life is the Lord himself—and not the power of people or of the male reproductive organ.

What small changes God makes! Abram becomes Abraham. In Hebrew the difference between the two names is only one letter. As for circumcision, the only difference is that the time is moved ahead.

These are simple changes, but we do not quickly exhaust their significance. What is great in the eyes of people is an abomination before God. O Christians, don't ape the world! The Lord is your portion.

As for the third assurance, it had to do with Sarah's name. Every attentive Bible reader must be struck by the fact that, by the time of the story recorded in Genesis 17, the Lord had never yet said that he planned to realize his promise to give Abraham numerous descendants by way of Sarai as mother. Or if he did, there is no record of it in the Bible. In fact, Sarai herself believed that because of her advanced age she would have to help the Lord fulfill his promise by means of the Hagar solution. Abraham agreed with her. Apparently the Lord had not said expressly that Abraham's lawful and official posterity would be born of Sarai, his own wife.

That promise came now. And to give Abraham an assurance that this promise could also be relied on, he changed her name to Sarah. Before then her name had been Sarai. The name Sarah means "queen": "Kings of people shall come forth from her." When Abraham heard the Lord talking about

Sarah giving birth, he again fell on his face. He laughed. He thought to himself, "Shall a man of a hundred years old father a son? And shall Sarah give birth at the age of ninety? Was this really what the LORD meant? But it wasn't necessary! Couldn't he just as easily keep his covenant with me by making use of Sarah's adopted son Ishmael? Wasn't Ishmael registered as Sarah's own son?"

But no, the LORD insisted on fulfilling his covenant with Abraham by means of Sarah herself as a mother. He would use a son born to Sarah. He even gave a command regarding the name of the son Sarah would bring into the world. Another name! The boy was to be called "Isaac." That was a clear allusion to Abraham's laughter of a moment before, for we are told, "And [he] laughed" (17:17, Hebrew: *wayyitskhaq*). The Hebrew form of the name Isaac is *Yitskhaq* (v. 21), which means "laughter." There is a play on words here.

Centuries later the name Sarah continued to speak of God's repeated rejection of any reliance on human power, calculation, knowledge, deliberation, and so forth. If there was to be any talk of laughter, it should be from God's side.

A Fourth Assurance

Shortly after these events the LORD came to Abraham again, this time specifically for Sarah's benefit. We could speak of the words he spoke on this occasion as the fourth assurance (18:1–15).

In the episode related in Genesis 17, the LORD said that Sarah would have a son by that time next year (v. 21). Those words are repeated in 18:10. So there could not have been much time between chapters 17 and 18. Still, the LORD showed Abraham again that his promise is unshakable. This time he made use of a surprising witness—Sarah herself! We won't say anything here about the deeply moving fact that God the LORD arrived at Abraham's tent as a dusty traveler and was willing to accept food and drink from his hand. How good the LORD is as he stoops down to us!

When the LORD sat down as a guest at Abraham's table, he repeated his promise: "About this time next year . . ." (18:10). But Sarah could hear what he was saying, since she was inside the tent near the table where the guests were seated. When she heard the LORD's words, she laughed, just as Abraham had laughed before her. Naturally she thought to herself, "My husband and I aren't exactly newlyweds anymore."

The LORD said, "Why did Sarah laugh and say, 'Will I truly bear a child even though I am so old?'" The LORD then came back to the point he had first mentioned in his discussion with Abraham in Genesis 17, where he had said, "I am God Almighty." This time he said, "Is there anything too wonderful for the LORD?"

Abraham and Sarah, and with them Israel and today's believers, must learn a lesson from this: God does not need the help of people in order to keep his promises.

Some time after that, the great miracle actually occurred: Sarah bore Abraham's son Isaac. Later the apostle Paul regarded the birth of Isaac from these two old people as such a miracle that he compared it to the resurrection of our Savior from the grave (Rom. 4:17, 24). We should therefore read the stories recorded in Genesis 17 and 18 in this light. With the LORD, all the power is present in abundant measure that is required for restoring our human life that has been corrupted by sin. He is all-mighty. Therefore we can calmly rely on him.

Already the people of Israel, for whom these stories were actually written in the first place, could learn about the faithfulness and power of God from them. From time to time the people were instructed through the stories about Abraham, Sarah, and Isaac, and they were confirmed daily in that instruction by the sign that every Israelite man and boy bore on his body—the sign of circumcision. That sign was a guarantee that God would surely keep his covenant with Abraham and his descendants. If only Israel would keep the covenant and not allow her heart to be divided between Yahweh and the gods of Canaan!

A Warning about Canaan

There was a good reason for mentioning the name Canaan just now. As we read through Genesis, it ought to strike us that just after the LORD God shows us how good and friendly he is in stooping down to his covenant partner Abraham and his wife by honoring them with a visit to their tent and patiently putting up with their weaknesses and shortcomings, we are told that he dealt very sternly with the Canaanite cities of Sodom and Gomorrah. What an instructive contrast for Israel!

When the covenant was made (Gen. 15), the LORD promised Abraham that he would give the entire area between Egypt and the Euphrates to Abraham's descendants. What the text says literally is "I have given" (v. 18). This is a manner of speaking that the LORD uses often in Scripture—and rightly so. When God promises something, he is so serious and definite about it that we can just as well speak of it in the past tense, as though that which is promised has already been received.

What was promised, however much it might still be wrapped up in the garment of his promise, had already been given. This way of speaking—describing God's promise as already given, even though its content was still wrapped in the garment of promise—occurs in various passages of Scripture (see Gen. 28:4; 35:12; Exod. 20:12; Num. 32:9; 33:53; Deut. 5:16; 9:23; 12:1; Josh 2:9, 14; 6:16; 18:3). It is from such passages that the church of the Reformation learned to speak the language of God's promises: "I have given it already." This is how certainly Israel had obtained the promised land. And we too should speak this way about God's promises that are sealed to us by baptism and the Lord's Supper.

When the LORD made his covenant with Abraham, he also told him that his children would not immediately come into possession of the land of Canaan, for the unrighteousness of the Canaanites had not yet reached its full measure.

We now know when that unrighteousness did reach its full measure in God's judgment: it was when Israel received the command from the LORD to strike all the inhabitants of Israel with the ban. The "ban" has nothing to do with "exiling" anyone. The word is used to translate the Hebrew *kherem*, which denotes a complete consecration to God that may not be sabotaged in any way, as Achan did, for example (Josh. 7). In Moses's days God commanded the Israelites to wipe out the Canaanites, whose wickedness he abhorred. (We will have more to say later about the wickedness of these Canaanites.)

But now there is something that should strike us here. Whereas in the days of Moses the LORD ordered his people Israel to proceed with the extermination of all the Canaanites, he himself undertook the extermination of one portion of the Canaanites, the inhabitants of Sodom and Gomorrah, during the time of Abraham. Apparently the measure of the unrighteousness of the Sodomites and their neighbors was already full by then (Gen. 18:20–21).

God's horrible judgment on those cities gave the Israelites an advance peek at the ban that they would later have to impose against all of Canaan. At least, that was how it should have been—and could have been. If the Israelites had lived in the faith of their father Abraham, they would have been able to do almost anything against the Canaanites despite their lack of power. After all, their God was almighty. But the books of the Prophets make it all too clear that the Israelites did not try to carry out their commission in faith. This becomes clear already in the first books of the Prophets. Faithful Joshua therefore had to admonish the people (Josh. 17:17–18).

For his part, the LORD did indeed keep his covenant. He did so through a whole series of miracles. First there was the birth of Isaac from parents with one foot in the grave, as it were. Then death and destruction struck some of the Canaanites in Sodom and Gomorrah. Later the doors of Israel's grave in Egypt were opened, and death struck the firstborn of the Egyptians. That was how the LORD, the God of Israel, acted on behalf of his people. He led them through the Red Sea and the Jordan. He fed them and gave them water in the wilderness. And he led the way when it came time to strike the Philistines.

But sad to say, Israel did not keep the covenant. The people did take up the battle against the Canaanites in faith, but they did not pursue, let alone finish, it in faith. Instead they wound up intermarrying with the Philistines. (We will have more to say about this later.)

How painful such stories as God's destruction of the Canaanite cities of Sodom and Gomorrah must have been for the Israelites to listen to later! How sensitively Genesis here reveals its character as a book with a certain purpose, namely, to remind people of God's covenant with Abraham and to introduce the rest of the Torah, including the covenant made at Horeb.

It must have been painful to read and hear that God himself had thundered against the Sodomites and wiped them from the face of the earth. It must have been painful to see that Lot had already gotten involved with the Canaanites and had almost perished with Sodom (Gen. 19:14). And then there was the shameful story of his daughters, into whose life the Canaanite wickedness managed to penetrate in such an abominable way (vv. 30–38).

It must have been painful to read and hear how faithfully Father Abraham watched over his covenantal responsibilities and how he made his servant Eliezer swear that he would never take a wife for Isaac from among the Canaanites (24:3). That was how things were supposed to be done.

But Esau already had taken two Canaanite wives. That is how things were not supposed to be done. And then there was the bitter disappointment of his parents (26:34–35). Therefore Isaac said to Jacob, "You must not take a wife from the Canaanite women" (28:6). That was how it should be done, and that was how it should remain. There were plenty of beautiful examples along with negative examples—already in Genesis.

But Israel failed to take these things to heart properly. Yet we as Christians do not have any right to look down on Israel on this account. Later church history has shown us time and again that God's church did not march ahead in the faith of Abraham, but felt safer relying on covenants of her own making than relying on the covenant the LORD made with her and her children. How completely different the world could have been!

CHAPTER 11

The Life of the Patriarchs

Faithfulness and Shameful Examples

When we read the chapters that follow the ones we have been discussing thus far, we see that they give Israel even more reason to feel ashamed—if that's possible. In the last part of Genesis (roughly chs. 20–50), the Israelites could read even more about the sins and miseries of their fathers as contrasted with the faithfulness of God. From these stories (e.g., Ishmael and Esau), they learned how some of Abraham's seed was alienated for good from the service of God, thereby sinking back into the paganism of earlier times.

Even when we turn to the most saintly figures, we read a story of falling and rising. As far as Abraham goes, we already pointed out earlier that there is no one without faults. Even though he was determined to stick to the path of faith in God, he often lost his footing, for example, in both Egypt and Gerar, when he sought refuge in his own cunning and calculations rather than in the LORD's promise to be a shield to him. Abraham tried to defend himself with the half-truth that Sarah was his sister. She was indeed his half sister, but much more important is the fact that she was his wife. That part Abraham did not dare mention.

We should be careful in how we judge this action on Abraham's part, for the man was indeed in a position of extreme peril. The demands of the power holders of that time were sometimes simply outrageous and scandalous. Instructive in this respect is a letter written by Labaya, the "king" of Shechem, which is one of the Amarna letters that were sent from Palestine and other areas to two of the pharaohs of Egypt. There letters date from about 1400 BC, which was only a few centuries after Abraham. Labaya writes to the pharaoh that he falls down on his face in the dust seven times and then seven times again before the king, "my lord and my sun." He also writes that he is not refusing to pay tribute and that he is wrongly being accused of unfaithfulness to the king. If the pharaoh gave the order, he would be willing to plunge a dagger into his own flesh. He is even prepared to give the pharaoh his wife if that should please him! Here we cannot help but be reminded of Genesis 12, 20, and 26, where this same topic is mentioned in connection with Abraham's life.

Abraham and Sarah were saved from their perilous situation in a manner that put them to shame. God intervened, saving the future of the church, and of the Christ who was to come forth from the church (Rev. 12:5). Furthermore, Abraham seems to have learned a lesson. After the defeat of the kings and the rescue of Lot, he was not so bold as to demand that all of Canaan recognize him at once. Rather, he gave tithes to Melchizedek, thereby obediently recognizing the authority of this Canaanite ruler, and to the king of Sodom he made it known that he fixed his expectations on God in faith, when he said, "lest you should say, 'I made Abraham rich'" (Gen. 14:20, 23). Finally, he seems to have been purified to such an extent that he was ready, at the LORD's command, to sacrifice his son Isaac, which meant the he would be left with nothing but the LORD and his promise. How pleasing Abraham's trust in God was to the LORD, his covenant God (Gen. 22:12; James 2:21)!

As for Isaac, Genesis does not conceal his stumbling from us either. Again the problem was a relationship with a "king"— the king of Gerar. But just as God had saved Abraham and Sarah, he now saved Isaac and Rebekah in a way that put them to shame. The LORD did not need their cunning to keep the oath he had sworn to Abraham. And the LORD elevated Isaac so magnificently from his perilous situation that Isaac's friendship was sought eagerly by those who had earlier threatened him. King Abimelech himself came to Isaac, along with his advisor Ahuzzath and his commander Phicol, to ask Isaac whether he would be willing to make a treaty with them (Gen. 26).

When we talk about Isaac's weaknesses, we can hardly keep silent about his attitude with regard to Esau and Jacob. It had been prophesied by what rule God would lead the future of Rebekah's twin sons. Those prophecies applied not just to the two sons as individuals but also to the nations that would come forth from them. Events would not unfold in accordance with the rule that we love to see followed (age, prestige, prominence), but rather in a way that shows that the real power belongs to God and not to people (2 Cor. 4:7). For this God had already prepared Isaac and Rebekah, the parents of the two boys, by making them wait twenty years before they received the blessing of children. When Rebekah was finally with child, God informed her, "The older one will serve the younger one." But later when Isaac helped to fulfill this divine initiative in blessing his sons, it was against his own will—that's how much he loved the bold figure of the hunter Esau and clung to the rule of the flesh, i.e., the rule of age and prestige first (Gen. 25:28; 27:1, 19, 32).

As for Jacob, we hardly need any reminders of his weaknesses. They are all too well-known.

Yet not one of them (Abraham, Isaac, and Jacob) ever became enamored with the godless world. Abraham never went back

to his fatherland and the idolatry prevalent there. Never did
the patriarchs shake off their status as pilgrims, the isolation
God had imposed on them, even though Abraham did call on
the help of the Amorites Mamre, Aner, and Eshcol (14:13, 24),
and Isaac made a treaty whereby he could live in peace with
Abimelech after years of quarreling. Neither Isaac nor Jacob
ever sought to mingle with the Canaanites. Many of their descendants did otherwise—even after they inherited the promised land. They followed the path of Esau and Ishmael, of
Ham and Cain. Therefore the Israelites who lived in Canaan
must have been very deeply impressed with what they read
in Genesis about the *toledoth* (origin and outcome) of such
figures as Ishmael and Esau (Gen. 25 and 36). Those figures
represent side roads that ran dead!

As the author of Genesis told his story, there was plenty of
"application" that came through. If only the Israelites would
understand what it all meant! Apparently the genealogy of
Esau was kept up by someone right up to the time of King
Saul (Gen. 36:31; 1 Kgs. 11:14). That way the readers and hearers would surely see where the path of forsaking the covenant
would lead.

God-Fearing Jacob

We can now conclude our introduction to the reading of
Genesis, even though very little has been said about Jacob
and nothing about his sons, those forefathers of the people
of Israel who must have been especially beloved. (One could
almost call them "popular.")

Think of the remarkable conclusion of the story of Jacob's
struggle with God at the Jabbok: "Therefore to this day the
people of Israel do not eat the sinew of the thigh that is on
the hip socket, because he touched the socket of Jacob's hip
on the sinew of the thigh" (32:32). Apparently such a unique
custom gave rise to questions from time to time; those ques-

tions could be answered by referring to the Peniel story in Genesis. God the LORD himself never forbade the eating of this tendon—at least, we do not read anywhere that he did.

In all likelihood the people adopted this prohibition voluntarily. In later times, unfortunately, it was elevated to a very important commandment, as though it were of divine origin. Just as in the case of certain rules adopted in the medieval Christian church, it became a troublesome vexation. A Jewish rabbi who has written a manual for butchers gives some pointers to be observed in the ritual slaughter:

> Some parts of a permitted animal, even if it is slaughtered in the proper way (after being inspected) are forbidden, such as the blood, some parts of the fat, and the so-called twisted muscle (the tendon attached to the hip socket) in the case of mammals. This prohibition is based on Genesis 32:32. . . . With regard to that "twisted muscle," the following must be observed. Because this tendon runs through the hindquarters of the animal and has many branches and can hardly be separated completely from the flesh, in most countries the hind legs are not eaten. The hindquarters are separated from the rest between the twelfth and thirteenth ribs.

If Jews really honor these rabbinical rules, practically the entire hind of the cow, the part we get our steaks from, is off-limits for eating, even if the cow is slaughtered in a kosher way. That's the kind of tangle we get into when we lift a Scripture passage out of its context, including the book in which it occurs. This is precisely what we are not to do. We must not set apart the beautiful story of Jacob at Peniel for some special Jewish purpose—and not for some special Christian purpose either.

We must not fall into the habit of speaking ill of Jacob; otherwise we wind up following the bad example set by Esau

(27:36). Esau gave Jacob an undeserved name, a name that sticks with him to this day. The Holy Spirit begins his story about Jacob by introducing him to us as a God-fearing man (25:27). Unfortunately, this text is often mistranslated: we are told that Jacob was a "quiet" man since he dwelt in tents. The Hebrew word used here (*tam*) is basically the same word that is used in 17:1, where the LORD says to Abraham, "Walk before me, and be blameless [*tamim*]." The idea the author of Genesis wants to get across is that Jacob was an upright man who lived in tents. That is to say, Jacob was a man who liked to stay close to his family, close to God's church, close to God himself. Esau, on the other hand, was acquainted with the inheritance of Abraham and was not always indifferent to it, but he was a man with a divided heart. Unlike Jacob, he wandered away from the path.

And yet, it was very weak of Jacob—and of his mother Rebekah as well—to suppose that the place God had assigned him in the great scope of his works had to be seized by trickery and cunning. Jacob seemed to think that God needed the help of sinful flesh.

Jacob relied on the same type of fleshly calculations in his relationship to Laban. The author of Genesis is surprisingly forthright as he tells the story of Jacob's descendants. Their great ancestor was not spared, and his descendants were hardly being flattered in the process.

But it pleased the LORD to give a place of honor in Israel to Leah, the one who was oppressed. He allowed her to be the mother of Judah, the royal tribe.

That is how the LORD is. This is simply his way of doing things, his style. Our human rules and preferences (based on age, prestige, power, greatness, charm, etc.) are not binding on him. Quite the contrary. Tamar was a Canaanite and played the role of a temple prostitute in order to gain her rights after her proper rights under marriage were denied her, but it did not please God that she should be oppressed, for she had earlier been included in Judah's family. God, who fiercely hates oppression, gave Tamar a place among the mothers of our Lord Jesus Christ. In Matthew 1:3 her name is even mentioned by Matthew in a last appeal to Israel to accept Jesus of Nazareth as the true Messiah—not despite his humility but precisely because of it. That he was nothing to behold was completely in line with his ancestry. Later, God made use of Jacob's son Joseph, the brother who was rejected, to keep a great people alive.

What happens when we suddenly place the story of Jacob at the Jabbok in the middle of this series? There God afflicted his servant, and from then on Jacob limped, which is hardly an attractive sight. Yet it was necessary so that we would learn to recognize the style God uses as he delivers us. That style is diametrically opposed to the one we so often admire.

But at the end of his life, on his deathbed, Jacob received the grace and light to be a preacher of this divine style. The oldest son of Joseph was not Ephraim but Manasseh. Thus, if Jacob had followed his own impulses, his right hand would have rested on the head of Manasseh. That was what Joseph expected as he presented his sons to Jacob. But the prophet Jacob crossed his arms and placed his left hand on the head of the older son.

The lesson was the same one we encounter earlier in Genesis, but this time the teacher was Jacob. How God hates our proud and sinful human nature! This nature is the source of our plotting and manipulating, and therefore the source of murder and death. As for God, he loves life.

Israel's Mirror

Genesis was written in the first place for ancient Israel. It was written so that this people would be introduced to the torah, the instruction that is first taught to us in the book of Exodus. Through the torah Israel is instructed in a way that not even the patriarchs were privileged to enjoy.

But first Genesis talks about some things that the people needed to know. It talks about creation and the garden of Eden, about human rebellion and divine grace, about the great flood and the Table of Nations. But it talks especially about Abraham's deliverance and God's covenant with him and with other patriarchs. More than half of Genesis deals with those patriarchs. And we also saw what kind of approach Genesis takes to the patriarchs. It certainly does not flatter them.

For the Israelites in Canaan, the book of the *toledoth* was in many respects a book that put them to shame. Let's not forget that the book was only an introduction to the Law. The books of the Prophets will show us what Israel did with the torah. The similarity between the central theme of Genesis and that of the prophetic books can only be described as striking.

Name and Subject Index

A

Aalders, G. C., 42, 219
Abel, 87, 132, 143–47, 149–51, 156
Abram, 191, 214, 230, 233
Adah, 148–149
Adam, xix, 29, 52, 53, 67, 84, 87,
    89, 91, 93–96, 104–12,
    116–19, 124–28, 131–40,
    145–47, 156, 157, 164, 177,
    179, 204, 211,
Ahab, 31, 179, 180
Alexander the Great, 43
Allah, 80
Amon, 21, 32
angel(s), 135, 157–59, 161, 177
    Michael, 180
    of the covenant, 181
    of Yahweh, 179–81
    of the Lord, 182, 210, 227
apostasy, 52, 159, 168
Apostles' Creed, 75
Apsu, 68
Aquinas, Thomas, 4
Aramaic, 6, 10
assurances, God's to Abraham,
    230–34
Assurbanipal, 44, 69, 199
Assyria, 192, 197, 203
Augustine, 4, 139, 178–79

B

Baal, 60
Babel
    city of, 175, 199, 228
    meaning of, 200
    tower of, 52, 177, 194, 196,
        201–3
Bähr, K. C. W. F., xvii, xviii
Barth, Karl, 107
Bathsheba, 174
Bavinck, Herman, xvii, 162, 219
Bedouins, 63
Bekker, Balthasar, 135
Belgic Confession, 9, 39, 135, 137
Berossus, 43
Bible
    anthropomorphism , 161–64,
        166
    divisions of, 17–20, 26, 27,
        33, 37–39
    genealogies, 176, 204
    Jerusalem, xvi, 9, 20
    King James Version, 37, 135,
        166, 177, 204
    Kittel's edition, 29
    Latin translation. *See*
        Vulgate
    Luther, 108
    meaning of, xv

Bible (*cont.*)
New Testament, xii, xiii, xv,
    xxi, xxii, 4, 7, 8, 11, 12,
    14, 16, 17, 18, 21, 22, 33,
    34, 39, 49, 114, 127, 169,
    181, 208, 215, 216
numbers, use of, 175–77
Old Testament, xv, xvi, xix,
    xxi, 4–14, 17–20, 22, 24,
    25, 27, 32, 39, 87, 125,
    149, 157, 179, 182, 186,
    220, 224
origin of, 3–6, 25
translations, 166
view of, 4
book of the law, 21, 22–24, 41
Brakel, Wilhelmus à, 135

C

Cain, xix, 51, 52, 84, 87, 119,
    143–58, 228, 244
spirit of, 172, 202
Cainites, 147–149, 152–53, 157
Calvin, John, 4, 85, 137, 140, 164
Canaan
land of, 237
religion of, 68–69
curse of, 172–74
Canaanites
punishment of, 174, 225, 238
wickedness of, 175, 192, 237
Canons of Dort, 137
Chaldeans, 208, 224
Christ
body of, 181
and the church, 182
Church, the Reformed, 135–36
circumcision, 231–233, 235
Clamer, Albert, 42
Code of Hammurabi, 227
covenant, xiii
cutting a, 223–25, 230

covenant (*cont.*)
God and Abraham, xii,
    30, 33, 46, 137, 213–14,
    221–39
God and Adam, 133, 138–40.
    See also covenant of
    works
God and David, 223
God and Israel, 30, 31, 34,
    45, 56, 59, 61, 67, 70, 79,
    81, 149, 223, 238
God and Judah, 32
God and Levi, 139, 223
God and Moses, 137
God and Noah, 46, 169, 171,
    223
new, 182
of law, 132, 133, 141
of nature, 133, 137, 140
of works, 132, 133–35,
    137–41
Sinai, 59
creation story, 46, 51, 72, 74, 81,
    84, 97, 98, 100, 106, 143
Babylonian, 68, 81
Cush, 172

D

Dan, 41
Daniel, 8, 18–19, 180
David, 153, 174, 215, 217–18, 223
death, 33, 55, 61, 106, 111, 115,
    124, 137, 165, 224
Abel, 156
Abraham, 29, 217, 225, 233
Adam and Eve, xxi, 123,
    125–27, 132–33, 150
firstborn Egyptians, 238
God's hatred of, xiii, xvii,
    xviii, xix, xx, xxii, 112,
    128, 130, 146, 150–51,
    196, 247

death (*cont.*)
    Holwerda, Benne, 163
    Jacob, 247
    Jesus, xxi, 13
    Joseph, 26
    Joshua, 27
    Josiah, 32
    Moses, 23, 28, 40
    Samuel, 27
    Witsius, 134
    See also Cain
de Bres, Guido, 39
de Groot, J., 42
Delitzsch, F., 41
deliverance, 30, 52, 146, 171, 228,
    248
    Israel from Egypt, xx, 80
Diaspora, 6, 177, 178
discipline, 141

E
Easter sermon, xviii, xix
Elizabeth, 139
Elohim, 80–81, 83, 85–86, 91,
    153, 168–69, 199
Enosh, 151–152
Epic of Gilgamesh, 69, 199
'erets, 71–73, 75, 170, 194
Esau, 53, 156, 238, 241, 243,
    244–46
eternal life, xiii
Eve, xix, 29, 74, 79, 87, 96,
    104–7, 109, 111–12, 116,
    119, 122–28, 132, 140,
    144–45, 147, 149–51, 156,
    164, 211

F
fall, the, 117
first Adam, 67
flood stories, 43, 52, 68–69, 73,
    84, 168–72, 175

flood, the, 168–72, 197, 208
    God's punishment, xix, 33,
    46, 52, 73, 202
Ford, Henry, 100–101
forgiveness, God's, 120
Fazer, J. G., 157
Friedrich, F., xvii

G
Genesis, book of
    audience, 55, 59, 62, 67, 99,
    130, 145, 148, 174, 149,
    151
    author of, 61–62, 66–72,
    78–79, 86, 97–98, 99,
    103–4, 109, 116, 148–149,
    151, 173, 176, 177, 190,
    195, 200–201, 204–5,
    244
    creation, 54, 70–71, 75–79,
    84–87, 89–91, 95–110,
    127
    genealogies, 56, 156
    heading, 70–72
    Israelites' reading of, 52–53,
    71–72, 77–79, 85, 97–98,
    101–3, 107, 110, 113–15,
    119, 126, 128–29, 145,
    152–53, 165, 166, 173,
    244, 248
    King James Version, 166, 177,
    204
    lessons of, 50
    literary styles of, 77, 113
    naming of, 54–55
    origin of, 64
    paradise, 74, 83–84, 90–95,
    145
    postscript, 74
    prologue, 81

Genesis, book of (*cont.*)
    purpose of, 54, 56–57,
        66–67, 69, 72–73, 101,
        103, 196, 248
    Satan, 114–15, 121, 140, 144.
        See also Satan
    science, in relation to,
        100–103
    structure of, 50–55, 80, 84,
        107, 143, 147, 155, 175
    toledoth, 51–55, 80, 83, 87,
        154–55, 209, 244, 248
    transitions in, 51–53, 113
Gentiles, God's plan for, 213–17
giants, 159
Gibeonites, 153
Gideon, 71
Gispen, W. H., 64
God
    image of, 84–90, 97, 105, 107,
        116, 133, 162, 164, 166
    names of, xvi, xvii, xviii,
        80–81, 83
    revelation of, xiii, xviii, 55,
        152, 209–11, 229, 234–36
    spirit of, 11, 13–14, 16, 73–74,
        216
God's
    judgment, 119–20, 122,
        125–27, 146
    love of life, xiii, xxi, xxiii
    patience, 159–160
    power, 80
    promises, xix, 33, 52–53, 89,
        118, 125, 133–134, 138,
        149–50, 167, 171, 208–10,
        213–22, 224, 226–31,
        233–36, 241–42. *See also*
        mother promise
    protection, 153–54
    sorrow, 160, 163, 167–68
    warnings, 125

Gomorrah, 92, 214, 236–38
Greek
    gods, 159
    Ionians, 185, 186
    islands, 186, 195
    language, 6, 7, 10, 19, 25, 54,
        161, 185, 224
    names, 25
    New Testament, 21, 39
    notion of the soul, 164–65
    Old Testament. *See*
        Septuagint
    origin, 25
    people, 159, 185, 195, 197,
        210
    writers, 38, 157
Greijdanus, S., 219

H
Hagar, 210, 226–228
Ham, 172, 174, 176, 183, 187, 192,
    195–96, 203, 244
Hamathites, 47, 186, 188–90
hatred, 144
Hebrew, definitions of, 191–92
Hegelian, xvii
Heidelberg Catechism, 75, 76,
    137, 140
Herodotus, 201, 231
Hoedemaker, P. J., 43
Holwerda, Benne, xvi, xvii, xviii,
    163, 164
Homer, 42
hunting, 198–99

I
idolatry, xix, 72, 121, 123, 206–11,
    215, 219, 243
incest, 147
Isaac, xix, 31, 53, 227, 234–35,
    237–39, 242–44

Ishmael, 53, 227–28, 234, 241, 244
Islam, 228

J
Jacob, xxii, 26, 31, 41, 42, 53, 60, 148, 156, 178, 179, 207, 211, 239, 243–47
descendants of, 177
Jager, H. J., 219
Japheth, 172–74, 176, 183–84, 186, 190, 192, 195–96, 203
Japhethites, 47, 185
Jehovah, xvii
Jephthah, 64
Jerusalem, 21, 23, 32, 153, 189
Jesus, as the true Messiah, 176
Joseph, 12, 26, 55, 247
Joshua, 27, 48, 70, 180, 207, 237
Josiah, 21–24, 30–32
Judah, 246
people of, 32

K
Keil, C. F., 41, 42
Kohnstamm, Philip, 89

L
Lamech, 84, 148–50, 202, 228
law
as torah, 20, 21, 24
book of, 41
of Moses, xv, xvi, xviii, xxii, 8, 18, 20, 21, 22, 24, 26, 27, 28, 32, 33, 40, 42, 136–39, 141
Old Testament, xx, 7, 8
Paul's discussion of, 30
shadows of, 34

law (*cont.*)
"the Law, the Prophets, and the Psalms," 9, 10, 18, 20, 125
Yahweh's, xxi
last Adam, 114
Lazarus, xxi
love, husband and wife, 126
Luther, Martin, 4, 26

M
Manasseh, 21, 32, 247
Marduk, 69
marriage, 96, 116, 148, 157–58, 226, 228, 232, 246
Mary, 33, 121, 122
Mesopotamia, literature of, 42, 168–69
messianic Scripture, 7, 10, 12, 14, 121–22, 124
Micah, 179–80
Mizraim, 172
Moses, 27, 28, 30, 40–45, 48, 49, 60–62, 65, 66–68, 70, 79, 80, 96, 99, 133, 136, 137–41, 158, 160, 164, 177–79, 182, 198, 210
mother promise, xix, 121–23, 127, 129
Mount Horeb, xx, 31, 34, 46, 59, 61, 62, 71, 74, 78, 79, 81, 96, 98, 103, 161, 198, 223, 238

N
Naamah, 148–49
Naaman, 32
nakedness, 110–12, 118–19, 128
names, 149, 175, 234
Abram, 230
Sarai, 233

Near East, 22, 40, 62–63, 67, 69,
        85, 92, 128, 168, 209, 232
    climate, 111, 119, 148
    marriage, 232
    people of, 209
Nimrod, 196–99, 202–3, 228
Noah, 29, 33, 46–47, 52–53, 84,
        159–60, 169–73, 203,
        208, 218, 223
Numbers, book of
    origin of, 64

P

pain, 150
    childbirth, xix, 126, 128
    God's, 163, 167–68
pagan(s), xix, 76, 134, 157, 172,
        241
    knowledge of God, 207
    literature, 158, 206
    viewpoint, 86, 109, 228
    worship, 59
Palestine, 6, 26, 49, 65–66,
        68–70, 72, 77, 90, 92, 119,
        231, 242
Pentateuch, xxii
    and Deuteronomy, xx
    audience, 59
    author of, 27, 28, 39–43, 65
    origin of, 25–27, 48, 65
    parts of, 44–45, 48, 84
    themes of, 28–33
    See also Torah
Pharaoh, 12, 42
pharaoh, 172, 187, 242
Phinehas, 222
Pirot, Louis, 42
poetry, Hebrew, 46, 97
polygamy, 148
protevangelion, 121, 123
Puah, 174
Put, 172

R

Rebekah, 243, 246
rebellion, 89
    according to Paul, 117
    consequences of, 121–24
    God's response, 118–19
    in the garden, 51, 74, 84, 95,
        96, 113, 117–18, 127, 147
    of Satan, 94, 114–16, 120–21
Reformation, 20, 136, 236
relationships, God and human-
        ity, 110–12
repentance
    God's, 160–63, 167–68
    human, 167
Ridderbos, J., 219
righteousness, 218–22
River, Jordan, 13, 41, 44, 49, 64,
        66, 187, 238

S

Sabbath, 7, 34, 46, 55, 59–62, 70,
        79, 96, 98, 134, 137, 148
sacrifices, 30, 34, 139, 143–46,
        242
Sadducees, xxi, 25,
salvation, 203
Sarah, 117, 128, 233–35, 241–43
    See also Sarai
Sarai, 226–28
    See also Sarah
Saul, 42, 161, 167, 176, 181, 244
Savior, xxi, 8, 9, 14, 176, 180, 215
    birth of, 33
    on earth, 4, 10, 12, 18, 24, 49,
        114, 115, 197
    resurrection of, 235
Satan, 156
    and the snake, 114–23, 127,
        144
    in the garden, 93, 114–23,
        127, 140, 144

Satan (*cont.*)
  tempting Christ, 114
Schilder, Klaas, 140
Septuagint, 6, 18, 19, 20, 25–27,
    54, 90, 91, 128, 159, 175,
    178, 179, 219
Seth, 51, 52, 87, 143, 147, 150–53,
    156, 158, 175
Sethites, 143, 147, 150, 152–53,
    156–57, 175
Shaphan, 22, 23, 31
Shem, 52, 172–77, 183, 190–93,
    195–96, 203–5
Shemites, 47, 192
Shiphrah, 174
sin, 29, 83, 89, 94–95, 106,
    118–19, 125, 128, 131–32,
    134, 137–41, 145–47
Sin (moon-god), 78
sixth day of creation, 104–6
    See also Eve
snake. *See* Satan
snakes, in the ancient world, 115,
    123
Sodom, 92, 211, 214, 236–38
    king of, 207, 215, 242
Sodomites, 237
sons of God, 87, 157–59, 178–79
sons of Israel, 176–78
soul, human, 164–65
storytelling, 62–65
Synod of Dort, 136
Syria, 63

T
Table of Nations, 47, 172, 175–78,
    197, 199, 203
    divisions of, 183–90, 192–95
Tamar, 128, 246–47
Terah, 29, 52, 207–9
thigh, sinew of, 244–45
Tiamat, 68–69

toledoth. *See* Genesis
torah, 20, 21, 30, 56, 81, 141, 247,
    248
Torah, xii, xiii, xxi, 8, 24, 28, 32,
    39, 56, 62, 130, 138, 141,
    158, 171, 238
    meaning of, 21
    themes of, 23, 29, 33
    See also Pentateuch
translation, Dutch, xv
tree of life, xxi, 94, 95, 116, 118,
    129–32, 134–35, 138, 147
tree of the choice between good
    and evil, 94, 116, 118,
    125, 129
Trinity, 133
Tubal-cain, 148

U
Uriah, 174
Ussher, James, 204

V
Van Andel, J., 219
Vlak, Johannes, 136–39
Vulgate, 19, 20, 25

W
wisdom, xxi, 14, 16, 33, 126, 131,
    216
Witsius, Herman, xxii, 132–34,
    136, 140–41
Woelderink, J. G., 219

Y
Yahweh, xiii, xvi–xviii, xx–xxiii,
    21, 80–81, 83, 85, 91, 103,
    107, 146, 14, 152–53, 169,
    172–74, 180, 196, 198–99,
    203, 210, 218, 236. *See
    also* Angel, of Yahweh

Yahweh Elohim, 81, 91, 113,
    173–74, 199

Z
Zechariah, 33, 139
Zedekiah, 176
Zillah, 148–49

Scripture Index

OLD TESTAMENT

Genesis

1 . . . . .xix, 72, 74–77, 81,
        83–84, 90, 99–100,
        102–7, 110, 127, 170
1:1. . . . . 70, 72, 74, 76, 80
1:1–2. 70
1:1–2:3 . . . . 84, 107, 143
1:1–2:4 98
1:2 72–74
1:3–2:3. 74–78
1:3–5 78
1:6–8 . . . . 78, 102
1:8 71
1:10. .71
1:11. 86
1:11–13 78
1:14. 70
1:14–19 78
1:20 .91
1:20–23 78
1:21. .91
1:24 . . . . 86, 91
1:24–25 78
1:26 . . . . 78, 85–86, 105, 107, 199
1:26–27. 87
1:26–28 105–6
1:26–31. 85
1:27. . . . . 97, 105

Genesis (*cont.*)

1:29 .78
1:31. . . . . 79, 106
1–2. 29
1–3. 29
2. . . . . 74, 84, 91–92, 95,
        104–106, 110, 113, 127
        133, 139–140, 187
2:2 79
2:3 . . . .46, 62, 76, 79–80, 96, 148
2:4 . . . . 51, 55, 80–81, 83–84,
        90, 95, 98, 154–55
2:4–4:26. 143
2:5–6 90
2:7 91
2:7–8 106
2:8 . . . . 91, 93, 98, 111
2:8–17. 90
2:15 93
2:16–17. 134
2:17. . . . . 90, 94, 140
2:18 106–7
2:18–25 95
2:19 109
2:22 . . . . .107, 111
2:24 . . . . 79, 96, 115, 148
2:25 . . . . .110–13, 119
3. . . . . 74, 84, 91, 106, 113–17,
        125, 127, 129–30, 139–40
3:1 . . . . .113, 115

Genesis (*cont.*)

3:3 118
3:8 . . . . .108, 111, 119, 123
3:14 120
3:14–15 127
3:15 . . . . xix, 121–22, 124,
                                   152–53, 158
3:16 128
3:18 131
3:19 . . . . 91, 93, 127
3:20 . . . . xix, 128
3:22 . . . . .85, 129–31, 199
3:22–24 129
4 . . . . .144–45, 148, 158, 202
4–11 29
4:4 143
4:9–15 145
4:21 190
4:26 . . . . 151–52, 155
5 87
5:1 . . . . 51–52, 87
5:1–2 .76
5:1–3 .87
5:3 156
5:4 . . . . 147, 150
5:5 131
6 . . . . .158, 160, 167, 202
6:2 . . . . 157, 159
6:3 159
6:4 159
6:4–5 160
6:5 160
6:7 . . . . 67, 76, 160
6:7–8 160
6:9 . . . . .52, 218
9 173
9:1–4 128
9:6 87
9:15 208
9:18–29 . . . . 173, 203
9:25 .172
9:26 . . . . .173, 203

Genesis (*cont.*)

10 . . . . 47, 172, 175–78,
                     183–84, 186, 190, 192,
                     195, 197, 199, 202–3
10:1 52
10:2 176
10:2–4 183
10:5 47
10:6 . . . . 176, 186
10:6–20 186
10:7 .188
10:8 .199
10:8–12 . . . . 196–97, 202
10:9 .198
10:10 201
10:13 205
10:13–14 188
10:14 189
10:15 186
10:15ff 195
10:15–19 189
10:20 .47
10:21 . . . . . . 176, 190–91, 196, 205
10:24–25 194
10:25 . . . . 192, 194
10:26–30 175
10:31 .47
10:32 .47
11 . . . . .175, 177, 200, 204
11:1–9 . . . .175, 196, 199–200, 202
11:2 .201
11:4 .201
11:4–5 201
11:5 203
11:7 .199
11:10 52
11:10–26 . . . . 175, 204–5
11:10–32 . . . . 56, 177
11:15 192
11:19 .67
11:20–26 190
11:26 209

Genesis (*cont.*)

11:27 52
12 242
12–15 216
12–25 29
12–50 29
12:1 208
12:1–3 214
12:1–15:6 215
12:3 xix
12:7 214
12:8 152
13:4 152
13:10 92
13:15 215
13:17 215
14 . . . . .47, 65
14:13 . . . . 191, 244
14:14 40–41
14:18 207
14:20 242
14:22 207
14:23 . . . . 215, 242
14:24 244
15 . . . . 215, 230, 236
15:2–3 217
15:4 217
15:5 217
15:6 218–19
15:6a 220
15:6b 219–20
15:7–21 224
15:12 224
15:13 225
15:16 225
15:18 . . . . 215, 224, 236
16 . . . . .210, 226
16:4 227
16:11 227
16:15 228
16:16 226
17 233–35

Genesis (*cont.*)

17:1 . . . . .229, 246
17:2 230
17:7 230
17:7–21 229
17:11 231
17:17 234
17:19 230
17:20 228
17:21 . . . . .230, 234
17:22 229
18 235
18:1–15 234
18:10 234–35
18:17–19 209
18:19 67
18:20–21 237
19:1 180
19:14 238
19:30–38 238
20 242
20–50 241
20:13 86
21:12 53
21:31 46
21:33 152
22:12 242
22:18 xix
24:3 238
24:57 166
25 244
25:12 53
25:19 . . . . .53, 55
25:27 246
25:28 243
26 242
26:4 xix
26:25 152
26:33 46
26:34–35 239
27:1 243
27:19 243

Genesis (*cont.*)

27:32 243
27:36 246
28:4 236
28:6 239
29:14 109
31:30 207
31:34 207
32. .182
32:32 244–45
34. 191
34:3 96
35:7 86
35:11. 42
35:12 236
36. 244
36:1 . . . . .53, 156
36:31 . . . . 40–41, 244
37:2 . . . . .53, 156
45:18. 144
46:27 177
50:10–11. 49
50:11. 41

Exodus

1:5 .178
1:15–21. 174
2:23 225
3. . . . . 79–80, 210
3:8 203
4:22 158
6. 80
6:6 225
6:12 232
9:28 198
11:3. 42
12:26–27. 64
17:14. 28
20. .106
20:8–11. 74
20:11. 98
20:12 236

Exodus (*cont.*)

20:18–21. 59
20:24 64
21:2 191
21:6 . . . . 87, 158
22:8 158
22:9 158
22:28 158
23:13 . . . . 72, 121
23:14–19. 45
24:4 28
28. .xix
28:42–43 111
31:16–17 59
31:17. 61
32–33. 160
33:20 164
34:18 45
34:22–26 45

Leviticus

4:1–5:6 xix
5:20–26 39
6:1–7 39
8. 139
11 170
17:7. 121
18:1–5. 138
18:5 . . . . 133, 137–38
23. 45
25:23 72

Numbers

12:3 42
12:8 164
13:33 159
21:14. 65
23:19–20 167
24:16 207
25:13 130
28. 45
29. 45

Numbers (*cont.*)

32:9 236
33:2 28
33:53 236

Deuteronomy

1:39 94
4:19 77
4:23 224
5:3 224
5:12–15. 61
5:16 236
5:23–31 59
6:4 81
6:7 64
6:25 219
9:23 236
10:16. 232
12:1. 236
14:1. . . . . xx, 158
14:21c xix
15 61
15:1–16:17 60
15:12. 191
16 61
16:20 219
17:8–13. 64
17:18. . . . . .23, 24
24:1–4 96
24:12–13. 128
24:13 219
27:26 . . . . 133, 137–38
28–29. 31
28:32 32
28:41 32
31:9 . . . . 20, 28
31:24 28
31:24–26 23
32:8 . . . . 177–78, 202
32:8–9 179
32:14 144
32:17. 121

Deuteronomy (*cont.*)

33:14 77
34. . . . . 28, 40
34:1 41

Joshua

1:7 20
1:8 48
2:9 236
2:14 236
5–6. 180
5:14–15. 180
6:2 180
6:9 224
6:16 236
6:17. 180
6:25 180
7. 237
8:31 48
9. .153
17:17–18 237
18:3 236
24:2 . . . . .207, 208
24:15 207

Judges

5:6–7 208
6. 71
11 64
18:29 . . . . .40, 41

Ruth

1:14. 96

1 Samuel

13:19. 191
15:10–11 161
15:29 . . . . .161, 167
19:24 128
27:12. 218
29:3 191

2 Samuel

1:24 91
12:10–11 174
19:35 94
20:2 96

1 Kings

10 188
11:2 96
11:12 218
11:14 244
11:34 218
14:8 218
15:5 218
17 31
19:8 131
22:20–22 180

2 Kings

5 32
6:29 .31
22:11 22
23:2 23

1 Chronicles

1:7 .186
1:10 197
12:22 198
16:8 153
16:30 153

2 Chronicles

34:14 21–22
34:30 30–31

Ezra

6:1 21

Nehemiah

2:8 91
9:14 .79
13:23–24 136

Job

1:1 194
1:6 . . . . 157, 179
2:1 .179
2:5 .109
5:12 115
9:6 .101
15:5 115
33:4 73
35:10 133
38 107
38:7 . . . . 157, 179

Psalms

2 . . . . xix, 129
2:4 202
8:5–6 78
15:2 219
16 . . . . xix, 14
16:4 . . . . 72, 121
18:20 219
19 7
22:29 144
24:2 .101
29:1 .179
33:6 73
36:8 .91
45:17 64
51:10 76
58:4–5 115
65:11–12 144
78:3–4 64
80:10 198
81:16 144
82:1 . . . . 88, 158
82:6 . . . . 88, 158
89:6 179
103:1 97
103:15 151
104:13–14 76
104:30 . . . . 73, 76
105:1 64

Psalms (*cont.*)

106:31. . . . . 219, 222
110 . . . . xix, 14
119 7
119:91 77
124:8 154
144:3 151
147:19–20. . . . . 60, 211
149:2 133

Proverbs

3:2 xxi
3:8 xxi
3:18 xxi
3:23 xxi
3:24 xxi
5:1–23 xxi
6:20–7:27. xxi
6:30 165
11:21. 122
13:12. 131
14:15. 115
14:18. 115
25:1 .15

Ecclesiastes

2:5 91
8:3 .145
12:1. 133

Song of Songs

2:17. 119
4:6 .119
4:13 .91

Isaiah

1:2 .158
1:4 .122
1:27. 219
6:8 86
7:15–16. 94

Isaiah (*cont.*)

24:21 180
29:8 165
29:22 208
40:18 86
40:26 76
40:28 76
45:7 .76
45:18. 78
51:1. . . . . 179, 206
54:1 216
54:5 133
63:10 161
63:11. 43
65:17–18. 76
65:25 121

Jeremiah

6:10 232
31:22 76
31:31. 137
34:18–19. 223
49:36 101
51:34 91

Ezekiel

20:12 79
31:8 93
38–39. 184

Daniel

3:26 207
4:2 207
4:24 207
5:18 207
5:23 207
9:11 20
9:13 20
10:13. 180
10:20–21 180

Hosea
6:7 . . . . 138, 140
8:12 24

Joel
2. 14
2:32 154

Amos
4:13 76
9:7 189

Jonah
3:3 198

New Testament

Matthew
1. 176
1:3 247
4. 114
5:17–18 10
5:20 219
7:12. 7
10:16. 115
11:13 7
22:31–32 xxii
22:40 7
24:38–39 158

Mark
4:7 126
7:13. 10

Luke
1:4 .15
1:55 33
1:72–73. 33
1:76. 181
2:32 214

Luke (*cont.*)
3:38 157
7:27 181
16:15. . . . . 197, 202
16:16. 7
16:31. 7
24:27 7
24:44 . . . . .xii, 7, 20

John
1:4 xii
5:39 10
6:35 xii
8:44 114
10:34–35 158
11:33. xii
11:35. xii
12:34 7
13:1. 12
14:6 xii
14:16–17 12
15:25 7
15:26 12
20:31 12
21:7. 128

Acts
1:5 .13
1:8 .13
2. . . . . xix, 193, 202
2:21 154
2:33 13
6:13 10
7:22 65
7:56 181
13 xix
14:17 213
17:24. 207
17:26. 197
17:27. 210
24:14 7

Romans

1 117
1:21 210
1:25 77
4:3 218–19
4:9 218
4:13 . . . . 209, 215
4:17 235
4:18 218
4:22 218
4:24 235
5 . . . . 114, 117
5:6 125
5:12 125
5:12–14 67
5:14 125
6:23 125
8:3 134
9:4 30
9:30 216
10 137
10:5 134
11:17–29 17
11:33 217
15:4 67
15:9–12 216
16:22 15

1 Corinthians

1:17–31 228
1:30 136
6:3 182
9:9 20
10:20 121
14:21 7
15 . . . . 67, 114, 125

2 Corinthians

3:14 17
3:15 7
4:7 243

2 Corinthians (*cont.*)

11:3–4 114
11:13–14 114

Galatians

3 . . . . .30, 137
3:6 218
3:8 214
3:8–9 33
3:14 33
3:24 141
3:29 214
4:27 216
6:7 160
6:11 15

Ephesians

1:4 217
2:12 30
2:14 34
3:4–5 216
3:10 217
5:25 126

Colossians

2:15 124
2:17 34
4:16 . . . . 12, 14

1 Thessalonians

5:27 14

1 Timothy

2:13–14 67
2:14 95

2 Timothy

1:9 217
3:8 208
3:14–17 11

Hebrews

1:14. 181
6:8 .126
10:1. 34
11:3. 78
11:4. 144
12:2 217

James

2:21 242
2:23 218

1 Peter

1:10. 66
1:11. 67
3:19–21. 172
3:21 208

2 Peter

1:18–21. 66
1:19. 34
1:19–21. 11
2:4 114
2:5 .160
3:5–6 170
3:15–16. 12

1 John

2:19 144
3. 144
3:8 . . . . 114, 124
3:12 144

3 John

4. .vii, 67

Jude

6. 114
9. 180

Revelation

1:3 15
1:5 181
1:13–15 180
4:11. 101
5. 181
5:5 181
7:1 .102
12 121
12:5 242
12:7. 180
12:9 . . . . .114, 116
20:2 114
20:8 . . . . 101, 185
22:2 . . . . 131, 138
22:14 138
22:18–19. 15

EXTRABIBLICAL SOURCES

Baruch

4:7 121

Book of Jubilees

12. 208

Ecclesiasticus

1:1. 9

Contributors

Cornelis Vonk (1904–1993) was a Reformed preacher and pastor in the Netherlands during the middle third of the twentieth century. His sermons and studies are widely known and appreciated today as a warmly devotional and pastoral treatment of the Bible text.

Frans van Deursen is an emeritus Reformed preacher and pastor in the Netherlands. He has authored a number of commentaries in this series, on both Old and New Testament books. He continues to preach regularly and to contribute volumes for this series.

Theodore Plantinga (1947–2008) was a Christian philosopher, born in the Netherlands, who worked as a translator, editor, secretary, professor, and writer in Canada for over 50 years. He taught philosophy at Redeemer University College from its founding in 1982 until his death.

Nelson D. Kloosterman serves as executive director of Worldview Resources International and labors as the translator of the volumes in this series. He is an ordained minister (PCA) and lives in Indiana.

Jordan J. Ballor is a research fellow at the Acton Institute for the Study of Religion & Liberty and serves as executive editor of the *Journal of Markets & Morality*.

Stephen J. Grabill serves as senior research scholar in theology and director of programs at the Acton Institute for the Study of Religion & Liberty.